The Father and the Feminine

The Father and the Feminine

Exploring the Grammar of God and Gender

SPENCER MILES BOERSMA

CASCADE *Books* • Eugene, Oregon

THE FATHER AND THE FEMININE
Exploring the Grammar of God and Gender

Copyright © 2024 Spencer Miles Boersma. All rights reserved. Except for brief quotations in critical publications or reviews, no part of this book may be reproduced in any manner without prior written permission from the publisher. Write: Permissions, Wipf and Stock Publishers, 199 W. 8th Ave., Suite 3, Eugene, OR 97401.

Cascade Books
An Imprint of Wipf and Stock Publishers
199 W. 8th Ave., Suite 3
Eugene, OR 97401

www.wipfandstock.com

PAPERBACK ISBN: 979-8-3852-0866-1
HARDCOVER ISBN: 979-8-3852-0867-8
EBOOK ISBN: 979-8-3852-0868-5

Cataloguing-in-Publication data:

Names: Boersma, Spencer Miles [author].

Title: The Father and the feminine : exploring the grammar of God and gender / Spencer Miles Boersma.

Description: Eugene, OR: Cascade Books, 2024 | Includes bibliographical references.

Identifiers: ISBN 979-8-3852-0866-1 (paperback) | ISBN 979-8-3852-0867-8 (hardcover) | ISBN 979-8-3852-0868-5 (ebook)

Subjects: LCSH: Femininity of God. | Masculinity of God. | Women in Christianity. | Wisdom (Biblical personification). | Trinity. | Holy Spirit. | Feminist theology. | Language and languages—Religious aspects—Christianity

Classification: BT153 B64 2024 (paperback) | BT153 (ebook)

07/30/24

Contents

	Introduction	1
1	Revelation and Liberation	21
2	Ineffability and Idolatry	42
3	Analogy and Narrative	62
4	Christ and the Cross	106
5	Spirit and Sophia	135
6	Trinity and Mutuality	182
7	Conclusion	222
Bibliography		243

Introduction

How we talk about God affects who we are just as much as what we believe about God, and how we talk about God with gendered language will have important effects on how we relate to others as gendered people. For a prime example (albeit a problematic one), the message of John Piper, a prominent Reformed Baptist pastor, shows how intimately connected patriarchal language for God is with the domination of men over women. He stated at a conference,

> God revealed Himself in the Bible pervasively as king, not queen; father, not mother. . . . The second person of the Trinity is revealed as the eternal Son, not daughter; the Father and the Son create man and woman in His image and give them the name man, the name of the male. . . . God appoints all the priests in the Old Testament to be men; the Son of God came into the world to be a man; He chose 12 men to be His apostles; the apostles appointed that the overseers of the Church be men; and when it came to marriage they taught that the husband should be the head. . . . Now, from all of that, I conclude that God has given Christianity a masculine feel. . . . And being God, a God of love, He has done that for our maximum flourishing, both male and female. . . . He does not intend for women to languish or be frustrated or in any way suffer or fall short of full and lasting joy in this masculine Christianity. From this, I infer that the fullest flourishing of women and men takes place in churches and families that have this masculine feel.[1]

For him, God, while transcendent of gender, has explicitly revealed himself as male in order to prop up a vision of the church that is male-led. Piper sees this as benevolent and biblical. Patriarchy is the rule of men as

---

1. Statements are reported by Alex Murashko, "John Piper: God Gave Christianity a 'Masculine Feel.'"

a social group over women (re-termed in some circles as "complementarianism," which is the notion of inherently different and hierarchical roles based on a theological understanding of gender in the family, church, and society). This, for Piper, is good.

Complementarians have always been quick to say that male headship, both in God and the church, does not cause abuse. Women are to submit to godly men in the church and home. Stated most generously, the best proponents of complementarian theology do not advocate violence against women (although excluding women from positions of influence for these theological reasons is arguably itself a form of violence against their dignity and agency). However, there are various tendencies that have continuously created a kind of elective affinity for the suppression and abuse of women.[2] The emergence of the #MeToo and, sadly but not surprisingly, the #ChurchToo movements have exposed the ramifications of this theology. Cultural historian Kristin Kobes du Mez has gone so far as to assert that the battle over patriarchy and women's equality goes right to the core of Christianity in the United States. In her book *Jesus and John Wayne* (2020), she charts the merger of a kind of cultural patriarchal nationalism with evangelical identity, at times in disturbing detail, documenting the correlation of a configuration of masculinity with power, femininity with submission, and how this has continually left male culprits unaccountable and female victims suppressed. If evangelicalism has internalized patriarchy and nationalism, it serves as an ironic and sad reminder that often there is a version of conservatism that is the mirror reflection of what it hates: an accommodation to worldly thinking.

Behind the vocabularies spoken about God are the victims to whom these paradigms have caused pain. As the stories of abuse and suppression have mounted, it is evident that there is an establishment, a cultural system of language and practices, that is deeply dismissive of women's voices and hostile to women questioning the authority of men in power, even when voicing evidence of obvious wrongdoing, as this cultural system is deeply committed to protecting its own power. Moreover, if this power is modeled in a literalistic manner on God's power, we can see why the response of the system to what is perceived as sinful resistance is sometimes wrathful force. Many in this debate do not think Father language reifies maleness into God's being, much less being against women.

---

2. Kevin Giles has drawn specific connections between the conviction of male headship and the susceptibility of women to abuse in Giles, *The Headship of Men and the Abuse of Women*.

INTRODUCTION

However, practically speaking, there is a reiteration of God's identity that very much reinforces this implication. How people treat women is connected with what "God" means.

I first became aware of this topic from the controversy surrounding the book *The Shack* (2007).[3] It, as well as its more recent movie (2017), ignited a theological firestorm as the author, William Paul Young, depicted the first member of the Trinity as a Black lady named "Papa" and the Holy Spirit as an Asian woman named "Sarayu," all in a process to help the main character, Mack, deal with his hurt and pain over the broken relationship he had with his father. Often missed by his critics, the main character is encountered by a motherly depiction of God in the process by which his understanding of God is healed. Only then is he able to picture God as a father fully again. With the pervasive popularity of a book like *The Shack*, it is clear that the book's appeal to the broader population far exceeded its critics' prowess in censuring it. In fact, the denouncement by many conservative pastors drove their parishioners toward the brouhaha out of curiosity. While the notion that God is male and exclusively a father is still the default setting of most people, atheists included, the question is being asked no longer in the safe and speculative classrooms of seminaries but in churches and small groups. (Sometimes these questions are heard and engaged in an open-minded way, and other times they are only superficially heard, and the defensive answers given are expected never to be questioned.) *The Shack* was, for millions of Christians, a provocation to thinking about gender and God.

Meanwhile, a resurgence of a kind of patriarchalism and anti-feminism has come as a surprise to many feminists who thought the culture was obviously bending in their favor. The popularity of the Canadian intellectual Jordan Peterson, who has sported a kind of popular conservativism of liberties and has achieved astounding popularity with his self-help books[4] as well as his YouTube channel, has contributed to a cultural anti-feminism. Peterson gained recognition for his refusal to use transgender pronouns, seeing this as an infringement of his liberty of speech. While an obviously talented psychologist and lecturer, his criticisms often display characteristic ignorance of the basic tenets of what he criticizes, whether socialism, Marxism, postmodernism, critical race theory, or feminism. His message has connected with audiences who feel

3. William Paul Young, *The Shack*.
4. For example, see Jordan Peterson, *12 Rules for Life*.

disenfranchised as he scapegoats feminism and other things for social ills that men face. Peterson has denied the gender pay gap, ignoring how women face a glass ceiling in the workplace, usually related to mothering. Peterson has defended notions of hierarchy with appeals to mythic symbolism of what the male and the female represent. Femininity represents chaos versus masculine order. These appeals show an outdated over-reliance on Jungian psychology, which ignores a great deal of nuance in studies of symbolism. Yet his simplistic binaries offer popular appeal, and they foster a kind of anti-feminism that will buttress conditions of patriarchy.

There are many other popular-level conversations, some of which we will get to in the following chapters, but what this sketch seeks to display is that a certain conversation about God, gender, and language is no longer restricted to the speculations of theologians. These are questions increasingly asked by people in the pew.

Thus, this book asks: Can God[5] be referred to as "Mother" or as female? Is God a "he" or a "she"? And what are the consequences of these words in the lives of men and women? What does this language mean for us as gendered creatures who seek to emulate God's character and treat each other in a godly way? Is the Bible thoroughly male in its characterization of God? Does it recommend an exclusive pattern? In Christian theology, there is rarely a topic that does not display a vast range of opinions, and this debate is no exception. This text will attempt to chart and assess the diverse debate on gendered language for God,[6] looking at how the different sides in the dispute appeal to patterns of biblical language and historic Christian imagery. Overall, the argument of this work is a modest proposal: while male language for God should not necessarily be taken as offensive (and thus will continue in the church), it also cannot be taken as exclusive (which in many cases it is). Feminine language for God exists in the Bible and church history and, thus, is more than permitted. Indeed, such language can aid in finding deeper authenticity in the Christian way of life.

---

5. The reader will note that I used the generic term "God" throughout the book, avoiding pronoun usage in an attempt for neutrality in the argumentation. This is also a usage for simplicity's sake, however clunky and contested. As the book proceeds, other possibilities and proposals will be unpacked and analyzed.

6. This work is the fullest treatment of thinking that began in a sermon but got fleshed out in two articles. See Boersma, "The Motherly Love of God"; Boersma, "Beyond Literalism and Liberalism"; Boersma, "Father and the Feminine."

INTRODUCTION

While the lines between culture and church, academic and popular, are blurred and interwoven, this book attempts to leave the popular battles to those soldiers who want to fight them and focuses instead on the primary academic arguments on the strict question of how one refers to God. (Further implications for what this means as gendered people will be tentatively touched on at the end of each chapter, anticipating further work.) To get oriented in this debate, a survey of some of the major voices and works, both feminist and those of a more conservative variety, is necessary.

IMPORTANT FEMINIST THEOLOGICAL WORKS ON LANGUAGE FOR GOD

First, there are several important figures who have advanced female-inclusive language in various ways. While feminism has several antecedents, the debate about gendered God language came to the fore first with the work of Mary Daly (1928–2010). Mary Daly denounces any male imagery as the cause of the enslavement of women in her primary work, *Beyond God the Father* (1973):

> The biblical and popular image of God as a great patriarch in heaven, rewarding and punishing according to his mysterious and seemingly arbitrary will, has dominated the imagination of millions over thousands of years. The symbol of the Father God, spawned in the human imagination and sustained as plausible by patriarchy, has, in turn, rendered service to this type of society by making its mechanisms for the oppression of women appear right and fitting. If God in "his" heaven is a father ruling "his" people, then it is in the "nature" of things and according to the divine plan and order of the universe that society be male-dominated.[7]

She continues:

> If God is male, then the male is God. The divine patriarch castrates women as long as he is allowed to live on in the human imagination. The process of cutting away the Supreme Phallus can hardly be a mere "rational" affair. The problem is one of

---

7. Mary Daly, *Beyond God the Father*, 13. This is considered her primary work, but it was preceded by *The Church and the Second Sex* and followed by several others, most notably, *Gyn/Ecology: The Metaethics of Radical Feminism*.

transforming the collective imagination so that this distortion of the human aspiration to transcendence loses its credibility.[8]

Daly, representing perhaps one of the furthest voices in the other direction from John Piper, sees the image of God the Father as a projection of patriarchy onto the transcendence of the divine. Patriarchy is the domination of men as a group over women as a group, which can exist in various forms—whether personally, in family, in society and culture, and, particularly for this study, in religion—and can appear in modes that explicitly allow and even encourage overt abuse to more subtle modes, like repression of female voices and representation. For Daly, Scripture, then, cannot be trusted as it displays this characteristic infection with patriarchy. In the interest of the liberation of women, this image and all its implications must be replaced forcefully. This means Christianity must undergo a drastic revision and re-symbolization if it is to be a religion that truly liberates women. Whether Christianity can do so and still retain that which is essential and particular to it is an issue. Daly was neither concerned that Christianity should retain any particularity (the patriarchal infection was total in her view) nor confident that it could be revised successfully and still be Christianity (she eventually renounced Christianity).

Rosemary Radford Ruether (1936–2022) wrote a formative feminist theological work, *Sexism and God-Talk* (1983).[9] This book looks at the major topics of theology (Christology, anthropology, eschatology, etc.) through what she sees as the iconoclastic lens of Jesus, who sought the liberation of all people, and in this case women. Thus, she discusses how each discourse has been oppressive to women and how it can be revised. Apart from her radically iconoclastic approach is a kind of pragmatic syncretism where she looked to any sources, whether different political philosophies or world religions, as sources to be used. These included looking to Gnosticism and various pagan spiritualities.

Sallie McFague (1933–2019) wrote important works on the nature of religion and metaphor, particularly as it relates to gender and justice. Her major project regarding gender is spread over three works that show her thoughts unfolding: *Speaking in Parables* (1975), *Metaphorical Theology* (1982), and *Models of God* (1987). These works advance a fervent

---

8. Daly, *Beyond God the Father*, 19.

9. She continued to write several important works, some of which are the following: *Gaia and God: An Ecofeminist Theology of Earth Healing*; *Goddesses and the Divine Feminine: A Western Religious History*; *My Quests for Hope and Meaning: An Autobiography*.

postmodern sensibility that theological realism is impossible. Instead, religious language is metaphorical all the way through, and the divine is then constructed using large constellations of metaphors, which she calls models. Fundamental to human change for the better is adopting models of God that are non-patriarchal and non-hierarchal, such as God as Mother, Lover, and Friend. After *Models of God*, she turned to more ecological matters (a move of concentration similar to Ruether's work), as she saw feminism and ecology as mutually intertwined.[10] Notably, she argued that the earth is the body of God, incorporating female imagery into the notion of the Creator that renders God not transcendent over the world but imminent within the world, a move she hoped would combat views of God where the earth could be neglected.

While standing within the feminist tradition, Catholic scholar Elizabeth Johnson (1941–) has offered formidable arguments for inclusive language. Her first book was in Christology, *Consider Jesus* (1990), where she offered a short defense for Jesus' masculinity as compatible with feminist concerns. However, her most substantive work is the award-winning *She Who Is* (1992). There, she argues for the ineffability of God as a basis for a refusal to allow masculine-gendered language to be dominant. From there, she uses biblical images and classic Catholic authorities like Aquinas to argue that linguistic approaches such as analogy support her thesis. She then uses these to offer a reading of the Trinity where each member, beginning with the Spirit, then the Son, then the Father, has female aspects. These, she argues, support the possible enrichment of the attributes of God with motherly qualities. The book culminates in her suggestion that God's name in Exodus 3:14, "The One Who Is" (as Aquinas saw it), can be productively understood as "She Who Is."

Catherine Mowry LaCugna (1952–97) is one of the modern giants of the doctrine of the Trinity. Her award-winning book, *God for Us* (1991), offers an exposition of the history of the doctrine of the Trinity, all to develop her argument of relational personhood. While the book does not deal with inclusive language, she argued for a feminist interpretation of the baptismal formula and the trinitarian persons in several essays before her untimely death from cancer.[11]

Two voices that have been very important for the construction of gender-inclusive liturgical resources are worth mentioning: Ruth Duck

---

10. Sallie McFague, *The Body of God: An Ecological Theology*.
11. LaCugna, "The Baptismal Formula."

(1947–) and Gail Ramshaw (1947–). Both have authored several liturgical resources, including lectionaries, hymns, prayers, and poems (which will be discussed further at the end of this project), but their academic work both have focused on the application of gendered language. Duck's work has looked at the Trinity and, more specifically, the baptismal formula. Gail Ramshaw-Schmidt has also been a forerunner of inclusive language in liturgies and lectionaries, and she spelled out the nature of gender-neutral liturgy in a few early essays[12] and then, primarily in her book, *God Beyond Gender* (1995).

In looking at these works, one should note the range and diversity that will appear in each chapter's discussion of these different sides. This project will seek to appreciate the more nuanced proposals while critiquing the more extreme.

IMPORTANT CONSERVATIVE RESPONSES

There have been several important responses to these works. These are a bit harder to map out since the arguments are often incorporated into more sustained treatments of classical topics. While feminism began and blossomed in the latter half of the twentieth century, the view that God is to be understood with exclusively male language has been the default setting of many. Some of the defenses of fatherly and male-exclusive language have merely been stated in the works of systematic theology, particularly when discussing the Trinity. Other defenses have been biblical studies that have analyzed the Bible and defended its language. Still, others have been more focused in their treatment of these issues.

One of the most important works for the conservative side came before Daly. Joachim Jeremias (1900–1979), in his book *The Prayers of Jesus* (1967), offers a pivotal description regarding Jesus and the Father. Jesus' prayer to "Abba," he argues, is novel to Jesus, a title of intimacy unmatched in the Judaism and the surrounding religions of his day. This, therefore, constitutes a kind of pinnacle revelation within the Gospels, something that transcends culture and time. Jesus' unique usage of the "Abba" and "Father" has been taken up in several notable defenses in biblical studies. John Hammerton-Kelly's study, *God the Father* (1979), carries Jeremais's insight further. Expanding the narrative insights from

---

12. Ramshaw-Schmidt, "Lutheran Liturgical Prayer and God as Mother"; Ramshaw-Schmidt, "De Divinis Nominibus"; Ramshaw-Schmidt, "An Inclusive Language Lectionary"; Ramshaw-Schmidt, "Naming the Trinity."

INTRODUCTION

Paul Ricoeur's powerful essay on the subject, "Fatherhood: From Phantasm to Symbol"[13] (which was an essay directed at Freudian objections to Christian father language), Hammerton-Kelly uses historical-critical scholarship, coupled with a narrative approach to argue that Jesus' usage of "Father" did not succumb to the trappings of patriarchy.

Evangelical theologian Donald Bloesch (1928–2010) wrote *The Battle for the Trinity* (1985) as one of the first full-scale responses to feminist re-symbolization. This was a follow-up to his previous book, *Is the Bible Sexist?* (1982), which stands as a very early defense of women's equality and ordination by a conservative evangelical. However, Bloesch is concerned with a full-scale re-symbolization of the faith by feminism that would cause it to lose its historical content. He notes that several of the more radical feminists, such as Ruether, argue for the incorporation of gnostic and pagan material. He sees this as potentially destructive, akin to how the Nazis called for the re-symbolization of Christianity to make it amendable to German culture. This is an extreme example, but the concern for revelation and the historical context of Christianity stands as Bloesch's primary concern. While Bloesch argues against a form of inclusive language, he actually admits there is a lot of female language in the Bible and even proposes his own prayers that include female and motherly references.

In the edited volume *Speaking the Christian God* (1992), Alvin Kimel Jr. brings together the most fulsome defense of the position ever found between two covers. Strangely, the book's cover features the famous icon of Andrei Rublev, "The Trinity" (also called "The Hospitality of Abraham," painted in 1411). Somehow, it escaped both the book's authors and its editors that Rublev depicts three angelic figures with female qualities. Thus, the volume is a strange mix; some essays are highly polemical, while others offer careful nuance, rebuttal, and even concessions. The book houses some of the principal thinkers of the position, including Thomas F. Torrance, Robert W. Jenson, and Colin Gunton. However, it also offers some of the worst arguments for the position. For instance, Elizabeth Achtmeier's essay, the first essay in the volume, is highly accusatory and seems to deny the existence of any passages in the Bible that use female bodily imagery. Thomas Hopko's essay overtly refuses, by his own admission, to interact with feminist scholarship, making an argument about apophatic theology that will be considered later in this

---

13. In Ricoeur, *Conflict in Interpretations*.

project. Meanwhile, the essays by Janet Soskice, Thomas Torrance, and J. A. DiNoia are careful pieces of scholarship that modestly argue for "Father" as an enduring reference.

Marianne Meye Thompson, in her book, *The Promise of God the Father* (2000), surveys the meaning of "Father" from the Old Testament into the New, furthering and updating the insights of Hammerton-Kelly. The book offers the most substantive exposition for the meaning of the "Father" in the Bible to date. However, as we will see, Thompson makes certain concessions previous authors refused to make, including admitting that "Abba-Father" is neither a name nor unique to Jesus (although she contends that the *usage* is unique).

Kathryn Green-McCreight argues, in her book *Feminist Reconstructions of Christian Doctrine* (2000), that some feminists (she sees a difference between "biblical feminists" and "mainline feminists," the latter more disagreeable) have imported concerns into Christian theology that do not cohere with the realism of the biblical narrative or its grammar of governing doctrines. While her book is a kindred spirit to my own due to her post-liberal approach, it uses narrative realism and doctrinal grammar to delegitimize female language. My own book, by contrast, takes a different path in analyzing the structure of Christian discourse and argues for a different conclusion.

Some of this conversation is now happening online. For instance, when the Presbyterian Church of the United States of America adopted the paper "The Trinity: God's Love Overflowing"[14] in 2006, this was attacked by many conservative reformed thinkers. The Baptist leader and president of Southern Baptist Theological Seminary, Al Mohler, wrote,

> Dismissive of doctrinal orthodoxy and biblical language as out of date, oppressive, patriarchal, and worse, the proponents of theological reformulation intend to restructure Christianity around an entirely new system of beliefs, playing with language even as they reinvent the faith. . . . The line here is not merely between traditional and imaginative language—it is the line between the worship of the one true and living God and the worship of idols.[15]

---

14. Migliore, "'The Trinity: God's Love Overflowing.'"
15. Mohler, "The God Who Names Himself."

INTRODUCTION

In Anglicanism, another recent move in the Washington Diocese to a more inclusive language was met with criticism from the bishop of Dallas, George Sumner.[16]

The conservative voice has been stated, whether with the polemical fire of Mohler or the sophistication of Sumner, Bloesch, or Torrance, in arguments along these lines: the first member of the Trinity was named Father by Jesus, the Son, and God has sanctified the pronoun "he" for God's own. Anything else is forsaking faithfulness to the Bible.

THE ROAD FORWARD

When these two sets of thinkers are compared and assessed, important questions arise: What is the role of Scripture in Christian doctrine, and what is the role of experience, namely the experiences of one's body, patriarchal oppression, and liberation? How are convictions, even biblically derived convictions, complicit in patriarchy? Is patriarchy inherent to Christianity or a corruption of it, a failure for many Christians to be faithful to what the faith is truly about? And how is the manner of talking about God bound up with all this? What is the essence of God? Is "Father" the revealed name of the first member of the Trinity? If so, does that bind Christianity to patriarchy? If not, why is it so widely held and used, and how should one go about replacing this symbol? Should there be minor supplements? Should there be full-scale re-symbolizations? Should it go so far as eliminating all male-gendered references in the Bible (as inclusive lectionaries do)? Should the pursuit of female liberation go so far as to include perspectives from outside Christianity, as Rosemary Radford Reuther advocates? How far is enough? And can it go so far as to lose what some see as the core of what Christianity is? One agnostic feminist scholar, Daphne Hampson, put it this way: "Feminism represents the death knell of Christianity as a viable religious option."[17] Is this true? Is the heart of Christianity at stake with this one word, "Father," as Thomas Torrance insists? He offers this important challenge: "What is at stake here is the question whether biblical statements about God—for example, his Fatherhood in respect to Jesus Christ his incarnate Son—are

---

16. Sumner, "Contra Washington: Ten Theses."
17. Hampson, *Theology and Feminism*, 1.

related to what they claim to signify merely in a conventional way . . . or in a real way."[18]

A kind of fleshing out of the argument for inclusive language has occurred in a few smaller but important works: Virginia Mollenkott's survey of female imagery of the Bible,[19] as well as Jennifer Heimmel and Caroline Bynum's books on feminine and motherly imagery used for the members of the Trinity throughout church history, have offered a rebuttal to claims that inclusive language is unbiblical and unwarranted in the Christian tradition.[20] Still, as already stated, this conversation is highly polarized, and these two poles pull to extremes that many find too far. As already stated, Alvin Kimel Jr.'s edited volume has offered the most thorough defense of the conservative position, but as his exchange with Catherine LaCugna over her review of the book has shown, both sides are talking past one another and highly dismissive of one another.[21] The conversation is tongue-tied and highly polarized, and often the extremes are seen as representative. This book attempts to walk an uncomfortable, tension-filled middle way between the extremes of "literalism" and "liberalism." According to the approach defended here, one extreme uses Scripture in a highly exclusive way, missing its richness and misunderstanding its context and its forms of dynamic usage, and the other extreme often abandons Scripture and any claims to particular revelation in the name of concerns that appear forced onto the religion from outside. While I do not pretend to resolve all the aspects of this multi-faceted debate, by a slow consideration of each criterion of meaningfulness in theological discourses, my hope is to show convergences and clarifications.

This project will use the extremes at times as foils to draw the reader into a middle-ground argument. Part of this dynamic is due to what is perhaps the most intriguing development of this debate, academically speaking: namely, that there is a notable diversity on either side. Is it possible that Father language is not patriarchal? Is it possible that getting rid of this language jettisons a redemptive potential bound up with it? Evidently, there are women and feminists who think so. Meanwhile, there are many men (myself included) who have seen the theological validity of motherly

---

18. Torrance, *Reality and Evangelical Theology*, 110.
19. Mollenkott, *The Divine Feminine*.
20. Heimmel, "God Is Our Mother."
21. LaCugna, review of *Speaking the Christian God*, 114–16. Kimel, "It Could Have Been . . . ," 389–94.

INTRODUCTION

and female language about God.²² Does Scripture allow for, perhaps even necessitate, female and motherly language? Can it be used to liberate not only women but men as well into deeper relationships with God and others? Evidently, there are men who think this is the case. Thus, while there is a gender divide in this debate, it is not total. Moreover, as this investigation will show, experience is important, but it is not necessarily obvious or clear. Thus, in order to move forward, a methodology that clarifies the meaning of Scripture and the data of experience is necessary.

SOME CLARIFICATIONS AND DELIMITATIONS OF THIS STUDY

While this project attempts an assessment of the grammar of gendered language about God, it must make clear the approach, which is fourfold: it is feminist in one sense of this word (although not radical feminist), seeing liberation from patriarchy as germane to Christian concern; it is catholic (small "c") in concern for the role of tradition (however, admitting its diversity and distortions), and Baptist or Free Church in ecclesial location, which stresses the liberty of conscience and local congregations in employing the Scriptures. However, primarily the approach of this work is postliberal in its analysis of religious language.

This study insists that "feminist" and "Christian" are not (or at least should not be) contradictory categories. No survey of feminism or history of its movements with its waves will be undertaken here,²³ only to note that within Christian feminism, there is a noted diversity; there are biblically minded feminists and mainline ones, reformist feminists and radical post-Christian feminists. It should become obvious which ones I am most in agreement with, but that comes with the need to recognize that more radical writers present important challenges. Their voices ought to be heard. Theology is best done when the theologian is willing to listen. While there is a radical form of feminism that does not take Christian self-description or the biblical narrative's claims to revelation seriously (or at least, it disagrees with Christian doctrines), the theologian's awareness of that should be coupled with the humility of realizing the rightful challenge feminism offers to the rest of Christian theology, a

---

22. Jürgen Moltmann, Leonardo Boff, Gerald O'Collins, Joe Jones, Paul Smith, and Clark Pinnock are all examples of theologians who espouse this position. They will be mentioned at appropriate times later.

23. For a short and accessible resource, see Walters, *Feminism*.

call to actually live out the vision of Jesus Christ and his counter-worldly, counter-oppressive kingdom. In that regard, there are challenges to theology that are rightfully offered and can be welcomed, for all Christian theology as such must seek to uphold the dignity and liberation of women. These challenges are deeply entangled with issues of race, as well as disability, sexuality, class, etc. Indeed, a holistic approach to life and life's problems must be complemented with an *intersectional* approach.[24] However, for the purposes of this study, language and gender must be isolated as the primary concern of this project (although one will see race as a necessary topic in clarifying the meaning of Jesus' flesh or culture, a necessary topic for discussing the meaning of the Spirit). Doing this is, admittedly, to take one piece of the puzzle out of the whole, but to keep the project manageable, it is necessary.

There is a concern here to be both willing to prophetically critique the church when it has failed to live out the kingdom of Jesus Christ, but also a trust that God's Spirit has not been unfaithful these many centuries. While the record of treatment of women warrants at times some turning over of tables, there is also a desire to hold on to that which is small "c" "catholic" in Christianity,[25] although what that is, in an ecumenical context, is often not obvious. So, while what that means is, of course, contested, it is held to in principle here. When some conservatives cite "this is what the church has always held to be true," a good historian will point out that history is rarely so uniform. A good "catholic" should point out that the rich history of the church has more to it. Thus, subsequent chapters will be peppered with examples of thinkers who have imagined God differently than the typical masculine-exclusive way.

This is a study done very much from a Baptistic perspective, although the findings of this study apply regardless of denominational location, or at least can. Of course, there are many types of Baptists, and this one reflects the convictions of the Canadian Baptists. One will see that this Baptist approach sees Scripture as the inspired rule for faith and practice, and what this means is held to generously, extending liberty to individuals and local congregations to interpret according to their conscience. The reflections of this project flow out of the Baptist conviction of the primacy of God's word over all tradition and convention. This does not dismiss tradition, as one will see, but sees all extrabiblical convictions as

---

24. See Kim and Shaw, *Intersectional Theology*.

25. Two Baptists that have written on this are Steven Harmon, *Towards Baptist Catholicity*, and Curtis Freeman, *Contesting Catholicity*.

permitted and configured by the rule of Scripture, properly understood through Jesus Christ, which the grammatical approach of this project will clarify (spelled out next chapter). Baptists hold to the possibility of congregations and interpreters who are able and responsible for choosing their convictions as their consciences are led. The Bible's authority means responsibility and liberty; the two cannot be separated. This leads to a kind of openness to contextual experience and prophetic revision that is germane to what Baptists, at least some communities of Baptists, have historically been about.

When this book appeals to "grammar," it is embracing a "postliberal" approach to theology. Postliberalism was pioneered at Yale Divinity School by a number of scholars like Hans Frei, George Lindbeck, David Kelsey, Paul Holmer, and others.[26] Postliberalism is really a refusal of modernity's attempt to legitimate Christian faith on something other than itself, seeking instead theological reasoning that could address contemporary challenges while remaining authentic to the community of faith's historical self-descriptions (its "cultural-linguistic system") rather than attempting to translate the convictions of the faith into some other schema. This entails things like reclaiming a hermeneutic of the Bible *after* historical criticism (while not denying historical criticism as some do) that sees Scripture as a canonical and unified whole. It could entail reading the narratives of the Gospels, for instance, as realistic narratives rather than as reconstructions, allegories, or myths. This also means thinking about Christianity as something like a language and culture with its own rules of "grammar" for its intelligibility.

Thus, this work will show both the meaning of fatherly language for God as well as the presence and legitimacy of female and motherly language for God. It will do so by looking at the "grammar" of Christian speech about God, namely that if religion is like a language system, then there are governing concerns and patterns that recommend ways these figures fit together. This work will attempt to balance the poles of reference and function in theological language. Both are important in thinking about God and our treatment of other people, but not always in straightforward ways. One approach of this investigation is strictly analytic and referential: does the Bible have motherly and female language for God? Do the biblical rules of Christian speech allow for further female figures (perhaps as suggested in church history)? However, on

---

26. For an explanation of postliberalism, see Fodor, "Postliberal Theology."

the other side, since language is meaningful when lived, it also must be asked, in what ways does this language encourage and form Christlike behavior or has it been co-opted and reappropriated in patriarchal ways? What are the criteria in Scripture for successfully living out the convictions this language forms? In this, we will see successful ways, both biblically and liberating, that one can refer to God as a "he" and "Father." However, when the biblical grammar is examined, we also have to admit that female and motherly language is permitted as well and can certainly aid in promoting Christlike behavior in the church.

Too often, the language is discussed as though men gravitate to male language and women to female language. However, this ignores how male language in the Bible has been employed to aid and enrich the experience of women and how female language has been used to speak to men, and not in ways reducible to the influence of patriarchy. For instance, as we will see, despite the patriarchy of the culture, a figure like Lady Wisdom has captured the attention of male writers. Thus, a constructive path forward begins by recognizing that this debate will not be solved by merely changing the language of the church from male to female based on the premise of a binary that male language is for men and female for women (or that one is obviously bad and the other obviously good). If language is meaningful through its context of usage, it is possible that there will be contexts in which highly masculine language does not necessarily get used in patriarchal ways (although it certainly has contributed to patriarchy in the current context). Patriarchy in the church will not be eradicated if there is a committee that assembles and insists all male language be changed to female imagery, or perhaps not even by a kind of 50/50 split in language. The whole notion that language about God is like a zero-sum game is about as problematic as viewing poetry as a competition between letters of the alphabet. While it will be stressed is the use of biblical language and figures in discursive practices that counter patriarchy. Now, while it will be argued that Father is not the name of the first member of the Trinity, thus warranting alternatives (the grammar of which will be explored later), it is also argued that we should be very cautious about attempts to cut out classic and historic expressions and about grand acts of iconoclasm. However, advocated here is the use of the diversity of Christian language from a scripturally patterned and Spirit-discerned community in worship, prayer, preaching, and witness. Male language will continue to provide the means by which people have fought patriarchy, but that does not rule out female language on principle. So, as I will reiterate through this work, the continued use of male language for God is not to be taken as offensive (provided its usage is configured by thematic centers like Jesus' kingdom teachings, the Spirit's liberty, and triune love). When the breadth of language in the Bible is investigated, we will see that it also permits female expressions that Christians are at liberty to utilize.

When Christians are attentive to how our language functions, we often have to admit that we are saying things in ways the Bible's fuller context would not permit or condone. It is always possible that God is honored with the lips while that heart is far from God. The same goes for language in this debate. We will see that while the incarnation of Jesus Christ, his cross, and resurrection are central to the Christian faith, sadly, this language can be confessed but not lived out in a Christlike way. A male Messiah can reiterate patriarchy even though the kingdom of God that Jesus proclaimed and lived is decidedly against it. The cross that is a sign of hope to the lowly and a call to those of high status, privilege, and power to lower themselves has been used to further abuse. In this regard, fuller and even provocative explorations of this imagery can aid in confronting these accommodations.

Thus, words must be understood by the contours of grammar that render them intelligible, where reference and function have intertwined capacities to offer meaning. This book is an attempt to clarify the different forms of grammar for the words this conversation has become tongue-tied over. In looking at several approaches (or "rules of grammar") to how Christian thinkers have classically commented on the structure of Christian discourse about God (following rules such as all discourse about God must be apophatic, analogical, narrative-driven, configured by thematic centers that are Christological, pneumatic, and trinitarian), a constructive middle ground arises. This, in turn, opens pathways by which we, as gendered people, achieve greater levels of authenticity.

PREVIEW OF CHAPTERS

This debate is really a clash between two rules in which Christians speak about God, namely the rule of revelation and the rule of liberation. This will be discussed in chapter 1, which suggests a postliberal or "grammatical" approach that brings together concern for biblical speech and liberating ways of life in the figural reading of the Bible. Chapter 2 moves on to the notion that God is ineffable. Both sides appeal to this notion as a rule for Christian speech but apply it in fundamentally different ways: one to say that only biblical speech is authorized, another to negate what it sees as idolatrous renderings of language. Chapter 3 discusses three patterns of language: metaphor, analogy, and narrative. To speak of God is to speak of one who is beyond human language, which in many cases warrants analogical and metaphorical speech. However, it will be shown that this does not undermine realistic reference to God, especially if situated in larger units of speech like the biblical narrative, which provides vital context for meaning. Chapter 4 discusses doctrinal themes more explicitly, namely the identity of Jesus Christ. The historic maleness of Jesus is contested by both sides in that the male figure is either used to prop up male leadership or dismiss female representation on the male-exclusive side, and on the other, there are feminist theologians who seek to bypass the historical Christ entirely, advocating for female representation. To this, it will be argued that a resolute commitment to the historical incarnation of Christ actually opens a pathway to think about female representation. Chapter 5 moves on to the portrayal of the Holy Spirit. While the Spirit is identified as the Spirit of Christ, there is also the figure of Lady Wisdom, the meaning of which will occupy a significant portion of this chapter. Chapter 6 brings the previous chapters together to discuss the nature of trinitarian discourse. Essential to this question is whether Jesus names the first member of the Trinity "Father" or whether Father is a title or metaphor. Also significant to the discussion is whether the "Father" is bound up with patriarchy (or whether, as we will see, the language is, in many ways, counter-patriarchal). From there, a fuller discussion will occur regarding female language and the Trinity and how this contributes to understanding the essence of God as love. In conclusion, it will be noted that many of the arguments made on both sides are simply too simplistic. The Bible, church tradition, and human experience in faith are all much richer than many appreciate. While thoughts will be sketched out in each chapter, what this means for humans as gendered creatures is a matter needing further study. This work primarily focuses on the already quite contested question of female language for God. I close the book with my own personal story of how I came to contemplate female language for God and what it meant for my relationship with my mother.

INTRODUCTION

WHY WRITE A BOOK ON THE POSSIBILITY OF FEMALE LANGUAGE FOR GOD?

I have no interest in fighting or finger-waving over a person's language in prayer or worship. At the same time, there are personal and intellectual reasons why this became a topic of study (which are explained at the end of this book). Suffice it to say, this has not been a merely academic interest of mine. Speaking as one who was at one point adamantly opposed to female language and egalitarianism, I have found contemplating the female imagery of God to be spiritually nourishing and necessary in confronting a literalized theme that was embedded in my convictions that legitimatized patriarchal practices. This was a part of my becoming convinced that the gospel of Jesus Christ implores a way of life where the dignity and agency of all people are upheld. This in turn concretely means combating patriarchy in ways like advocating women's ordination, etc. Confirmation that I needed to write this book came when I taught about these issues in class. Often, the women in the class expressed to me how much these topics were encouraging and empowering, how often many of them did think about God in feminine ways but learned to keep these things to themselves for fear of condemnation. Meanwhile, men found thinking about these figures aided in deepening their spirituality as well. Thus, the intention of this study is *enrichment*.

When doctrinal answers are messy, and issues are complex and confusing, there is always a need for grace and patience, as well as a need to allow the parameters of fellowship to be generous as people are given the space to work out, live out, differ, and discuss various convictions. So, what this study intends is to offer the gracious parameters, the "generous orthodoxy," to borrow Hans Frei's phrase. Unity cannot come with the denial of the truth, but it can allow for a center that makes possible liberty for a gracious circumference. This comes with the rejection of extremes on either side. These acts of saying "No" to certain exclusive or totalized claims on either side are made based on hopefully a broader, truthful, and loving "Yes." This is a "Yes" to Scripture, revelation, the church, Christ, the Trinity, and the Spirit, as well as a "Yes" to listening to the experience of women, to healing the emotional wounds of both men and women, to seeking the liberation of all people, and to affirming self-giving love and the pursuit of truth wherever it is found.

This study will demonstrate by the end that Father language is not offensive, but that does not mean its supplementation with motherly and female language is not permitted. It most certainly is, but as I will show, there really is no hard and fast rule for just how much or how little (beyond leaving it up to the liberty of the conscience). Nevertheless, worshiping God in all the richness of Scripture with all the richness of tradition and all the voices of the people of God should not lead to the impasse of mutual offense either side has taken toward each other. Language about God flows out of God's generosity and plenitude to speak and be spoken with, to be worshiped and praised, and to encourage and exhort. So, considering all the facets of gendered God-language should not be a challenge for the church so much as an opportunity and privilege.

1

Revelation and Liberation

THERE IS A POLARIZATION over how and why Christians can speak of God, split into those who assert *reference* versus those that look to *function* as the site of meaning. This reflects a deeper clash in theology over the rule of revelation in Scripture and those who assert the rule of liberating action as authoritative. However, what becomes apparent is that both sides manifest extremes; the concern for revelation can fall into literalism, and the concern for liberation can fall into liberalism. This should suggest that more is needed than merely simple proof texts or appeals to experiential pragmatism. A deeper analysis of the way Christians talk about God—its "grammar"—is needed.

THE CONCERN FOR REVELATION

Conservatives have typically asserted that God is a "Father" and a "he" because this is the language of Scripture. God in the Old Testament is described as "he," and Jesus, who is male, more importantly, uses "Father" in addressing the first member of the Trinity. "Father" is thus the name of the first member of the Trinity and not merely a title or metaphor among others. This argument, quite simple in form, is utilized by dozens of scholars.[1] In this, the baptismal language of the "name" of the "Father,

---

1. Some examples are as follows: Packer, *Knowing God*, 183; Geffe, "'Father' as the Proper Name of God," in Chen, *God as Father?*, 44; Bloesch, *Battle for the Trinity*; Pannenberg, *Systematic Theology*, I:259–64; Kimel, ed., *Speaking the Christian God*; Cooper, *Our Father in Heaven*; Biggs, "Gender and God-Talk."

Son, and Holy Spirit" (Matt 28:19) is essential to the identification of God. To attempt to supplant this language is tantamount to undermining what God has revealed.

So, the concern of this perspective is that any language about God must be done on the basis of the Bible, which records revelation and, in turn, reveals. God acts in events in history and speaks to the prophets and other people the Bible's narratives record. Revelation is historical and verbal and thus offers certain content. Its texts reveal not merely a sense of wordless awe of God's presence but God himself in Jesus Christ. The Bible's writings are inspired (2 Tim 3:16), and the canon of Scripture is then doctrinally regulative. The words of Scripture are, in the church today, words that are spoken by the Spirit of Christ, just as they came together in the Bible by the providential action of the Spirit. Whether by explicitly giving a writer a prophetic oracle or implicitly guiding the minds of ancient sages, chroniclers, and canonical editors, they continue to speak beyond their origin. Thus, when Scripture speaks, God is speaking through the text written by ancient human authors.[2] Some within this perspective then see the Bible as inerrant, for Scripture is spoken by the Spirit, and God cannot lie; therefore, the Bible does not falter on any statement it makes, whether about science, history, or gender. Others would say that God can speak using the author's fallible words as God has sanctified them for God's own perfect purposes.[3] In other words, what the Bible said to its original context is what the Bible is saying to today's context.

Now, there is a diversity of perspectives within this view as to the meaning of the term "Father." Next to none would argue that God is truly male, but gendered personal pronouns are seen as preferable to the depersonalized "it." The male is not essential, but it is exclusively ordained for usage. Most would see God as Father by revelation, but of course, God is no created thing and thus is not male in a sense to be reduced to a creature. Without God revealing God's very being, God is unknowable, and so is salvation. The implicit rule of this position might be stated that since the Bible legitimates the language that is permissible, and since Jesus did not refer to the first member of the Trinity as Mother, this is not language the church today is allowed to use.[4] God is named by revelation, and speech about God is regulated by Scripture.

2. See Goldingay, *Models of Scripture*.
3. Webster, *Holy Scriptures: A Dogmatic Sketch*.
4. Some essays that state that God is beyond gender but that God cannot be referred

There are, of course, practical implications bound up with this. Some see this discussion connected to women in leadership. Particularly in Roman Catholicism, a female priest cannot represent Christ (who is male) the way a male priest is called to do.[5] Or, in some conservative Protestant theology, a woman cannot lead (whether in the church, home, or society—there is a spectrum of what is allowable) because this forsakes a headship God has installed. Male headship coincides with divine headship (a trinitarian issues that will be take up later).[6] There are plenty, however, who are convinced equalitarians who do not see Father language bound up with restricting women in leadership.[7] Individuals like Donald Bloesch and Stanley Grenz stand out for their thoroughly evangelical convictions of Scripture and their ardent defense of egalitarianism, the two, in their view, being directly connected.

It is important to keep in mind that while this project splits the debate up into two sides down the fault line of whether inclusive God-language is permitted, there is, nevertheless, a range of approaches in each group. Within the conservative side of this debate, there is a concern for the reality of revelation, the authority of Scripture, and the social implications bound up with these, although there is a diversity of what each means.

THE CONCERN FOR LIBERATION

Nevertheless, many feminists worry that the use of male imagery alienates women and makes patriarchy more plausible. Mary Daly famously said, "If God is male, then the male is god."[8] By this, male imagery is bound up with patriarchy, as it suggests that God is closer to men, and that men can be comfortable asserting domination over women. It has the effect of delegitimizing female experience in various forms, whether subtlety or in overtly abusive ways. Therefore, that which oppresses women must be negated and supplanted.

---

to as Mother seem to display a characteristic failure of integration of the biblical grammar, for example, McGregor-Wright, "God, Metaphor and Gender."

5. See "Declaration *Inter Insigniores* on the Question of Admission of Women to the Ministerial Priesthood," sect. 5.

6. See for example, Grudem and Piper, eds., *Recovering Biblical Manhood and Womanhood*.

7. A good example of this would be Bloesch, *Is the Bible Sexist?*

8. Daly, *Beyond God the Father*, 18.

The feminist approach then begins with the assumption of the dignity of women and the evils of patriarchy, which it uses as a lens by which the Bible, Christian language, and everything else are judged. Ruether writes,

> The critical principle of feminist theology is the promotion of the full humanity of women. Whatever denies, diminishes, or distorts the full humanity of women is, therefore, appraised as not redemptive. . . . The negative principle also implies a positive principle: what does promote the full humanity of women is of the Holy.[9]

Daly and Ruether's axioms have led to revisions to traditional language about God in order to prioritize female language as a counter against patriarchal language. Such a move is made possible by an appeal to the idea that all language about God is metaphorical, as God is radically transcendent from reference. In other words, in contrast to conservatives, there is an insistence on revelation being non-verbal or non-propositional as the divine is completely ineffable in these accounts.

Since no language essentially refers to God, language about God is really about humans. Theological language is functional. Thus, for Sallie McFague, all images have their place, but certain ones like "king" or "father," which have held a dominant hegemony in Christianity, should be de-prioritized and replaced with others like "mother, lover, and friend,"[10] since these encourage more humane ways of life. Ruether advocates using the term "God/ess."[11] In the current climate, this must be done to achieve pragmatic ends in both thinkers' estimates, namely, to achieve liberation. One can see in this position a metaphorical approach that uses pragmatic concerns of liberation as its rule for how to speak of God: "The truth of theological formulation lies in its effects."[12] So this approach tends to see God as radically transcendent, all language about God as metaphorical, and in light of how masculine language has been used to oppress women, reflecting the Bible's patriarchal culture, female language ought to be used instead to achieve a liberating effect.

Now, there is diversity within this approach as well. Some advocate much stronger revisions than others. For instance, Mary Daly and

---

9. Ruether, *Sexism and God-Talk*, 18–19.
10. McFague, *Models of God*, 165.
11. Ruether, *Sexism and God-Talk*, 68.
12. Carr, *Transforming Grace*, 109.

Rosemary Radford Ruether have both advocated supplementing the language of the Bible with concepts from other religions, such as paganism and Gnosticism.[13] Mary Daly called for the demon of patriarchy to be exorcized from Christianity, but it came with the realization in her view that the possession was total.[14] Thus, the only exorcism possible was also a "castration" of the phallocentrism of Christianity, but instead, Daly left Christianity formally. Ruether has seen her approach more as a radicalization in line with the prophetic approach of the Bible. While primarily grounded in Christian language, Ruether, however, gleans from other religions as well in a syncretistic fashion. Meanwhile, Sallie McFague views language as metaphorical, and while she does not display quite the syncretism Ruether does, she abstracts the language of Christianity heavily, divorcing Christology from the historical Jesus and the Trinity from the biblical narrative. On the other hand, Elizabeth Johnson has argued that God is ineffable and all names about God are metaphors in some way, but she still seems to hold to the historicity of Jesus' life and how his life, death, and resurrection reveal God, who is inclusive of both genders.[15] This subtlety and diversity are often lost by many of feminism's critics (a critical book like Kimel's *Speaking the Christian God*, for instance, has essays that almost entirely attack McFague as representative). While this project shares similar concerns with Kimel's book, it also has agreements with some feminists, such as Johnson and Fiorenza, on other points.

So, it is important to emphasize here the diversity of implications the rule of liberation yields. This mirrors the diversity of implications within the rules of revelation.

LITERALISM AND LIBERALISM

Extremes on either side are apparent. The primary conservative weakness is that this strict appeal to the Bible ends up with a kind of literalism, where feminists have often resorted to a kind of liberalism (for lack of a better word).

Literalism often seeks to uphold the "letter" so tightly that it ironically misses the "spirit." The best aspect of this position asserts that the

---

13. Ruether, *Sexism and God-Talk*, 20.
14. Daly, *Beyond God the Father*, 10.
15. See for example, Johnson, *Abounding in Kindness*, particularly the essays "A Theological Case for Naming God She" and "Resurrection: Promise of the Future."

Bible prioritizes "he" and "Father" because this is the content of revelation. The notion that God reveals God's very self is certainly fundamental to the Christian faith. However, characteristic of literalism, there is often an emphasis on one detail that neglects others. A young-earth creationist will insist that Genesis 1 is a concrete, realistic description, but a creationist has to ignore details in the text of a flat, domed cosmology. Similarly, a literalization of God as Father often downplays or ignores how the Bible uses motherly language in an analogical fashion along with fatherly language, as will be shown in a later chapter. Literalism, ironically, misses a lot of what the Bible says and how it says it.

If the Bible is the word of God, as it is a witness to Christ, where the Spirit speaks through it to proclaim salvation and equip Christlike action (as the biblical writers attested to hearing), the question of whether the Bible can contain corrupted texts, texts tainted by patriarchy, is a notion that is often quickly dismissed. The Bible has been used to suppress women, an abuse that has a constituent and long history. Thus, as Bloesch humbly admits, with any attempt to hold the conservative approach to Scripture must come the terrible admission that authority has been easily misused.[16] While Christians do not believe in the Bible so much as they believe in Jesus *through* the Bible, central to the Christian faith is the authority of the Bible and its role in conveying the subjects of concern to the Christian faith. However, any doctrine of the Bible has to take into account the history of its pervasive misuse by those who hold its statements as revelatory and inspired. The existence of "dark" texts is a recalcitrant fact that anyone who holds to the authority of the canon must recognize. It is possible to merely blame the abuse on irresponsible interpreters, but that only goes so far. One scholar pointed out that if Scripture is accommodated to an ancient world to any significant degree, then how Scripture is an inspired authority must be nuanced in ways evangelical theology has often failed to do.[17] One does not need to go any further than Jesus' own description of divorce laws as evidence of aspects of the Bible being accommodated to fallenness: "Moses permitted you to divorce your wives because your hearts were hard" (Matt 19:8). If Scripture reflects its culture, then Scripture cannot be straightforwardly appealed to as a timeless authority, where its statements are always and immediately applicable. Most interpreters know this intuitively in many

---

16. Bloesch, *Battle for the Trinity*, 65.
17. See Boyd, *Inspired Imperfection*.

matters, whether it is head coverings or cosmology, but the question is whether something as cherished as the language of God as Father is content directly revealed from heaven or a notion that finds its meaning in the conventions of patriarchy (or passages around headship and submission in marriage). That possibility is unsettling for some (the truth of the matter is more complicated, as it will be explored).

On the other side, there is a persistent tendency to downplay the authority of the Bible and realistic accounts of revelation. The notion that Scripture is rife with male language for God warrants, in this estimate, a sort of correcting or bypassing of it, seeing the Bible not as revelation or in any realistic sense as the word of God.[18] Rosemary Radford Ruether defines revelation in highly experiential terms: "By revelatory, we mean breakthrough experiences beyond ordinary fragmented consciousness that provide interpretive symbols illuminating the means of the whole of life."[19] Ruether states that her interpretive principle entails that only those aspects of the biblical text that are useful to women's liberation are authoritative, the rest are to be "set aside and rejected."[20] Hers is a prophetic and iconoclastic approach that turns on the Bible's language and goes beyond it. McFague states that the "authority of the Bible is the authority of a classic poetic text."[21] Furthermore, she says, "The Bible as a model can never *be* the word of God, can never capture the ways of God."[22] Fiorenza's approach holds to the dignity of women and the experience of liberation as central, which she sees as a facet of the kingdom of God in Scripture (Fiorenza, however, calls it the "basileia" vision of Jesus to avoid male language).[23] From that vantage point, she sees a feminist approach as using that liberating biblical kernel to critique the rest. Feminist biblical scholarship holds to that experiential and liberating core and, from there, engages in an interpretive pursuit to expose the influence of patriarchy even within the canon. While exposing patriarchy, a feminist hermeneutic listens and remembers lost or suppressed voices of women in the Bible and Christian tradition, empowering women today

---

18. See Schneiders, "The Bible and Feminism." She argues for a "metaphorical" account of the Bible as the word of God as central to feminist biblical interpretation in general.

19. Ruether, *Sexism and God-Talk*, 13.

20. Ruether, *Sexism and God-Talk*, 23.

21. McFague, *Metaphorical Theology*, 59.

22. McFague, *Metaphorical Theology*, 62.

23. Fiorenza, *In Memory of Her*, 118–30.

for emancipatory action. So, some hold to a highly de-particularized understanding of revelation and the Bible, while others do so less. While all critical scholars need to consider the patriarchal influences on the writers of the Bible and even the canon of Scripture, the worry here is this: If revolution cuts off revelation, does it not also cut off its own roots?

The worry is that if the Bible reflects aspects of the culture of patriarchy that surrounded it, how does a person know whether or not it is infected all the way through? If it is infected, what is left, and how does one tell the difference? These are valid questions. If the language of the Bible is thoroughly de-actualized, without a definite claim to revelation, metaphorical language has the potential to slip into a projection of the human mind onto God, as Feuerbach accused theists of doing. Nietzsche once argued that morality was nothing more than the disadvantaged in society trying to manipulate the powerful into giving in to them. "Slave morality," he called it, and he thought that such pity was misplaced. Equality between all people, whether between men and women—and he clearly thought men were superior—or between the less capable and the more, whoever that might be, served to disadvantage those truly exceptional from achieving their true potential.[24] Is he correct? If not, on what basis does all human life, regardless of gender (or race or status), have dignity and count as worthy of emancipation? If the writings of Scripture come completely out of the conventions of their time, whether or not one should care, let alone sacrifice for the dignity of another, is a matter of preference, perspective, or pragmatics. When it comes to the Bible, why one image is prioritized over another can potentially come down to one person's vision of liberation over another. The fact that someone like Jordan Peterson's highly hierarchical and male-dominant understanding of society is seen as appealing to many shows that liberation without realism of revelation can end up being perspectival and preferential and is at risk of devolving into Nietzschean self-assertion rather than the more counter-intuitive task of self-renunciation, compassion, and solidarity. If John Piper's vision of a male, all-powerful God is indeed an accurate portrayal of the God of the Bible, the God who will save his elect, isn't resisting this all-determining God futile? The meaning of gendered language cannot rest on function alone, for the criteria for the success of action are divergent. In fact, positing the effectiveness of one's own metaphor for God based on one's own preference of functional language, as McFague

---

24. For an overview on Nietzsche's dislike for notions like human dignity and equality, see Gushee, *The Sacredness of Human Life*, ch. 8.

admits, "is obviously something of a circular argument,"[25] which she sees as inevitable. Yet this is at times what Sallie McFague seems to admit of her own radically metaphorical approach: "I do not know who God is," she writes, "but I find some models [that is complex presentations of metaphors like mother, lover, and friend] better than others."[26] Some metaphors for love do not speak of a real concept of love but "project a possibility: that God's love can be seen through the screen of these human loves." She says in her treatment of the story of Christ: "Does this mean that each age reads into the story what it needs to, what it must, in order to make it speak to the deepest crises of its own time? Perhaps."[27] Without a trustworthy claim to revelation, measures of function can be nothing more than subjective projection. This is, ironically, not practical.

There are lots of forms of "liberal" theology today, some quite stimulating and insightful, but there are also unproductive forms that seek to undermine (or at the very least fail to uphold, or bypass) a robust sense of the place of revelation and Scripture, imposing what seem to be concerns foreign to the biblical narrative upon theology. Some approaches to God as "Mother" are this kind of liberalism.[28] Nevertheless, what must be asked is whether there is a consistent account of Scripture and its contents—both its passages of emancipation and its "dark" passages that have been used to abuse—that is constant with Christianity's central claims about itself as Christians have reflected on the nature of faith over the centuries. Donald Bloesch rightly worries that if the core of Christianity is lost, its redemptive potential is lost, too. Where Christians have re-symbolized their faith to match their culture, it is here that Christian faith is often so historically diluted that it lacks the capacity to critique political ideologies.[29]

25. McFague, *Models for God*, 192n37.
26. McFague, *Models for God*, 192n37.
27. McFague, *Models of God*, 49.
28. It should be noted that some versions of feminism are quite critical of liberal political discourses that treat man and women as generically the same, emphasizing individual equality without social equity. In that regard, theological liberalism, as a very broad category for all theologies that use methodological foundations based on independent reason and experience, is different from political liberalism.
29. Bloesch offers the example of Nazi Germany, where Christianity was resymbolized in line with Germanic culture. The concern is correct, but Bloesch's example is surely more extreme than feminism. Feminism is not Nazism. Another example is Americanism where American white nationalism has glossed the Bible. Again, the concern is correct, but feminism seeks to liberate oppressed people, where white nationalism seeks to keep people suppressed. Bloesch, *Battle for the Trinity*, 69–82.

While the primary concern of Christian feminism is to uphold the dignity of women as bearers of God's image, same as men, and in this regard, all Christians should be broadly feminist, there are forms that are not concerned with being authentic to Christian faith or the kind of descriptions the Christian community attempts of itself and its narratives. This, admittedly, will look very different depending on which ecclesial community one is a part of. This discussion will look very different in Canadian Baptist churches or the Baptist Union of Great Britain, where neither the literalism of biblical inerrancy nor motions against women in ministry have succeeded, as opposed to the Southern Baptist Convention. It will look very different in Anglicanism than in Roman Catholicism. This will look very different for Free Church traditions that have autonomous churches that choose their own ways of worship by congregational vote than in high church traditions, where the liturgy is decided by a hierarchical body. However, then, it should also be noted that some theological institutions and communities have made decisions that exclude women's voices and suppress viable criticisms of the community's convictions. In this regard, some feminist criticism of certain convictions asserts that these exclusions are inherent to the structure of Christian discourse and thus, in doing so, ironically, concede their own marginalization as coherent to that discourse. Mary Daly notably left Christianity, deeming it inherently patriarchal.[30] This is not rhetorically effective, especially if it is not true. The fact that women have been suppressed in this way, however, is even more tragic, and it is incumbent on all Christians to work against it.

When revelation is literalized and liberation accommodated, more sophisticated ways of discerning Christian speech are needed, which uphold both the inspiration of Scripture as well as the task of safeguarding the dignity of all people against oppressive forces like patriarchy.

THE NEED FOR A DEEPER GRAMMAR

Both approaches require a deeper "grammar." It is through a grammatical approach that the concerns of revelation and liberation are best integrated, particularly in the typological forms of interpretation of Christian Scripture.

---

30. Daly, *Beyond God the Father*, xii. She describes later in the book the coming revolution of women "as anti-Christ and its import as anti-church," 140.

In linguistics, grammar delineates the constraints that allow language to be meaningful in structure and composition. Grammar includes morphology (how words are formed), syntax (how words are arranged meaningfully), and phonology (how language forms sound). Grammar is closely related to phonetics (the study of how linguistic sound is made and perceived) as well as semantics (how words generate meaning, reference, and offer truth) and pragmatics (how context contributes to meaning). The philosopher Ludwig Wittgenstein said in one of his philosophical aphorisms, "Grammar tells us what kind of object anything is. (Theology as grammar)."[31] Wittgenstein spoke of "surface grammar" that merely renders words coherent on the page. For example, one thinks of the rules that govern whether to use the indefinite article "a" or "an." But in philosophy, Wittgenstein saw some arguments only resolvable by appeal to the "deep grammar." These are the deeper principles of meaningfulness that structure a discourse in the midst of life. Wittgenstein noted that propositional statements find their fuller meanings in their forms of life, and this necessarily completes the assessment of what this deeper grammar truly is and means.[32]

The theologian George Lindbeck went further to suggest that doctrines functioned like rules and could be clarified similarly. He called his approach the "cultural-linguistic" approach, suggesting faith language functioned like a cultural language, enveloping the speaker like the water a fish swims in, providing the means for Christians to function in the world. Christian doctrine is a form of speech, but in order for it to be meaningful as *Christian* speech, according to this analogy, theology assesses statements with grammar to see if something is spoken well.

Doctrines in conservative and liberal theology generally follow two schemes, as Lindbeck pointed out, which both, while not entirely wrong, are deficient in making sense of the diversity of theological statements and the holistic nature of the language itself. One he saw as cognitive-propositional and the other as an experiential-expressive approach; both have problems that appear in this debate. Conservative approaches use a highly "cognitive-propositional" approach, where statements are timeless, universal, purely referential, and, thus, often conflict at face value. Scripture and tradition yield a diversity of statements. While theological statements do make correspondent claims to reality, Lindbeck wanted

---

31. Wittgenstein, *Philosophical Investigations*, Book I: §373.
32. See Wittgenstein, *Philosophical Investigations*, Book I: §111, 112, 373.

to point out that often doctrines between, for instance, Lutherans and Roman Catholics, would be worded in such a way that put them in antithesis to each other but were not all that different at all in ostensive reference. For example, in ecumenical discussions, arguments over transubstantiation versus consubstantiation views of the Eucharist can notoriously shed blood over semantics all to, in essence, largely agree. In this regard, Lindbeck felt that offering a "deep grammar" of a doctrinal problem could help build consensus between the particular views and see the proverbial forest through the trees.

Scripture norms Christian speech about God, but how one brings together biblical statements is less than straightforward sometimes, and this is why "grammatical" reflection is important. For instance, the statement in theology that "the Father is greater than I" (John 14:28) is found in the Bible, attributed to Jesus, but has been used often to appropriate a problematic Christology, if "greater" is taken in a way to reflect on the full deity and consubstantial nature of the Son with the Father. Here, the statement is biblical in *some* way, but its *usage* often is not. Lindbeck recommended three Christological rules to govern statements about Jesus: (1) statements about Jesus had to conform to Jewish monotheism, (2) statements of Jesus must refer to the historical person, and (3) there is a "Christological maximalism" where every possible importance is ascribed to him that coincides with these other two rules.[33] By this, the unique historical and human identity of Jesus is upheld, but also the high Christology that sees Jesus as the fulfillment and embodiment of Israel's God in the flesh. The Father's greatness is typically viewed as Jesus' humility and obedience to the mission the Father has given while still being fully equal to the Father: "I and the Father are one" (John 10:30). Jesus is "very human and very God," and the two natures need to be reflected upon to understand how both are properly upheld. There is a vital interpretive function that theology places in making sense of how and why the Bible says what it says. In the history of theology, words like "begotten" had to be clarified so that they spoke well of the realities to which they pointed. Referring to the first member of the Trinity as "Father," for instance, while biblically accurate, had various conceptual misuses if that was taken to mean that, literally, the Father was causally or temporally prior to the Son.

Regarding the present investigation, two statements like "God is Father" and "God is Mother" at face value contradict, but if the biblical

---

33. Lindbeck, *Nature of Doctrine*, 94.

canon functions like a dictionary or glossary of the Christian way of speaking (or better yet, a kind of grammatical guidebook, showing the patterns and concerns that govern Christian speech), then a Christian speaker may employ both meaningfully and faithfully in different ways. The rules and contexts of usage would be central, however. This approach has been taken, although not by name, by those who do not see female or motherly language as normative. For example, Richard Briggs's insightful article delineates three aspects to the language: what the Bible says, what the Bible says in historical context (in other words, where and how it says it), and, most importantly for this study, what the *Bible could allow one to say*.[34]

On the other hand, liberals, as Lindbeck criticized, tend toward a highly "experiential-expressive" notion of theological language. In this regard, some liberal theology treated religious language as so functional and non-referential that in interreligious dialogues, Buddhist nirvana could be abstractly considered the same thing as Christian salvation. This really does not take into account how the language of Christian faith structures and constructs experience and does not merely express realities.[35] Thus, Lindbeck recommends the notion that doctrine functions as "communally authoritative rules of discourse, attitude, and action."[36] For example, a moment of intellectual epiphany can be psychologically similar to the moment of conversion, but with the language of the gospel being heard and accepted, a conversion moment and a general moment of epiphany are not the same. Christian prayer may have very similar qualities to mindfulness techniques, but with obvious differences in that one is directed to God in relationship and the other is not. In that case, they are physically nearly identical, but they are doing different things based on the pattern of meaning they follow.

Lindbeck is concerned that an experiential-expressive approach also meant that the Bible would be subsumed into something other than the core of Christian faith. In liberal theology, certain epistemological criteria have been used to legitimate Christian faith in order to make it more credible to the modern world. While there is nothing wrong with apologetics done well, the result often has been to filter Christian faith into a schema that does not fit or cannot fully reckon with all of what biblical revelation claims to be about. While Christianity ought to offer

34. Briggs, "Gender and God-Talk."
35. Lindbeck, *Nature of Doctrine*, 37.
36. Lindbeck, *Nature of Doctrine*, 18.

clarification of what it believes, it is another thing to change Christianity for the purpose of clarification. This does not mean faith premises are immune from criticism or revision, but it does mean that what the Christian faith espouses is not based on what the world ultimately thinks. Lindbeck says, "Intratextual theology redescribes reality within the scriptural framework rather than translating Scripture into extra-scriptural categories. It is the text, so to speak, which absorbs the world, rather than the world the text."[37] This means Christianity is not trying to be necessarily traditional or progressive but to be faithful to what is authentically Christian, reformulating doctrine when needed while standing firm on the faith's center. As it will be shown in this book, Scripture offers its own criteria for evaluating theological judgments that allow believers to evaluate female figures and experiences and goals of liberation in ways that are germane to the Christian faith.

Lindbeck considered his approach "postliberal" in that he rejected both the conservative flatly propositional view and the liberal flatly functionalist or expressivist view. Language is much more complex than that, and there are certain complexities that must be appreciated for this investigation to continue further.

First is that there can be innovated convictions in the Christian faith that are not stated in Scripture but are faithful to Scripture's deeper grammar. There are some creedal statements—like referring to Jesus as "fully human and fully God" or as having "two natures in one person"—that are not found directly in the Bible but that Christians have found to be helpful encapsulations of Scripture's content such that they are even considered defining rules of orthodoxy. Anyone who is against new vocabulary beyond the Bible must contend with the fact that one of the achievements of orthodoxy is the development of a new philosophical vocabulary that reflected on Scripture productively in its time. The question today might be: To what degree is this language transferable to a world that is culturally very different? To deny that Christianity or Christian doctrine "changes" is not historically possible. However, what stays the same is important.

Second, to speak as a Christian is to inherit a tradition of familiarity, which one is called to take up potentially in new ways in order to be faithful to it. Tradition is the vehicle by which the word of God is faithfully passed along. The ongoing examples of ways Christians have sought

---

37. Lindbeck, *Nature of Doctrine*, 118.

to be faithful to the Bible's message are what comprises tradition. While some Protestants, for instance, do not consider tradition to be authoritative, most contemporary Protestants consider tradition in some way important for the understanding of how the historic church has received and transmitted the Bible and its core convictions.[38] If Christians hold that the Spirit has been at work in the church, while the church is not infallible, there ought to be a commitment that the work of revision will co-inside with what the church has in some way always believed everywhere (as Vincent of Lerins has suggested). In this regard, this project will note examples from church history, admitting them as evidence and suggestions for possibilities of Christian grammar. However, while there is a center that holds, most Christians take for granted that Christianity has, in fact, changed by often prophetic voices that believed deeply in its core in such a way as to call for change. For example, democracy is preferable to a theocratic monarchy, the scientific cosmology of a heliocentric universe is more evident than a geocentric one, and the complete abolition of slavery is a necessary moral good. All of these are examples of revisions that are often taken for granted. The Bible, in the time of its writing, does not hold to these things, but its principles certainly suggest the compatibility of these advances with what Christianity is all about. It is not *whether* scientific discoveries or philosophical-cultural achievements can augment the Christian faith; it is really the question of how it can be done *right* so that what is truly central to Christianity is preserved. When there is a cultural amelioration like the civil rights movement or a discovery like heliocentrism, these are things that Christians have participated in, and thus, these revisions were not external to the church as if to say the church's culture and society's culture have no overlap.

This poses significant questions for the relationship of men and women and how one speaks of God. Fatherhood meant something more in ancient times than today, just as women's social mobility is very different today than before. How do these affect Christian speech in a way that holds to the core concerns of Scripture? As Luce Irigaray has noted in her linguistic studies (in this case, French-speaking subjects), masculine

---

38. See Grenz and Franke, *Beyond*, ch. 4. The authors define the role of tradition as follows: "The Christian tradition is comprised of the historical attempts by the Christian community to explicate and translate faithfully the first-order language, symbols, and practices of the Christian faith, arising from the inner-action among community, text, and culture, into the various social and culture contexts in which that community has been situated" (118).

vocabulary affected the female-speaking subject and her agency.[39] This leads Irigaray to conclude that a feminine language is necessary for female liberation. Certainly, when one looks at Scripture, one sees an overwhelming majority of male references to God and human characters in the Bible. However, to think of the Christian faith as a language and Scripture as a book that offers the paradigms for this language, this project seeks to move between two strategies. The first strategy is to merely reiterate male language as exclusive, and the other is to do away with male language and replace it with female language. Instead, when one looks at the structures of language in the Bible, there is the possibility that one (such as Father language, the figure of Jesus Christ, etc.) offers space for the other (notable female and motherly language) in such a way that does not require purging or revising classic language. Rather, it opens up a space of liberty to use the others alongside.

Third, the practiced site of language is essential to its meaning. Wittgenstein wrote, "To obey a rule is to follow a practice."[40] For example, while a North American and a British person might have the same descriptions of cars, driving in the right-hand lane means decisively different things, as the rules of driving differ in cultural context. Thus, while doctrines make truth statements, in light of there being a plurality of statements, it is necessary to ask how their practical and contextual dimensions contribute to their meaning. In some cases, this contextual dimension resolves the difference, but in others, it demonstrates incommensurability. Surely, a Mormon and a Roman Catholic believe "in Jesus" is quite different ways, yet use the same words. Lindbeck gives the example that during the Crusades, the battle cry of the blood-thirsty Crusaders as they killed innocent Muslims was "*Christus est Dominus!*" ("Christ is Lord"). As a proposition, if a certain classic Christian meaning is the reference here, the statement is correct, but in the context of usage, if "Christ is Lord" implies that one ought to kill innocent lives, the usage means the phrase is incorrect.[41] The Lord that advocates the murder of innocent lives is not the same as the one identified by the Gospel narratives, despite the name being the same. Similarly, an interpretation or employment of the Christian language that results in women being demeaned, silenced, or oppressed is simply not a truly *Christian* use of that language, regardless of whether it is backed with proof texts. Understanding this

---

39. See Irigaray, *I Love to You*.
40. Wittgenstein, *Philosophical Investigations*, I:200.
41. Lindbeck, *Nature of Doctrine*, 64.

means that one can be "biblical" (in the sense of backing one's theology with Scripture) while failing to be centrally Christlike, the very concern that Scripture implores. This aspect makes speaking about God as Father (or Mother) particularly tricky, as it necessarily begs a question: What *kind* of Father? And, what does this mean when *practiced*?

Fourth, often neglected in doctrinal discussion, is the affective or emotive dimension of a statement.[42] Why can, for example, a church meeting on what color to paint the foyer potentially erupt into shouting matches when technically no issues of orthodoxy are being contested? A simple assertion like "The foyer should be painted blue" can be a front for deeper convictions concerning what a church ought to be, how the church needs to grow, and how the church honors its past. There are often highly personal, sentimental, and emotive dimensions to a statement, which can mean critiquing it can constitute for the person who espouses the conviction nothing short of a personal attack on their identity. If something as relatively banal as the color of a foyer can do this, something like examining racial or gender prejudice will surely do so in more visceral ways. Talking about these subjects will quickly reveal highly subconscious and subterranean convictions, for some never put into words but existing connotatively behind what, for example, a "safe" neighborhood as opposed to a "shady" neighborhood looks like or what an "authoritative" leader ought to look like, etc. Theology must name these affective dimensions to verbalize them and to allow them to be assessed by our deepest convictions of faith (and to realize that sometimes our deepest convictions of faith can be inadvertently formed and intertwined with them). Similarly, even considering the notion of female God-language will make some people uncomfortable or even cause them to erupt. This may be nothing to do with "what the Bible says," even for a self-described devout believer. For what is "feminine" or "masculine" may take on a host of connotations based on past memories or aspects the believer has taken as part of their identity. Is female language avoided because of negative connotations about femininity, a view that the female is "weaker" or that the female body is tainted somehow, or is the female associated with hurts or frustrations someone has had in their love life, etc.? Thus, for the present investigation, if Christianity does hold to the dignity of men and women and to the eradication of those things that

---

42. James McClendon (with James M. Smith) have used speech-act theory to note that there are affective conditions of speech that are important to consider if a conviction is to be successful or problematic, see *Convictions: Defusing Religious Relativism*, 59.

have obstructed that equality, whether personal or systemic, any employment of Christian language that generates a form of life that harms women or sees men as superior, should obviously be exposed and rethought, but such an exercise is admittedly not easy. One must be attentive to the *affective* side of doctrine, even though it so often is like an iceberg, living largely under the surface.

Fifth, the scriptural grammar commands actions like listening to the experiences of others, such as women, as integral to following scriptural commands to love. In other words, Scripture and experience ought not to be taken as at loggerheads. It is important to reiterate why gendered experience is important for theology. Pamela Dickey Young offers good nuance in this regard in stating that "women's experience" means several things for theology: (1) women's bodies are different from men's (thus, care for both will be different); (2) women's social experience is sadly characterized by both submission of women to men and sexual objectification of women by men; (3) there are experiences of direct oppression and harm based on gender (thus understanding these dynamics will be central to following God's will to overcome them); (4) women's historical experience is often "lost" or suppressed (thus, a fuller account of the church involves listening to these voices); finally, in culmination, (5) women's experiences, all of the data from the preceding points, can thus be the catalyst for social change.[43] Scripture cannot be read without experience. (The idea that it can be is a modern assumption that is simply inhuman.) Scripture is always read from a particular social location and read through paradigmatic experiences (such as the event of conversion, experiences of oppression, etc.). Experience, as we have said, is fallible and ambiguous at times, but is meaningful as it is brought into conversation with Scripture and configured, allowing the person to see their life in relationship to God. Thus, listening to the Bible can only be done by listening to others as well. One cannot treat another in a Christlike way if one refuses to hear the various ways one might have neglected to do so.

Sixth, it also must be appreciated that Christian language is highly fallible.[44] Nothing about Christian faith makes a human any less fallible, and there is nothing about the Christian faith that makes the Christian less human. Christian faith has sometimes been invoked to find an infallible pattern of life or a certain set of ideas. While there are practices of

---

43. Young, *Feminist Theology/Christian Theology*, 53–56. Serene Jones offers similar criteria in *Feminist Theory and Christian Theology*, 1–22.

44. McClendon, *Doctrine*, 33.

the Christian faith that are virtuous and ideas that have stood the test of time as trustworthy, grounded on the figures of Scripture, this does not mean the Christian has surmounted fallibility, nor does it mean that these ideas, interpretations, and practices can never be modified or perverted. Thus, there is fallibility in the act of believing that must be considered. Disciples with even the best intentions can get things wrong. Nor does every correct belief terminate in the right action. Jesus warned the Pharisees, quoting the prophet Isaiah, "They honor me with their lips, but their hearts are far from me" (Matt 15:8). There is a perennial danger that orthodoxy on paper does not result in an orthopraxy in life. While factuality must always determine functionality, there is a big difference between those who believe in all right things and those who believe in the right way.

Lastly, central to this investigation is the possibility that the Christian language is governed by multiple schemas of grammar, and one set of rules can actually result in more than one way of saying things. A word like "love" or a symbol like water can have layers of rich connotations. Love can remind people of both the most ecstatic and joyful times of their lives as well as the most painful, just as water has the power both to sustain life or destroy it. If Scripture contains more than one pathway of referring to God and more than one way words have meaningfulness, a grammatical analysis can aid us not in recommending a definite answer so much as prescribing limits and goals by which different articulations can be performed better. Reflecting on the full extent of the Christian religion will admit a kind of bounded pluralism where, as Eugene Rogers notes, its language will then provide a space of disagreement.[45] Thus, words like "Father" or "Mother" might not have as straightforward references or usages as the dichotomy of conservative and feminist seem to suggest. However, as the following reflection on the rules of Christian discourse will show, all Christian grammar manifests a convergence in Jesus Christ.

One can imagine that taking a grammatical approach can, in some way, be disagreeable to both conservatives and feminists. A conservative may dismiss this exercise and go with their own proof texts or toe the party line of their church tradition. Many grant possibilities of female language in theory but shy away from practice because it will rock the proverbial boat of their church. Such methodological analysis like this

---

45. Rogers, *Essentials of Christian Thought*, 7.

might be perceived as just a way of making them question what they do not want to question. Meanwhile, a feminist might roll their eyes at this technical deliberation when the answer might be experientially obvious. Daly once said, "One of the false gods of theologians, philosophers, and other academics is called Method."[46] Some have retreated into Scripture from the world in the hope of finding a place where all things are clear and black and white; some retreat from Scripture into the realm of pragmatism in the hope that things are obvious and evident. By contrast, this project reflects an appreciation that both Scripture and human experience are beautifully multifaceted.

Baptist theologian James McClendon writes, "Our task is not only to clarify the grammar of faith but to furnish a tongue-tied world with language adequate to Christ's presence in its midst."[47] So, likening theology to grammar has been a way of commenting on the capacity of doctrine to do several things: structure and norm religious speech and practice, interpret and construct experience, and correctly discern the interplay of fallibility and innovation. Each of these is important for the task of this investigation as they attempt to speak well of the mystery of the infinite love shown in Jesus Christ in a deeply complex world.

CONCLUSION

So what exactly is a name, grammatically speaking? This is not straightforwardly answered. While there are "proper names" like "Jesus" or "Yahweh," there are lots of other words that name God in a secondary sense, such as the general word "God" or "El," titles like "El Shaddai" or "Christ," qualities such as "Being" itself or "Goodness,"[48] and still others that do not fit neatly into any category, like Jesus being called "Immanuel." Are names arbitrary (or merely aesthetic, as in today's culture), or are they irreducibly particular (and thus irreplaceable)? Or are names in the biblical narrative indicative of a certain denotation?[49] It seems that biblical names carried an important denotative function. Even a proper name

---

46. Daly, *Beyond God the Father*, 11.

47. McClendon, *Doctrine*, 430.

48. In that regard, Janet Soskice has advocated the recovery of the traditions of naming God based on different titles and attributes. This is different from "proper names," a distinction in this project since that is what is in question in regards to the identity of, for instance, the first member of the Trinity. See Soskice, *Naming God*.

49. Grenz, *The Named God and the Question of Being*, 271–80.

like "Jesus" (which is, of course, not culturally accurate, as it is actually "Yēshu") carried the connotation of being a Joshua-like savior figure, saving Israel. Is "Father" a name, a title, a metaphor, or a symbol? In some sense, it can be all of these. Can a name be unisex? One of the oddities of the conservative position is the insistence that "Father" be understood as a name that transcends gender but nevertheless insists on pronoun usage that is specifically gendered. What this book seeks to show is that there are multiple pathways by which God is named, or at least spoken of, that do not replace the proper names "Yahweh" and "Jesus." This aids us in understanding masculine and father language as well as permitting female and mother language, as both are holistically understood through the various grammars that offer deeper meaning to the divine identity.

When the grammar that structures Christian discourse about God is analyzed, one will see that its language has layers that fill out the two sides of the Bible and liberation. This investigation takes its starting place in the canon of Scripture and the dignity of human beings, assuming these two criteria are not ultimately locked in a zero-sum game. It begins by looking at ineffability and negation but supplements these with the rules for analogy and metaphor, then takes all of these and shows how they come to fuller meaningfulness in narrative. Narratives in Scripture find their fulfillment typologically in the incarnation, cross, and resurrection of Jesus Christ. Thus, the grammar moves from the structures and operations that govern speech to the figural themes of what Christians speak about. Furthermore, Christ cannot be properly understood without the witness of the first and third members of the Trinity. These figures are studied from Scripture, praised in worship, and followed in ministry; each of these practices orient the conditions of speech. These together form a holistic account of speaking of God.

2

Ineffability and Idolatry

THE FIRST APPROACH IN clarifying the grammar of gendered speech about God might be called "apophatic" (which means "negation"). The rule might be stated as follows: all discourse about God must recognize that God is transcendent and ineffable, therefore, names and other ways of speaking about God must be "negated" to prevent misconception. That is to say, for instance, if God is powerful, God's power is so beyond human comprehension that we must say God is *not* powerful (at least not in the way a finite mind is prone to thinking about power). What does this mean for speaking about God as Father (or Mother)? On either side of this debate, the ineffability of God is upheld, but in different ways. So, the task of this chapter is to analyze the ways Scripture and Christians have talked about God's ineffability and how these relate to revelation and the threat of idolatry.

COMPETING MEANINGS OF INEFFABILITY AND THE THREAT OF IDOLATRY

As stated, proponents of male-exclusive language (usually conservative voices) and female-inclusive language (usually feminist voices) appeal to these notions in two different ways.

Conservatives appeal to ineffability and transcendence to assert that God is beyond gender, but nevertheless, through realistic revelation, God is usually to be spoken of in exclusively male terms. This influences mentalities; for instance, the Southern Baptist Convention's resolution in 1992 states, "God is beyond human gender . . . [but] has uniquely and explicitly revealed Himself to us as Father."[1] T. F. Torrance takes a more developed route, arguing that the ineffability and transcendence of God become the basis of the authority of God to authorize speech regardless of human offense, for if God is transcendent, without the words that God reveals who God is in God's very self, nothing is known. Therefore, the revealed words are all the church can say.[2]

Now, when one looks at the scholarly literature, one will see also that there is strong resistance to mystical accounts of ineffability in Barthian scholars (a point to be explored shortly). Yet Eastern Orthodox theology, for instance, would not have the same prejudice and would be shocked to think mysticism and Scripture were somehow incompatible. Nevertheless, there are those that delineate ineffability differently, some arguing against the inclusion of female language and others for. Thomas Hopko looks at several early church thinkers (such as Dionysius) and states that while God's being is ineffable and thus "supraessential" in God's transcendence, the trinitarian names are not negated in apophatic theology. They flow from this "supraessential" and "supragood" quality and not from the essence and goodness of the world. Hopko writes, "For the mysterious Dionysius, the supraessential, supradivine, supragood Divinity whose nature is beyond all names and includes them all in God the Father with his only begotten Son and Word, and his most holy Spirit."[3] He goes on to say,

> Orthodox theological and liturgical texts unanimously affirm the conviction that the three divine hypostases of the Godhead, with their proper names of Father, Son, and Holy Spirit, are not subject to apophatic qualification as are all metaphysical properties and metaphorical images attributed to God's essence.[4]

Attributes cannot be negated with their opposite (so Father cannot be negated with Mother): "The Holy Trinity admits no opposites or contraries to itself."[5] Hopko's account warrants a further look at Dionysius.

---

1. Thus reads the Southern Baptist Convention's resolution. See "SBC Executive Committee Revision of Report of Committee on Resolutions."
2. Torrance, "The Christian Apprehension of God the Father," 121.
3. Hopko, "Apophatic Theology a," 156.
4. Hopko, "Apophatic Theology," 158.
5. Hopko, "Apophatic Theology," 150.

Meanwhile, some feminists have used ineffability to emphasize the radical transcendence of God from all language and knowing. Thus, McFague writes, "no language about God is adequate,"[6] and thus, religious language applies "only to our existence, not God's."[7] This is important for later chapters as McFague argues that all forms of literal language about God are idolatrous.[8] McFague likens her project to the work of negative theology. She sees her project as having much in common with Jacque Derrida's philosophy of deconstruction, criticizing "our nostalgia for Presence." She writes further,

> The desire for full presence, whether in the form of nostalgia for the garden of Eden, or the quest for the historical Jesus, or the myths of God incarnate, is a denial of what we know as adults to be the case in human existence such innocence, certainty, and absoluteness is not possible. . . . This is not a completely new insight . . . for a long tradition of negative theology has accompanied the tradition of presence.[9]

In metaphor, a figure of speech vital to this discussion that will be taken up next chapter, McFague sees a kind of interplay between the "is and is not" that is similar to positive and negative theologies, with what seems to be a gradual accentuation of the "is not" through her project. This is taken to the point where in her later book, *Models for God*, McFague seems to indicate that any revealed realism is also problematic, leaving language about God potentially agnostic. Sallie McFague writes,

> I do not know who God is. . . . God is and remains a mystery. We really do not know: the hints and clues we have of the way things are—whether we call them experiences, revelation, or whatever—are too fragile, too little (and more often than not, too negative) for much more than a hypothesis, a guess, a projection of a possibility that, although it can be comprehensive and illuminating, may not be true. We can believe it is and act as if it were, but it is, to use Ricoeur's time, a "wager." . . .[10]

One can clearly see an extreme account of transcendence and ineffability that is so total as to refuse possibilities of imminence in revelation.

6. McFague, *Models of God*, 35.
7. McFague, *Models of God*, 39.
8. McFague, *Metaphorical Theology*, 4.
9. McFague, *Models of God*, 25.
10. McFague, *Models of God*, 192–93n37.

However, it must be noted that there are other accounts of ineffability in feminist theology. Elizabeth Johnson states agreement with McFague's feminist project, but she is much more self-conscious to argue that her theology is in line with what the church has consistently held about God's ineffability:[11]

> No human concept, word, or image, all of which originate in the experience of created reality, can circumscribe the divine reality, nor can any human construct express with any measure of adequacy the mystery of God, who is ineffable. This situation is due not to some reluctance on the part of God to self-reveal in a full way, nor to the sinful condition of the human race making reception of such a revelation impossible, nor even to our contemporary mentality of skepticism in religious matters. Rather, it is proper to God as God to transcend all direct similarity to creatures, and thus never to be known comprehensively or essentially as God.... It would be a serious mistake to think that God's self-revelation through powerful acts and inspired words in the Jewish tradition and through the history and destiny of Jesus Christ which give rise to the Christian tradition, removes the ultimate unknowability of God.[12]

She continues in her book, *She Who Is*:

> The holiness and utter transcendence of God present throughout all creation has always been an absolutely central affirmation of the Jewish tradition and its grafted branch, Christian faith. God as God, ground, support, and goal of all, is the illimitable mystery who, while immanently present, cannot be measured, manipulated, or controlled.[13]

Johnson builds her account of ineffability using Scripture and Christian tradition in conjunction with feminist concerns. She continues on to argue that this essential ineffability and incompressibility applies to "all names"[14] as an implication of God, revealing that God's essence is "I Am that I Am" (Exod 3:14).

---

11. One should note that this is also the starting point for some feminists, such as Johnson, *She Who Is*, 105.
12. Johnson, "The Incomprehensibility of God," 441.
13. Johnson, *She Who Is*, 104.
14. Johnson, *She Who Is*, 113.

If Johnson is correct, she is giving a resolute reading of the apophatic tradition in negating male imagery as idolatry of God, which has a correlation to the harm of others, particularly women. She writes,

> The experience of women today provides a powerful catalyst for reclaiming this classic wisdom as an ally in emancipating speech about God. Feminist critique of patriarchal discourse is surfacing the false assumptions that underlie insistence on exclusively male symbols.... God can be pointed to in symbols shaped by women's reality.... Not doing so has allowed one set of symbols to become a block to the remembrance of the incomprehensible mystery of God.[15]

Johnson states, "Use of 'God-She' immediately indicates the inherent inadequacy of 'God-He.'"[16] Thus, the mystical is appropriated to counter patriarchal language as she sees it.

However, one should note that there is a concern for idolatry on the conservative side as well. If God has revealed God's very self in a certain way, to make an image based on preference and then to project it onto God would be, by definition, idolatry. Elizabeth Achtemeier states,

> The feminists, believing themselves divine, think that by their own power, they can restructure society, restore creation, and overcome suffering. But the tortured history of humanity testifies to what human beings do when they think they are a law unto themselves with no responsibility to God.[17]

Thus, the worry for idolatry goes in both directions. Both referring to God as Father and referring to God as Mother can fall into a kind of Feuerbachian slip if the grammar of revelation is not clarified. If Johnson is correct, what can be made of Hopko's assertion that the name of the Father cannot be negated?

What is characteristic of feminist negations is the usage of counter-images, while conservatives seek to reiterate a non-patriarchal meaning of male language. Which is the desired strategy? To answer this question, the ineffability of God and the possibility of the negation of names must be clarified.

---

15. Johnson, *She Who Is*, 112.
16. Johnson, "The Incomprehensibility of God," 444.
17. Achtemeier, "Exchanging God for 'No Gods,'" 16. Achtemeier makes this accusation against Dorothee Solle, who speaks of God manifested within, but then uses this as a blanket condemnation of all feminism.

GOD'S INEFFABILITY IN SCRIPTURE AND TRADITION

Scripture bears the revelation of God; that is, it preserves stories, accounts of events, and messages of revelation, and it functions to convey that revelation to others. The content of the Bible upholds that God is ineffable, which Christian tradition has attested to. There are a number of ways Christian discourse is "mystical" that are linked together: God's transcendence over creation, the essence of God revealed in the divine name, as well as God's incomparability, beauty, hiddenness, and silence. These can be seen in both the Old and New Testaments, and, as we will see, themes from these appear in major theologians, who offer important insights into this discussion.

This dynamic, however, goes back to the very beginning, as God is the Creator of all things, and therefore, if God is the Creator at the beginning, God cannot be reduced to the creation in any sense that prevents God from being God.

The central text of God's ineffability is Exod 3:14. Moses is called to the burning bush and asks what God's name is. In the ancient world, knowing a god's name was a way of invoking it in incantations to placate the god in one's favor. Yet the voice out of the burning bush answers, "I Am who I Am." While the meaning of the name has many interpretations, commentators agree that this speaks of a liberty of being that cannot be reduced to a name like other gods: unlike them, this God simply is who God is. This name mirrors the action of God, who is later described as having "mercy on whom I shall have mercy" (Exod 33:19) when Israel disobeyed and made idols. Thus, Exodus provides important clues to the meaning of both ineffability and idolatry.

Similarly, the *Shema*, the prayer of Israel, "Hear O Israel, the Lord your God the Lord is One" (Deut 6:4), has received mystical interpretations. This prayer is a repudiation of polytheism and, in doing so, a repudiation of any reduction of God to the humanly projected pantheon. If God is truly one, God is a unity without limitation, composition, or division, and thus, God is beyond all things.

Throughout Scripture, God is described in terms that resist reduction to language, concepts, or images. God's form cannot be seen (Deut 4:12), and this explicitly resists God being reduced to any image:

> Since you saw no form when the LORD spoke to you at Horeb out of the fire, take care and watch yourselves closely so that you do not act corruptly by making an idol for yourselves in the form of any figure—the likeness of male or female, the likeness of any animal that is on the earth, the likeness of any winged bird that flies in the air, the likeness of anything that creeps on the ground, the likeness of any fish that is in the water under the earth. (Deut 4:15–18)

While God is said to be light, other passages speak of God's transcendence being like darkness: "Then Solomon said, 'The LORD has said that he dwells in thick darkness'" (1 Kgs 8:12 cf. Pss 18:11; 97:2). God is incomparable: "To whom then will you liken God, or what likeness compare with him?" (Isa 40:18, cf. v. 25). God, in acts of salvation even, always possesses a mystical hiddenness: "Truly, you are a God who hides himself, O God of Israel, the Savior" (Isa 45;15). God's ways cannot be fathomed (Job 36:26). God's acts are awesome (e.g., Ps 47:2). While God reveals in words, as Elijah finds, God speaks in the "sound of sheer silence" (1 Kgs 19:12). God is the Holy One (holiness indicating God's difference and separation from human sin and human expectation), and this God is God and not a human being (Num 23:19; Hos 11:9)

In the New Testament, even with the incarnation of Jesus Christ as the "visible image of the invisible God," these descriptions do not disappear. For example, God dwells in "unapproachable light" (1 Tim 6:16). Paul prays, "How unsearchable are his judgments and how inscrutable his ways!" (Rom 11:33). This does not speak of a mysticism where revelation is obscured, but rather a mysticism whereby God reveals something definitive, and in so doing, God's goodness is so beautiful it renders the believer in awe.

Has the church, then, maintained the compatibility between mysticism and revelation? As one can see from the Christian tradition, this truth is upheld consistently by many in different ways. Justin Martyr maintained that God is nameless: "For no one can utter the name of the ineffable God; and if anyone dares to say that there is a name, he raves with a hopeless madness."[18] Clement of Alexandria spoke about God's unknowability and, thus, the need for God's revelation to be able to speak of God. He writes,

---

18. Justin Martyr, *First Apology*, ch. 61. This chapter deals with baptism and continues on to say that baptism is in the name of the Father, the name of Jesus, and the name of the Holy Spirit.

> This discourse respecting God is most difficult to handle. For since the first principle of everything is difficult to find out, the absolutely first and oldest principle, which is the cause of all other things being and having been, is difficult to exhibit. For how can that be expressed which is neither genus, nor difference, nor species, nor individual, nor number; nay more, is neither an event, nor that to which an event happens? No one can rightly express Him wholly. For on account of His greatness He is ranked as the All, and is the Father of the universe. Nor are any parts to be predicated of Him. For the One is indivisible; wherefore also it is infinite, not considered with reference to inscrutability, but with reference to its being without dimensions, and not having a limit. And therefore it is without form and name. And if we name it, we do not do so properly, terming it either the One, or the Good, or Mind, or Absolute Being, or Father, or God, or Creator, or Lord. We speak not as supplying His name; but for want, we use good names, in order that the mind may have these as points of support, so as not to err in other respects. For each one by itself does not express God; but all together are indicative of the power of the Omnipotent. For predicates are expressed either from what belongs to things themselves, or from their mutual relation. But none of these are admissible in reference to God. Nor is He apprehended anymore by the science of demonstration. For it depends on primary and better known principles. But there is nothing antecedent to the Unbegotten. It remains that we understand, then, the Unknown, by divine grace, and by the word alone that proceeds from Him.[19]

For Clement, names like Father and Lord are general titles common to religious discourses, which fall short of God's essence, and so, only the grace of Christ is the means of true knowledge. However, notice that Clement also uses masculine titles (Father, etc.) but sees them as inadmissible as references to God. He calls for a plurality of "good names" so that the mind has a point of reference. Basil writes against Eunomius that God's essence cannot be known and that God is known in God's activities or energies:

> We say that we know the greatness of God, His power, His wisdom, His goodness, His providence over us, and the justness of His judgment; but not His very essence.... For they confess themselves that there is a distinction between the essence and

19. Clement of Alexandria, *Stomata*, Book V: ch. 12.

> each one of the attributes enumerated. The operations are various, and the essence simple, but we say that we know our God from His operations, but do not undertake to approach near to His essence. His operations come down to us, but His essence remains beyond our reach....[20]

Basil's brother, Gregory of Nyssa, follows Basil in upholding this distinction. One could say that Nyssa deepens this. He comments in his book *The Life of Moses*,

> This is true knowledge of what is sought; this is the seeing that consists in not seeing, because that which is sought transcends all knowledge, being separated on all sides by incomprehensibility as by a kind of darkness. Wherefore John the sublime, who penetrated into the luminous darkness, says, "No one has ever seen God," thus asserting that knowledge of the divine essence is unattainable not only by men but also by every intelligent creature.[21]

For Nyssa, the ineffability of God is a darkness a believer is invited into as true knowledge beyond knowing. It is not something one surmounts on the spiritual journey to supposed knowledge. Augustine, preaching on John 1:1, insisted that the god that we can comprehend would not be God.[22] Thus, he maintains that God in God's revelation cannot be truly or finally grasped. Anselm of Canterbury, in his *Proslogion*, contemplates God as "that than which nothing greater can be thought," all to realize that God is even greater than that. Only then does he assert that God dwells in unapproachable light, being of ineffable beauty.[23] The Fourth Lateran Council in 1215 said of the perfection of Creator and creature: "Each perfection of course in one's own way, because between them no similarity can be found so great but that the dissimilarity is even greater." Thomas Aquinas (1225–74), perhaps one of the most important thinkers in Christian history, wrote, "The divine substance surpasses every form that our intellect reaches. Thus, we are unable to apprehend it by knowing *what it is*. Yet we are able to have some knowledge of it by knowing *what it is not*."[24] This survey can go further, but it suffices to say that the

---

20. Basil, *Epistle 234*, sect. 1.
21. Gregory of Nyssa, *Life of Moses*, Book II, sect. 163.
22. Augustine, *Sermons on the New Testament*, Sermon 67.
23. Anselm, *Proslogion*, chs. 15–17.
24. Aquinas, *Summa Contra Gentile*, I.14.2 (italics belong to the original).

ineffability of God, which takes many forms in these writers, is a staple of Christian theology.

What is important to note about these biblical texts and church thinkers is that God's ineffability means a couple of things. First, God is, apart from specific revelation, unknowable (an assertion similar to what Torrance has argued), but also, second, even with divine self-revelation, God's mystery and incomprehensibility remain. In fact, they are deepened. God is veiled, even in revelation. Thus, Johnson's claim is verified:

> Revelation, however, cannot and does not dissolve the mystery of God; in its light, we see ever more clearly the incomprehensibility of God as free and liberating love, love which chooses us without our deserving it, bears and removes our bondage, gathers us in. Even and especially in revelation, God remains the wholly other, conceptually inapprehensible, and so God.[25]

Thus, wrapped up with the conservative critique of feminism, oddly, is a wariness of mysticism, characteristic of certain Barthian thinking, that simply does not hold up to a wide consensus of church thinkers. Karl Barth once said, "Mysticism is esoteric atheism."[26] While Barth's theology has many virtues, his opinion of mysticism is not one of them. He saw mysticism as rising out of Platonic philosophy, foreign to the Bible, and employed in liberal quests to elevate private religious experience to deny biblical authority and theological accountability. It seems this sensibility has been carried on by a number of the scholars in this debate (in fact, a good deal of the proponents of Father-only language are Barthians in one way or another: Colin Gunton, T. F. Torrance, Robert Jenson, etc.). This assumption must be corrected. Historically, there is a strong consensus of theologians who have not seen the ineffability of God and revelation to be at loggerheads; rather, they are one and the same.

INSIGHTS FROM DIONYSIUS

To clarify this rule further, the nature of apophatic theology was first and still perhaps best developed by the figure who wrote under the name of Dionysius the Areopagite (a character from Acts 17:34). This writer from the late fifth to early sixth century was really the first to devise a fully mystical approach to contemplating God, beautifully explained in

25. Johnson, "The Incomprehensibility of God," 442.
26. Barth, *Church Dogmatics*, I/2, 322.

several works, namely his *On the Divine Names* and *Mystical Theology* (as well as his *Celestial Hierarchy* and *Ecclesial Hierarchy*). While a full treatment of this writer's profound work cannot be taken up here, a short sampling of some of his major concepts exposes some problems in the extremes found on either side of this debate.

If God is truly ineffable and incomparable, one implication for Dionysius concerning the disclosure of God's name to Moses, "I Am who I Am" (Exod 3:14), is that all language for God in some way is inadequate. For Dionysius, God names God's self as unnameable, the "Nameless Name."[27] Even the divine names for God must be negated to aid the believer in truly understanding how much more God is than human thinking. However, he sees this as a discourse that flows out of Scripture, not despite it: "We use only what Scripture has disclosed."[28] Thus, Dionysius contemplates the words of Scripture, which he surely regards as revelation, but understands the deep grammar of this language. In this, he sees God being named in transcendentals, such as goodness, being, life, beauty, etc., which is important since God's name is not merely a proper name. For each name, he is constantly aware of the fact that God is always so much more than any single biblical description. When God is described, an apophatic approach seeks to contemplate how God is also "not" that in order to respect God's ineffability. While a more explicitly apophatic approach is developed in his *Mystical Theology*, this is already seen in Dionysius's *On the Divine Names*. For example, he states that one of God's names is "being."[29] However, he argues that God is "not existent" or "not being," as God's being is simply beyond all existence as humans know it. This makes for a rather interesting mystical interplay as God both "exists" and does "not exist" as God is being, yet *beyond* being. He writes,

> Hence, with regard to the supra-essential enlightened after this blessed union, they discover that although it is the cause of everything, it is not a thing since it transcends all things in a manner beyond being. Hence, with regard to the supra-essential being of God—transcendent Goodness transcendently there— no lover of the truth which is above all truth will seek to praise it as word or power or mind or life or being. No. It is at a total removal from every condition, movement, life, imagination,

---

27. Ps. Dionysius, *On the Divine Names*, 1.1.
28. Ps. Dionysius, *On the Divine Names*, 1.2.
29. Ps. Dionysius, *On the Divine Names*, 1:1.

conjecture, name, discourse, thought, conception, being, rest, dwelling, unity, limit, infinity, the totality of existence.... Realizing this, the theologians praise it by every name—and as the Nameless One.[30]

Dionysius goes on to state that God is beyond the name "God" and even the shorthand name from Exod 3:14, which he reads as "I am being."[31] In other words, Dionysius is quite comfortable with negating what can be understood as proper names of God. When it comes to symbols such as "Father" and "Son," he does not see them as non-negatable (contra Hopko). They are irreducible in that they point to the unity-in-diversity of the activities of the ineffable God, and thus they mutually negate each other in the paradox of the Trinity, one yet three.[32] So, he sees the work of the Trinity as even negating its key terms: "it is the work too of the Father and of the Son who supremely transcend all divine Fatherhood and Sonship."[33] Notice, then, that the triune symbols are not negating merely "human" notions but rather negating even "divine" ones for the sake of ineffability.

Dionysius, for many of the names, uses opposites to negate and fill out the account of divine ineffability. For example, when thinking about God's being and temporality, Dionysius is quite content to see God as both being and becoming, past and future:

> He is the reality beneath time and the eternity behind being. He is the time within which things happen. He is the being for whatever is. He is coming-to-be amid whatever happens. From him who is come eternity, essence and being, come time, genesis, and becoming. He is the being immanent in and underlying the things which are, however they are. For God is not some kind of being. No. But in a way that is simple and indefinable he gathers into himself and anticipates every existence. So he is called "King of the ages," for in him and around him all being is and subsists. He was not. He will not be. He did not come to be. He is not in the midst of becoming. He will not come to be. No. He is not. Rather, he is essence of being for the things which have being.[34]

30. Ps. Dionysius, *On the Divine Names*, 1.5–6.
31. Ps. Dionysius, *On the Divine Names*, 1.6.
32. Ps. Dionysius, *On the Divine Names*, 2.3.
33. Ps. Dionysius, *On the Divine Names*, 2.8.
34. Ps. Dionysius, *On the Divine Names*, 5.4.

He continues this approach in his smaller work, *The Mystical Theology*, where he is more explicit in the negations of imagery. God's light is so "beyond" that it appears as "darkness";[35] God's word speaks, but speaks as silence, etc. The book ends with stating that God is even conceived to be beyond every assertion, but then also, God is beyond every negation as well.[36]

Dionysius has many applicable insights. God's name is the "Nameless Name," and even still, God is beyond every name, including God's own. Ineffability is total, but not as a contradiction to revelation. This is an ineffability found in and through revelation in Scripture. Dionysius is a kindred spirit in reflecting on the structure of Christian speech about God using the rules of Scripture, just not in a literalistic fashion. What does Dionysius do? Dionysius uses metaphysical opposites to correct or fill out one another, not seeing them as opposites. In the Trinity, he is aware of how God is beyond even "divine fatherhood and sonship," as his doctrine of the Trinity has reciprocal negation from one to three and three to one. Sadly, Dionysius's treatment of divine symbols for God is lost (one of the great tragedies of theological history), and the mentions of other conceptual names of God neglect awareness of female imagery (although he may have done this in his lost works).[37] However, to extrapolate, one could argue that it is fully consistent with Dionysius's approach to upholding both that God is Father and beyond fatherliness, and to negate or fill this out, he might have used "Mother" (not that male-female is equivalent to the other binaries discussed). But all of this is understood in realizing that God is also beyond both assertions and negations.

Thus, in sampling Dionysius, there is the possibility of negation in regard to God's ineffability that does not undermine revelation but rather flows from it, one that goes to the very core of revelation: to divine sonship and fatherhood. To pair feminine and masculine, father and mother language in contemplating the God who is the being and becoming of all existence and yet beyond existence is not unwarranted.

---

35. Ps. Dionysius, *Mystical Theology*, ch. 1: sect. 1.
36. Ps. Dionysius, *Mystical Theology*, ch. 5.
37. Ps. Dionysius, *On the Divine Names*, 1.6 and 1.8.

INEFFABILITY AND IDOLATRY

THE NATURE OF IDOLATRY AND ITS REMEDIES

While Dionysius is not concerned about idolatrous speech about God per se, these negations are relevant to how feminists have insisted male language needs to be negated to prevent idolatry, the reduction of God to the creaturely, a concern Dionysius and others would share. But what is an idol? Can patriarchy be an idol? Can a biblical symbol like God as Father become an idol? Should correction of this idol involve the use of an opposite image, like God as Mother? Or should it merely be corrected by reiterating a non-patriarchal reading of God as Father? Adversely, can female experiences projected into the Christian religion be idolatrous? In order to apply these insights regarding the apophatic further, the nature of idolatry (something Dionysius never addresses) must be clarified.

As Edward Curtis notes, idols in the ancient Near East were statues or pictographic representations of a god or goddess, but more than that, they were considered living sites of divine presence, believed to be able to eat sacrifices and smell incense offerings or infuse worshippers with blessings like protection in battle or fertility in marriage.[38] Israel was categorically opposed to this exercise. Exodus 20 and Deut 4 refuse the possibility of rendering God in an image. They read,

> I am the LORD your God who brought you out of the land of Egypt, out of the house of bondage. You shall have no other gods before me. You shall not make for yourself a graven image or any likeness of anything that is in heaven above, or that is in the earth beneath, or that is in the water under the earth; you shall not bow down to them or serve them; for I the LORD your God am a jealous God. (Exod 20:2–5)

> You saw no form of any kind the day the LORD spoke to you at Horeb out of the fire. Therefore, watch yourselves very carefully, so that you do not become corrupt and make for yourselves an idol, an image of any shape, whether formed like a man or a woman, or like any animal on earth or any bird that flies in the air, or like any creature that moves along the ground or any fish in the waters below. And when you look up to the sky and see the sun, the moon, and the stars—all the heavenly array—do not be enticed into bowing down to them and worshiping things the LORD your God has apportioned to all the nations under heaven. (Deut 4:15–19)

38. Curtis, "Idol, Idolatry."

One cannot help but see the prohibition of images in either "a man or a woman" as critical. God cannot be reduced to a thing (or a gender). This command coincides with the people's stubbornness in Exodus. They wanted to worship a god they could see, and so they got Aaron to craft a golden calf, which they proceeded to worship. What is wrong with having an image? The rebuke of images is so strong in Scripture because of its tendency to coincide with delusion. Psalm 135:15–18 reads,

> The idols of the nations are silver and gold,
> made by human hands.
> They have mouths, but cannot speak,
> eyes, but cannot see.
> They have ears, but cannot hear,
> nor is there breath in their mouths.
> Those who make them will be like them,
> and so will all who trust in them.

God alone must be worshipped because God alone is God. Anything else is a delusion that will not save the person. Here, there is a vital connection between belief in God's transcendence, God's ability not to be limited by this world or reduced to God's creation, and the quality of human life.

Idolatry is not merely bowing to an object. It is treating anything in this world as a god or using it to fulfill a need only God can and should fulfill. The brilliance of the Hebrew prophets is their adaptation of the rebuke of idols and their application of it socially. For instance, Habakkuk looked at the Babylonian army, saw its power, and remarked, "Their might is their god" (Hab 1:10). The trust the nation had in violence to procure safety and status was a kind of idolatry. Similarly, Paul warns the Colossian congregation: "Put to death, therefore, whatever in you is earthly: fornication, impurity, passion, evil desire, and greed (which is idolatry)" (Col 3:5). In other words, all sin, as loving something more than God, loving something more than it should be loved, is idolatry.

One can see two applicable warnings in Habakkuk and Paul. Habakkuk warns that trust in social power can be like an idol. Certainly, the culture of patriarchy, its destructive endorsement and upholding of male power over women, is an idol. Moreover, if the language of God as male and as a father has been used to do this, these symbols, quite apart from the reality to which they point, become something like idols, reductions of God to the created order, and examples of human trust in human power. They can also merely be symbols that believers have placed more significance on than is biblically appropriate.

Edward Curtis notes that even the things of God can be turned into idols.[39] The bronze statue of the serpent, used to heal the Israelites in the desert, was eventually worshipped, and so it had to be dismantled (2 Kgs 18:4 cf. Num 21:4–9). Similarly, Gideon's ephod was worshipped (Judg 8:26–27). More significantly, the ark of the covenant itself, the site of divine presence for Israelite worship, was turned into something like an idol (1 Sam 4–6). It was being brought into battle as a way of ensuring victory even when God was not properly honored by the people. As a result, God allowed the ark to be captured. A similar attitude persisted in regard to the city of Jerusalem and the temple; both were promised sites of divine presence, and yet both were destroyed because of the people's hubris. Thus, there is evidence that the things of God can be treated in an idolatrous manner, and God does respond iconoclastically.

What does this mean for masculine imagery? While God promises in Jesus Christ a constant presence to the church (Matt 28:10), this should not be turned into a kind of secure presence that ignores misuse, for Matthew warns that there are those who see Christ as Lord that will not inherit the kingdom of heaven due to their refusal to do God's will (Matt 7:21). Feminists have often overstated their case in insisting that all male language for God is idolatrous, nonetheless, there is ample evidence in church communities that male language has been used to reinforce male power.

The question then becomes, how are idols corrected? Surely, with repentance, but this does not necessarily proscribe what language then ought to be used. One will note different pathways. The typical strategy of the more conservative position is to reiterate a non-patriarchal understanding of the Father symbol, insisting that it remain normative. This pathway can often be disingenuous, particularly in ecclesial traditions that still bar women from the clergy because of a theology of male representation. Meanwhile, the feminist strategy is to counter the male images with feminine or motherly ones, the proscribed degree and regularity of which there is no definitive proposal. Again, both strategies have their assumptions. For the conservative, female language is not permitted by Scripture. For the feminist, male language is, for the most part, patriarchal. Yet, in this project, a holistic permission of both is being pursued, where male imagery is not essentially offensive, but neither is it exclusive.

---

39. Curtis, "Idol, Idolatry," 379.

THE PROPHETIC AND THE CONTEMPLATIVE PATHS

While the strategy of reiteration will be discussed further in other chapters (in other words, what a non-patriarchal understanding of the Father symbol might mean), the strategy of negation can take two forms: the prophetic and the contemplative.

One response to the kind of merging of patriarchy with male imagery that culminates in harm to marginalized people, particularly women, may call for a kind of prophetic iconoclasm. Rabbi Abraham Joshua Heschel once said, "The prophet is an iconoclast, challenging the apparently holy, revered, and awesome. Beliefs cherished as certainties, instructions endowed with supreme sanctity, he [or she] exposes as scandalous pretension."[40] While the theology and practices of the temple find their origin in none other than Moses, essential to understanding the presence of God with the people, the prophets' message overtly negated and contradicted these institutes as they were used to foster apathy, arrogance, and neglect of justice. In the face of the promises of God to protect and be with the people, the prophets proclaimed messages such as the oracle of Hosea: "You are not my people, and I am not your God" (Hos 1:9). They did not hesitate to negative convictions central to Israel's revealed testimony, whether affirmations of God's character, God's promises, the laws, and the temple when their function caused the neglect of sincerity, humility, justice, and righteousness. Jesus similarly continued these prophetic critiques of the temple sacrifices and purity laws. Thus, Scripture does permit the reflection on and revision of its own symbols and images in light of their intended purposes. If God can be Father but not Mother, moreover, if our language for the Divine functions to prioritize the male over the female, that might be a good indication that God has been reduced to a thing. The accusation that such language can be "idolatrous" may be harsh but accurate. If Father language is used to overtly or implicitly reinforce patriarchy, the necessity of prophetic iconoclasm is made possible, just as the temple needed to have its tables turned. God's transcendence is given realistically in imminence, but this does not mean it can be grasped so as to be taken for granted. Prophetic discourse, as Ricoeur notes, inherently "reorients by first disorienting" through hyperboles and iconoclastic negations.[41] Here again, theology can and must

---

40. Heschel, *The Prophets*, 1:10.
41. Ricoeur, "Naming God," in *Figuring the Sacred*, 229.

look to those willing to call out injustice and lampoon images that have become morally lax. As Ruether states, "Feminist theology is not asserting unprecedented ideas; rather, it is rediscovering the prophetic context and content of Biblical faith itself when it defines the prophetic-liberating tradition as norm."[42] The key to a feminist theology, properly understood, is not to minimize the word of God, properly understood, but to speak prophetic truths through it as the Spirit calls discerning thinkers to do.

However, there is always a challenge. Using inclusive language can give the impression that biblical revelation is being subverted by human assertion in some people's view, and thus, doing so may be counterproductive in some congregations, even those that would be fully willing to engage in an egalitarian way of living. Vital will be the subsequent grammars that discuss the meaning of male imagery and the evidence for feminine imagery. Thus, inclusive language can be counterproductive, but only because a community of disciples has been taught a way to hear and interpret such language. Prophetic zeal should be tempered with patient teaching and persistence when one finds oneself in a community of disciples who intend to do better but often do not know how. As stated in the last chapter, male images in their context often provide the grammar for speaking of the female. When this is understood, female and motherly figures supplement in conjunction rather than polemicize iconoclastically.

The second strategy is the purging of patriarchal ideas of God through the work of prayer and contemplation. However, before one can contemplate the various analogies and metaphors of God that are female (to be discussed in the next chapter), it is necessary simply to sit in silence, in the negation of all words into the presence of God's ineffability, reminding oneself that God's being exceeds all existence. These are the lessons of the mystics. Thomas Merton writes, "If nothing that can be seen can either be God or represent Him to us as He is, then to find God, we must pass beyond everything that can be seen and enter into darkness. If nothing that can be heard is God, to find Him, we must enter into silence."[43]

To affirm that God is ineffable and that God is Spirit also has profound implications for humans as gendered creatures. The root of human life is the Spirit. It is the Spirit of God, the breath of life, that makes

---

42. Ruether, *Sexism and God-Talk*, 31.
43. Merton, *New Seeds of Contemplation*, 131.

humans living souls (Gen 2:7). While the nature of the Spirit will be discussed more fully later, to understand that the root of the soul, the energy of life itself, is the Spirit is also to realize that there is a dimension of the person that longs for union with the ineffable, propelled by primordial goodness. This does not commit believers to a dualistic notion of body and soul but rather expresses the depths of the self, the true self, which longs to break through all the ideological distortions of patriarchy and sin—false constructions of gender—refusing to be reduced to these things. This does not speak of a kind of complete, autonomous self "underneath" or latent in the person. Rather, to be a created being is to be finite, awaiting completion by God in union with God in the eschatological Sabbath.

In this way, to negate one's images of God in silence is also to negate the present self as well. In silence, in the presence of the ineffable God, one is invited by God, who is both the root of the soul and the goal of all true human subjectivity awaiting resurrection, to sift one's consciousness. Thomas Keating calls this the "divine therapy,"[44] where in the silence painful memories are brought into healing light, past wrongs are confessed, and deep anxieties are named as to be released in trust. All of this is the work of prayer that begins in the stillness and silence, listening for God's ineffable presence.

Thus, in identifying the possibility that male language for God is often used in idolatrous ways, there are two possible pathways to addressing it. The first is prophetic, and the other is contemplative. While feminism has tended toward the former, one should not bypass the latter as an essential component of a spirituality that negates the ways the human mind has reduced God to things but also how believers have reduced themselves to distorted notions of the self.

CONCLUSION

In this investigation, we have seen the ineffability and transcendence of God utilized to do two different things: if God is ineffable, God's revelation enables speech about God and prescribes what speech is permissible (which in one side's estimate is exclusively male); meanwhile, the other side insists that to speak of God exclusively as male, in fact, is idolatrous, violating God's ineffability. This chapter has surveyed Christian

---

44. Keating, *Open Mind, Open Heart*, 95.

tradition and found that there is a consensus on the ineffability of God, and when we looked at one of the apophatic tradition's most important thinkers, Dionysius, we found that the divine names could be negated. Metaphysical names were negated with their opposites, and the trinitarian threeness is negated with oneness and vice versa. Moreover, all names are negated into the divine darkness of God's presence, which is beyond word and even beyond negation itself. This challenges both sides but also yields further questions: Yes, it seems that all the names of God can be negated as all are inadequate. However, the ineffability of God is not against biblical reflection but rather is founded by it. Thus, proposals by both Hopko and Sallie McFague are problematic: Hopko for reading the tradition so narrowly and McFague for denying the reality of revelation. As to the nature of idolatry, we found that idolatry is to reduce God to a created thing, but more than that, it can be treating something like a god or even treating something with more concern than God wants. While God promises God's presence and speaks with humanity, it seems that the things of God can be treated as idols, and when they are, they are negated by the prophets. So, in principle, the symbol of the Father can be turned into an idol. The question is whether the symbol should be negated with its opposite (with female and motherly language) or negated in such a way that purges it of improper connotations. As we found, these are contingent on whether the Father symbol is thoroughly patriarchal and whether the Bible does have female imagery, warranting its use to flesh out divine language. In practice, it is suggested, one way or another, that the healing of the self as a gendered being wounded by patriarchy begins in contemplative prayer. More will be said about this in the next chapter, but here, it is insisted healing begins in the silence that centers the self—the self that has been reduced, objectified, and oppressed—on the God who refuses to be reduced or objectified.

3

Analogy and Narrative

IN SCRIPTURE, THERE ARE many statements about God and the life of faith that are deeply poetic and beautiful. Psalm 18:2 says, "The LORD is my rock, my fortress, and my deliverer . . . my shield and the horn of salvation." God is a "potter" in Isa 64:8. Hebrews 12:29 says that "our God is a consuming fire." Jesus uses several important ones in the Gospel of John. Jesus is "the bread of life," "the light of the world," "the door," "the good shepherd," or "the true vine."[1] Of course, all of these descriptions are not literal, but they are all ways God has communicated in the canonical Scriptures. An important way people think and refer to things in life, and thus also God, is by analogies and metaphors. But in what way is a metaphor or an analogy true? The next classic way Christian language has been organized is the way of analogy (comparisons using "like" or "as," communicating meaning based on a corresponding partial similarity) and metaphor (the creative application of similarity to two dissimilar things to describe one through aspects of another).[2] What this rule ends up showing is that since creation is good and God is the goodness of all goodness, there are ways to speak of God using analogy and metaphor. How this is done appropriately, however, comes down to the context of a statement, which, particularly for Christian theology, is determined by the biblical narrative.

---

1. Examples of each, respectively: John 6:35; 8:12; 10:7; 10:11; 15:1.
2. This essay uses basic definitions of metaphor, but for more in-depth treatments, see Soskice, *Metaphor and Religious Language*; as well as, Ricoeur, *The Rule of Metaphor*.

COMPETING VIEWS OF METAPHOR, ANALOGY, AND NARRATIVE

As with the other rules that structure Christian speech about God, analogy, metaphor, and narrative have competing accounts in conservative and feminist theologies. Each makes definite claims that require further testing. It is important to emphasize that terms like analogy and metaphor are developed in different ways. For instance, to use an analogy as a linguistic convention is vastly different from a theological articulation of religious language as analogical or metaphorical. These are, in turn, set within two different ways narrative informs how analogies and metaphors have meaning and reference.

Within the male-exclusive perspective, there is a notable diversity of what is and is not an analogy and metaphor. There are some that are completely dismissive of the relevance of female analogies and metaphors for God in the Bible. For instance, David Clines's recent article goes through twenty-two passages that suggest a female ascription to God, dismissing all of them since nowhere is God actually understood as female, in his view. Rather, God is resolutely male who acts in occasionally female-like ways. He writes,

> The fact is, though, that the Yahweh of the Hebrew Bible is a thoroughly male God and there is simply no benefit in failing to recognize that fact and accept its consequences. For my part, I regret the damage done to the feminist cause by the repeated claim that the Bible is less masculine and less sexist than it actually is.[3]

However, are the female analogies for God so inconsequential to God's being? While Clines is correct that a male personality can act like a mother at times while having no relevance to one's actual physical sex, Cline's argument seems to completely dismiss classic ways of thinking about God that both refuse to reduce God to the created order (or to gender) as well as seeing God's being as being participated in by all created being (what is understood as the analogy of being).

For others, God is not literally male, but male metaphors still carry significance that female ones do not. Roland Frye, for instance, notes that motherly languages for God "illustrate some specified phase or facet of divine attitude or intent as defined by the simile's context, but they are

---

3. Clines, "Alleged Female Language," 249.

not and do not claim to be, a transparent equivalent to personal identity as are predicating metaphors such as 'the good shepherd' and 'the lamb of God' and, even more broadly, God 'the Father' and Christ 'the Son.'"[4] Frye sees the Father symbol as a naming metaphor, where motherly language is a mere simile, thus placing stronger redistributive power in metaphor.

Male-exclusive accounts tend to acknowledge analogy and metaphor but often apply them with restraint. For example, Colin Gunton grants metaphorical language and analogy, but he does so from a basis of underlying realism concerning historical revelation.[5] Concerning the atonement, for instance, which is wrapped in metaphors of sacrifice, military victory, healing, and exchange, Gunton writes, "These biblical metaphors, then, are ways of describing realistically what can be described only in the indirect manner of this kind of language. But an indirect description is still a description of what is really here."[6] Gunton is aware, far more than Frye, of the flexibility of metaphor (a point that will be reiterated shortly) and, thus, notes the need for criteria to clarify them. In this case, he argues for the events of revelation in history.[7] This is something he sees as entirely absent in McFague's account. He accuses her of what he calls "protean" employment of different metaphors for God (that is, flexible and dynamic changes in metaphors for God) as a symptom of a fundamentally "procrustean" attempt to force a different notion of the gospel into Christianity, one that cannot even affirm God's saving revelation. In this regard, Gunton's patience wears thin: "Let me compound the offense. Christianity is necessarily 'patriarchial' in the sense that it concerns the relationship in time of the eschatological rule of God the Father over creation. Is that authoritarian? Yes, in the sense that we cannot alter the facts, it is, I believe, 'the God we are going to get.'"[8]

When it comes to the title "Father," for Donald Bloesch, this is not metaphorical. It is a divine name. Donald Bloesch states this explicitly: "Such words as Father, Son, and Lord, when applied to God, are analogies, but they are analogies *sui generis*. They are derived not from the

---

4. Frye, "Language for God," 39–40.

5. Gunton, "Proteus and Procrustes." Gunton offers in many ways an agreeable critique to McFague but goes too far in insisting that everyone who seeks to permit mother language denies realistic revelation the way she does.

6. Gunton, *Actuality of the Atonement*, 65.

7. Gunton, "Proteus and Procrustes," 69, 70.

8. Gunton, "Proteus and Procrustes," 74.

experience of human fatherhood or sonship or lordship but from God's act of recalling himself as Father, Son, and Lord."[9] The standard strategy, then, is to state that God's Fatherhood is not based on human fatherhood.

There is a common appeal to Aquinas in these discussions, particularly how Aquinas understands analogy. J. A. DiNoia gives his argument using clarifications from Aquinas's theology.[10] For example, God loves "like a Father," but this does not mean God is a father the same way a human can be a father. DiNoia points this out with the two statements, "God is faithful" and "Kristen is faithful." Language about humans and God takes on a certain quality that needs distinguishing. First, there is the Thomistic notion of the *res significanta* (that which is being referred to, namely a quality in the person, Kristen). Second is the *ratio nominis* (the concept that is being attributed, namely faithfulness). The third is the *modus significandi* (the manner of the utterance). A term can be univocal (that is, one meaning applied in both cases) if its *ratio nominis* applies in the same manner to both ("Jack and Kristen are faithful"). It can also be equivocal (that is, not the same meaning or ambiguous in meaning) if the *ratio nominis* is fundamentally different. For instance, the "bark" of a dog and the "bark" of trees are equivocal. Sometimes two utterances share the same *ratio nominis* but in different ways ("Chocolate is good and Kristen is good"). As this relates to God, something like "goodness" must be analogical as its *res significanta*; while it shares the *ratio nominis* and *modus significandi* of statements made about human goodness, the reality of God's goodness is perfect. In regard to human and divine fatherhood, DiNoia maintains that the disparity between *res significanta* and *modus significandi*, as well as the fallibility of the *modus significandi*, provides a rule that prevents God's fatherhood from being reduced to human fatherhood. DiNoia writes, "To insist that the *modus significandi* of such predications of God differs from predications of created beings is to provide a linguistic rule that continually corrects for implications of our way of speaking that can never be true of God." In layperson's terms, these concepts create a kind of fail-safe device for speech about God, stopping harmful projection.

The possibility of referring to God as Mother, even metaphorically, or having female qualities and body parts, has been routinely critiqued as edging on paganism, polytheism, and pantheism. Elizabeth Achtemeier

---

9. Bloesch, *Battle for the Bible*, 35.

10. DiNoia, "Knowing and Naming the Triune God," 178–79. Aquinas, *The Summa Theologiæ*. This is particularly spelled out in Part 1, Question 13.

argues that feminine language cannot be used because it is prone to paganism, undermining God's transcendence.[11] Wolfhart Pannenberg argues that sexual differentiation in God would mean polytheism.[12] Gunton sees female language as pantheistic.[13] Roland Fyre associates feminine language with "Gnosticism," "animism," and "polytheism."[14] These are not the only accusations made against female God language, but they suffice to illustrate the reception has often not been warm.

Meanwhile, the feminist case for inclusive language makes very strong appeals to metaphor, and this is done in diverse ways. Sallie McFague argues that metaphors seek "similarity in the midst of dissimilarity," where a symbol works analogically and "rests on similarity already present and assumed."[15] Religious language is entirely metaphorical,[16] emphasizing that even the divine name is metaphorical to the point that it is a human construction that humans can preferentially change.[17] The anti-realist dimension of McFague's theology has already been noted in the previous grammatical rule, but it is worth exploring her statements a bit deeper.

McFague asserts in her first work, *Speaking in Parables*, that metaphor and parables (as extended metaphors) in the Gospel stories are really the fundamental linguistic units of the New Testament.[18] McFague would insist, in agreement with her critics, that the realities of the Gospels were communicated with rich metaphors, but there is disagreement over what these realities are. This is brought to the point of insisting that Jesus himself is a metaphor and a parable for God.[19] What this means for narrative and Christology will be explored further in the next chapters, but it should be noted that metaphor here, as Gunton suspects, is extended beyond merely a literary trope into a full account of what Christianity is essentially about. Metaphor is not just a way the Gospels communicate their truths. She writes, "Metaphor is not only a poetic device for the creation of new meaning, but metaphor is as ultimate as

11. Achtemeier, "Exchanging God for 'No Gods,'" 8.
12. Pannenberg, *Systematic Theology*, 1:261.
13. Gunton, "Proteus and Procrustes," 76.
14. Frye, "Language for God," 26.
15. McFague, *Metaphorical Theology*, 17.
16. McFague, *Metaphorical Theology*, 99, 134.
17. McFague, *Metaphorical Theology*, 15–16.
18. McFague, *Speaking in Parables*, 38.
19. McFague, *Speaking in Parables*, 2–3.

thought. It is and can be *the* source for new insight because all human discovery is by metaphor."[20] With this comes a kind of sensibility that faith is unconcerned with history, that the historicity of the Gospels is minimal, and thus, who Jesus was really is a literary identity that points, like a parable, not to Jesus' own historical life rendered in the narrative, but to something else.

McFague continues in her book, *Metaphorical Theology*, to expand the scope of metaphor. For instance, she further claims that Scripture is not the word of God in the traditional sense but is a metaphor as well. By this, metaphor heavily de-actualizes the Bible as a revelation: "The Bible is a metaphor of the word or ways of God . . . but as a metaphor, it cannot be absolute, 'divinely inspired,' or final."[21] Instead, Scripture functions like a poetic classic of a community, something irreplaceable but also able to be reinterpreted.[22] Furthermore, doctrines in the tradition are likened to "models." Models are larger metaphorical schemas that, as they are used in science, can organize data, mediating root metaphors for concepts. She sees creedal statements as doing something like this.[23] How are these judged? McFague admits to a great deal of plurality and fallibility to models but settles on three criteria. One is comprehensiveness and internal coherence. The second is a model's ability to manage anomalies when experience or evidence is presented that does not conform to the expected results of a model. Lastly, a model is judged by the experiential-pragmatic criteria (which bring up issues discussed in chapter 1 of this study). She states,

> We do not *know* that our models of father and mother, of liberator and friend, of creator and redeemer, really reflect the structure of the divine-human relationship. At most, we can say that given our experiences of healing, of liberation, or renewal, and so on, they appear to be apt or appropriate to the most profound dimensions of human experience.[24]

These conceptual clarifications lead her to her more pointed proposals about replacing the model of God as Father with alternatives.

---

20. McFague, *Speaking in Parables*, 56.
21. McFague, *Metaphorical Theology*, 54.
22. McFague, *Metaphorical Theology*, 61.
23. McFague, *Metaphorical Theology*, 111.
24. McFague, *Metaphorical Theology*, 143.

While she begins this work in *Metaphorical Theology*, she fleshes it out in *Models for God*, where she argues that God ought to be understood with the models of Mother, Lover, and Friend, and all three of these are vital to the survival of humanity as humanity faces the nuclear and ecological threats. In the face of these threats, she posits that the world must be understood metaphorically as God's body, and she sees this as a proposal to correct the mythological notion (in her view) of Jesus' resurrected body.[25] The world as God's body is the sign of the continual presence of God with all creation. She continues on to further add depth to her proposal of viewing God as Mother, Lover, and Friend. She sees these models as offering ways of understanding redemptive events in people's experiences. God as Mother can be used to understand agapeic love, the activity of creativity, and an ethic of justice. God as Lover can be used to understand the goodness of erotic love and this love as saving and healing. God as Friend sees the goodness of filial love and speaks to the phenomena of sustaining and companionship. McFague's proposal begs a lot of questions. Chief among these questions is whether religious language being metaphorical prevents the language from referring to reality.

It is worth noting diversity within this position, which is not all as extreme as McFague. Elizabeth Johnson appeals to analogy in important ways, and she does so by appropriating dimensions in Aquinas's doctrine of the analogy of being. Elizabeth Johnson appeals to a different set of concepts in Aquinas to legitimate her program of female God-language than DiNoia. For her, God can be referred to in a female way as the goodness of femininity finds its source in God, the goodness of all goodness. She writes,

> Analogical predication rests on an interpretation of the doctrine of creation that sees all things brought into being and sustained by God, who is cause of the world, causality itself being an analogical notion. . . . All creatures participate to some degree in "being," the very dynamism of existing which God in essence is. Thanks to this ontology of participation, every creature in some way participates in divine perfections, although in no way does God resemble creatures. Looking at creatures we glean clues about the characteristics of that primordial fire which is their origin and substance. Hence it is possible to speak positively about God, creator of all, thought terms drawn from

---

25. McFague, *Models of God*, 70.

our knowledge of creaturely qualities, but always with the proviso that the reality which we speak cannot be contained in this language.[26]

She continues on to say,

> The understanding that all speech about God is analogical assumes a strongly critical function when the androcentric character of traditional speech is faced with the question of naming toward God arising from women's experience today. Introducing female symbols makes it acutely clear that analogy still has a job to do in purifying God-talk of its direct even if unintentional, masculine literalism.[27]

While she grants metaphorical language as well, theological analogy is most important to her program. As this opening account suggests, further clarification is required to understand the usage of metaphor and analogy, and for this, this study will look at the thoughts of ancient minds (like Aquinas) and modern ones.

The meaning of any metaphor or analogy is bound up with the larger linguistic units that deliver them. In other words, one cannot speak meaningfully about these without speaking about the narratives they are found in. Again, there is a stark polarization here. Does the narrative render events or allegories of the reader's experience? This debate is wrapped up in debates on the level of historicity of Scripture, with conservatives resting their convictions on a historical core and liberals tending to see the narrative as highly mythological and its narrations as poetic symbols of experiences. Certainly, there is a characteristic lack of openness to historical criticism in conservative circles. Meanwhile, on the other side of the debate, there is often a denial of historicity of revelation. Sallie McFague sees the biblical narrative as mythological and thus "fiction."[28] This makes it possible to dismember the narrative: if the events are de-actualized, their symbolizations in the narrative are more open to being pliable. Blanche Jenson asks, "Can feminists live with the biblical narrative?"[29] It seems that the fallibility of the biblical narrative but also its reliability as a realistic revelation needs proper explanation as

---

26. Johnson, *She Who Is*, 114.
27. Johnson, *She Who Is*, 117.
28. McFague, *Models of God*, xi.
29. Jenson, "The Movement and the Story," 276.

the meaning of narratives necessarily flesh out the meaning of analogies and metaphors.

Thus, both the nature of metaphors and analogies as ways of speaking of God need to be clarified along with the nature of narrative. A part of this must be the question of the content of the Bible and the nature of its language, both motherly and fatherly.

DO METAPHORS IMPLY ANTI-REALISM?

To offer a metaphor about metaphors, Joseph Jones once said that the notion of metaphor has turned into a great genie in a bottle for modern theologians, essentially allowing them to do all that they wish.[30] This insight makes the careful work of Janet Soskice quite valuable as she has clarified a good deal of the matters surrounding metaphor in her book *Metaphor and Religious Language*. If something is metaphorical, does it undermine realism and history? She makes the following clarifications:

"Metaphor," she defines, "is that figure of speech whereby we speak about one thing in terms which are seen to be suggestive of another."[31] This is a very minimal definition, and she cautions against attempts to overextend and read into it. There are rhetorical and philosophical implications thinkers have drawn about the nature of metaphor, but these do not necessarily follow from the definition. McFague, for instance, is overreaching when she draws conclusions about the alleged mythic and non-referential discourse of the Gospels, for such conclusions do not follow from the fact that the Gospels make use of metaphor.

There are other clarifications that problematize the program of McFague. Metaphors, as a linguistic phenomenon, are not mental or metaphysical events. In other words, metaphors cannot be attached readily to mental or physical processes that go beyond language. While the human power of language involves the power of creativity necessary for metaphors, the claim that perception or thinking itself is "entirely metaphorical" cannot be sustained. There are fundamental extra-linguistic dimensions to thinking that form the prior conditions for metaphors to be created. Thus, thinking is not entirely metaphorical. Also, objects cannot then be metaphors.[32] To claim that Jesus is a metaphor is really saying

---

30. Jones, *Grammar of Christian Faith*, 1:155.
31. Soskice, *Metaphor and Religious Language*, 15.
32. Soskice, *Metaphor and Religious Language*, 16–18.

something about the portrayal of linguistic imagery about Jesus in the Gospels, but that is reducing the Christian truth claims to its language as if metaphor itself is a source of theology.

However, metaphors cannot form a source for theology in and of itself, as metaphors are employed in contexts that condition their truth claims. Soskice is fond of using the example of when Winston Churchill said, "Mussolini is a spoon." To make this claim does not destroy the actuality of either the person or the thing. Thus, to say that "Jesus is a metaphor of God" is problematic. Not only because Jesus is a person and people cannot be metaphors (only the language about them can), but also because this says nothing of whether Jesus is a historical person or how language describes him. What Soskice goes on to point out, then, is that metaphors do not inherently prevent realistic statements, as one can have a highly metaphorical statement that nevertheless, in its context of usage, refers to real historical events or even scientific facts: "We may justly claim to speak of God without claiming to define him and to do so by means of metaphor. Realism accommodates figures of speech, which is reality depicting without claiming to be directly descriptive."[33]

What McFague is doing, then, is assuming certain things about the Gospels in order to assert something about their language. McFague assumes the Gospels have little usable historicity and that they are not actually about the historical reality of Jesus' life but about something else. What McFague has claimed here is guilty of exactly what Gunton accuses: she has stretched a literary insight to hack away and insert a very different set of claims about Christianity. As Gunton notes, these exact an "ontological and moral price."[34] What is interesting is that it is not only Gunton, a conservative, who realizes this problem, but those sympathetic to McFague's enterprise do so as well. Without a sense of realism, as Gordon Kaufman wonders, should it not be asserted also that God as a person and personal, God as a being and even as existing is metaphorical too?[35] For him, the answer is yes, but this answer does not fully understand the negative theological tradition that the previous chapter's grammar spelled out. The essential paradox that anti-realist theology cannot uphold is that wonder, awe, mystery, and ineffability are grounded *because of*, not despite, realistic revelation. Without definite

---

33. Soskice, *Metaphor and Religious Language*, 148.
34. Gunton, "Proteus and Procrustes," 80.
35. Kaufman, review of *Models of God*.

claims to God's existence and actions, one is not even able to engage in metaphor at all.

Thus, the appeal to metaphor in McFague's theology makes assumptions that her theory of metaphor attempts to ratify, but the fact that humans speak metaphorically about God does not prevent that language from having high degrees of realism.

TENSIONS IN AQUINAS AND ANALOGY

From metaphor and critiquing McFague's proposal (one where Gunton's suspicions have been vindicated), the proposals of DiNoia and Johnson—particularly their employments of analogy and, more specifically, their employment of analogy in Aquinas—need further illumination.

Aquinas has several concepts in his thinking that create tensions in this debate, which, by exploring them, set this study up for our discussion on narrative. What is detected here is a kind of tension between analogical language and the analogy of being. If Aquinas's doctrine of the analogy of being is prioritized, the goodness of femininity and motherhood can name God, but if Aquinas's view about the sources of analogical language about God is correct, it cannot. The question for Thomistic thinkers is whether his appeal to analogy really reflects biblical usage.

Again, while Aquinas, like Dionysus, was largely unconcerned with female language in the Bible and the contemporary questions feminists are asking, examining Aquinas is really to ask whether his understanding of religious language about God prevents motherly and female imagery or whether they are compatible. Aquinas himself was deeply indebted to Dionysius. In so doing, Aquinas held that God was ineffable as well, but if God is the "I Am," Aquinas saw God as perfect being, "the One Who Is."[36]

Aquinas proposes his famous resolution to the problem of univocal and equivocal use of language for God with his development of analogical language and its philosophical schema, the analogy of being. By this, God's being is what holds all being together. God's goodness is the goodness of all beings, who are essentially good as created things despite displaying characteristic privations of goodness from the fall. This means that any goodness in nature, if it is truly good, is good by virtue of the fact that it participates in God's goodness.[37] If something is, for instance,

---

36. Aquinas, *Summa Contra Gentiles*, I:22.10.
37. Aquinas, *Summa Contra Gentiles*, I:34.1.

beautiful, it is such because it participates and finds its being in God, who is beauty itself, and thus it is beautiful because in some way it is like God's beauty. Yet, since God is beyond all beings, the analogical way incorporates Dionysius's negative way: God's goodness is *like* the goodness of created beings but is *not equated* with them.[38]

As a note, we should take the advice of Soskice and say that the concept of analogy, as a figure of speech, does not offer an ontology; rather, the participatory ontology of God warrants this analogical operation of contemplation. This is not to say that every word to God or from God is an analogy (doxological language will be discussed in a later chapter) but that every description of God has this characteristic similarity and dissimilarity due to God being the being of all beings and yet beyond all being.

Nevertheless, can this analogical way of referring include motherhood and femininity? If God is exclusively like a "he" or a "father" and simply can never be like a "she" or a "mother," this may indicate convictions that deny an aspect of God's goodness in creation. However, this is especially problematic since the Bible portrays humans, both male and female, as created in the divine "image" (Gen 1:26–27).[39] Exclusive use of Father language implies that fatherliness as a quality participates in God's being and goodness to a higher degree than motherliness. Now, motherhood and fatherhood are relations, not substances (a point we will explore shortly), but the point stands: if God is the being of all beings, the goodness of every good, if God is exclusively a he and not a she, a father and not a mother, if motherhood and femininity are illegitimate for thinking about God's goodness, one is given a distinct impression that motherhood and femininity are not as good. In addition to analogies, Aquinas also delineates how metaphors can be used to refer to God:

> Since it is possible to find in God every perfection of creatures, but in another and more eminent way, whatever names unqualifiedly designate a perfection without effect are predicated of God and of other things: for example, goodness, wisdom, being, and the like. But when any name expresses such perfections along with a mode that is proper to a creature, it can be said of God only according to likeness and metaphor.[40]

38. Aquinas, *Summa Contra Gentiles*, I:14.2.
39. McFague, *Models of God*, 98. Also see Jewett, *God, Creation, and Revelation*, 323–25.
40. Aquinas, *Summa Contra Gentiles*, I:30.2.

Aquinas gives an example in the next section after discussing metaphor where a stone is not a proper name of God the way wisdom is. Nevertheless, a stone "imitates God as its cause in being and goodness."[41] This more than makes possible references to God using the female (even from the animal world, as we will see), but the question is really whether these are of the same importance as male images.

For Aquinas, they are not. This is indicative of a larger defect in Aquinas's thinking. Aquinas seems to prioritize males in God's image over females. Aquinas locates the image of God in the rational powers of the soul. He notes that the image of God, that is, the rational soul, is in both men and women. However, since the man in Genesis 2, by Aquinas's reading, is the origin of the creation of woman, women are to be naturally subservient to men as a part of good social order, and these are coupled with how women are equated strongly with their ability to generate offspring, creating an imbalance. Since women are captive to their capacity of generation, the rationality of the male is superior. Genevieve Lloyd notes,

> For Aquinas, then, woman does not symbolize an inferior form or lesser presence of rationality. But her meaning is bound up with the reproduction of human nature, in distinction from those operations—including noble intellectual functioning—which define what human nature is. Despite Aquinas's insistence that she is "made in the image of God" in respect to the "rational principle," she is symbolically located outside the actual manifestations of Reason within human life.... Aquinas is committed not only to the naturalness of woman's existence, but also to that of her subordination; and he sees it as grounding in the predominance of Reason in the male.[42]

Thus, Aquinas explains the subservience of women to men,

> Subjection is twofold. One is servile, by virtue of which a superior makes use of a subject for his own benefit; and this kind of subjection began after sin. There is another kind of subjection which is called economic or civil, whereby the superior makes use of his subjects for their own benefit and good; and this kind of subjection existed even before sin. For good order would have been wanting in the human family if some were not governed by others wiser than themselves. So, by such a kind of

---

41. Aquinas, *Summa Contra Gentiles*, I:31.2.
42. Lloyd, "Augustine and Aquinas," 96.

subjection woman is naturally subject to man, because in man the discretion of reason predominates.[43]

Like much speech about God, while the explicit claim is that God is not male, the resulting associations suggest otherwise. This is evident in Aquinas's analogical language, particularly when it comes to God's name. In wondering whether "Father" is the name of the first member of the Trinity, Aquinas offers several reasons for thinking it is. In contrast to the name "begetter," Aquinas offers the case for "Father" because of the perfection and end of generation that fatherhood performs:

> According to the Philosopher [i.e., Aristotle], a thing is denominated chiefly by its perfection, and by its end. Now generation signifies something in process of being made, whereas paternity signifies the complement of generation; and therefore, the name "Father" is more expressive as regards the divine person than genitor or begetter.[44]

One may ask, why cannot God be a mother as well? For Aquinas, as he quotes Aristotle on procreation (who espouses that women are in procreation "misbegotten males," a point Aquinas distances himself from), motherhood is strictly passive and thus incapable of naming God's generative capacities:

> As regards the individual nature, woman is defective and misbegotten, for the active force in the male seed tends to the production of a perfect likeness in the masculine sex; while the production of woman comes from a defect in the active force or from some material indisposition, or even from some external influence; such as that of a south wind, which is moist, as the Philosopher observes (De Gener. Animal. iv, 2). On the other hand, as regards human nature in general, woman is not misbegotten, but is included in nature's intention as directed to the work of generation. Now the general intention of nature depends on God, Who is the universal Author of nature. Therefore, in producing nature, God formed not only the male but also the female.[45]

Aquinas's analogical view of language strongly asserts that God's proper names, particularly the Father, do not come from human convention.

---

43. Aquinas, *Summa Theologiae*, I: Q 92, A 1.
44. Aquinas, *Summa Theologiae*, I: Q 33, A 2.
45. Aquinas, *Summa Theologiae*, I:92.1.

This creates a kind of check valve from the analogy of being's possible susceptibility to project God from human convention. While it should be noted that there should be a scriptural discernment of appropriate analogies to properly understand what is good and what is not, what is true beauty and what is a distortion, etc., it is established on the basis of Scripture that both men and women are in the image of God, and thus, in some way able to reflect God's being. But when addressing whether "Father" is properly the name of the divine person, Aquinas answers with the distinction DiNoia notes. Furthermore, Aquinas cites Eph 3:14 as evidence that the term "Father" is a name for the first member of the Trinity and thus the name is not, he thinks, based on human convention.

> The terms "generation" and "paternity" like the other terms properly applied to God, are said of God before creatures as regards the thing signified, but not as regards the mode of signification. Hence also the Apostle says, "I bend my knee to the Father of my Lord Jesus Christ, from whom all paternity in heaven and on earth is named" (Ephesians 3:14). This is explained thus. It is manifest that generation receives its species from the term which is the form of the thing generated; and the nearer it is to the form of the generator, the truer and more perfect is the generation; as univocal generation is more perfect than non-univocal, for it belongs to the essence of a generator to generate what is like itself in form.[46]

Sadly, Eph 3:14 is a common proof text for the conservative side in this debate. However, the nature of this text is routinely missed. Paul prays, "For this reason, I bow my knees before the Father (*pros ton patera*), from whom every family (*pasa patria*) in heaven and on earth takes its name" (3:14). This passage is often incorrectly translated as "from whom all fatherhood . . . takes its name." This passage does not demonstrate that all true fatherhood is derived from God's fatherhood in the ontological sense, nor is "Father" the name of God eternally, uninfluenced by cultural convention. It is a play on words that is really only applicable in Greek, and its employment in the greater context of Ephesians is very much about a convention—Greco-Roman families, governed by a *paterfamilias*—which is being used metaphorically to describe the new reality of gentiles and Jews joining together in the household of God (this will be discussed further in a later chapter). In this regard, Aquinas's line of reasoning does not succeed in defending his assertions.

46. Aquinas, *Summa Theologiae*, I:33.2.

Soskice has noted that analogies, like metaphors, are entirely contextual in how they deliver meaning. She also warns that linguistic tropes cannot be made into philosophical processes so easily. Aquinas's massively influential philosophy of analogical language and the analogy of being yields tensions in this debate. If his account of God as the goodness of every goodness is correct, the goodness of femininity can be used to point back to God. On the other hand, his account of how language arises for God and his understanding of femininity preclude it. However, the question is whether analogy, like metaphor, really encompasses all the ways of speaking about God (we will cover narrative patterns shortly, but as we will see in a later chapter, conversive-doxological language is another way of thinking about divine language).

BIBLICAL ANALOGIES AND METAPHORS FOR GOD AS FEMALE AND MOTHERLY

While this debate has instrumentally appealed to analogy and metaphor as concepts that perform certain functions for their respective theologies, these appeals can do little to deliver on their expectations apart from looking at the Bible's actual usage of analogies and metaphors. Thus, a survey of the gendered symbols in the Bible will be undertaken with the questions of each side in mind: Do these symbols arise independently of human convention? Is there an absence of female and motherly imagery (as some assert)? Is feminine imagery to be equated with paganism, polytheism, and pantheism? (This survey will focus on the motherly and female symbols to clarify some of these questions, as fatherly imagery will be discussed with narrative description.)

While it may be a surprise for some, there are notable female and motherly references to God in the Bible. There are both important analogies as well as metaphors. First and foremost, there are explicit usages of motherhood and birthing metaphors, which directly contradict Aquinas's assumptions regarding providence and procreation. Deuteronomy 32:18 refers to God "bearing" and "birthing" Israel, which Israel has forgotten God in its disobedience: "You deserted the Rock, who bore you. You forgot the God who gave you birth." The metaphor of birthing is continued in Job 38:28–29: "Has the rain a father, or who has begotten the drops of dew? From whose womb comes the ice? Who gives birth to the frost from the heavens . . . ?" Notice the occurrence of the fathering and birthing images set together. Isaiah 46:3–4 continues this metaphor and applies it to the beginning and sustaining of Israel: "[Y]ou whom I have upheld since you were conceived, and have carried since your birth. Even to your old age and grey hairs, I am he, I am he who will sustain you. I have made you and I will carry you; I will sustain you and I will rescue you." Note, again, in this passage, the pronoun "he" is used alongside the metaphor of birthing.

The mother image is again employed analogically in Isaiah 66.

> Rejoice with Jerusalem, and be glad for her,
> all you who love her;
> rejoice with her in joy,
> all you who mourn over her—
> that you may nurse and be satisfied
> from her consoling breast;
> that you may drink deeply with delight
> From her glorious bosom.
> For thus says the LORD:
> I will extend prosperity to her like a river,
> and the wealth of the nations like an overflowing stream;
> and you shall nurse and be carried on her arm,
> and dandled on her knees.
> As a mother comforts her child,
> so I will comfort you;
> you shall be comforted in Jerusalem. (Isa 66:10–13)

This is a peculiar passage since Jerusalem is personified as a woman nursing the people whom God has restored, but then God identifies with this analogy. God is like the mother (Jerusalem) that comforts the people. The parallelism in the final verse seems to treat the mother, Jerusalem, and God as the same identity: "As a mother comforts her child, so I will comfort you; you shall be comforted in Jerusalem." Other passages suggest that Zion is the dwelling place of God (cf. Isa 8:18; 4:5–6; this foreshadows later discussion on the Shekinah of God). The presence is used in this passage as a kind of metaphorical identification. Isaiah 49:15 talks about a nursing mother but then suggests that God's love exceeds this:

> Can a mother forget the baby at her breast
> and have no compassion on the child she has borne?
> Though she may forget,
> I will not forget you!

As will be shown in the next section, these metaphors and analogies also have an apophatic quality to them, which is shown in the sweep of the narrative. The narrative is the source of apophasis as the acts of God form the basis of why no human conception of God can properly encapsulate the boundlessness of God's being in goodness and grace.

The motherly metaphor is vividly used to speak of God's wrath and then restoration:

> For a long time I have held my peace,
> I have kept still and restrained myself;
> now I will cry out like a woman in labor,
> I will gasp and pant.
> I will lay waste mountains and hills,
> and dry up all their herbage;
> I will turn the rivers into islands,
> and dry up the pools.
> I will lead the blind
> by a road they do not know,
> by paths they have not known
> I will guide them.
> I will turn the darkness before them into light,
> the rough places into level ground.
> These are the things I will do,
> and I will not forsake them. (Isa 42:14–16)

What is fascinating about this reference is that wrath is usually considered a male trait, but here, it is used to talk about the anger of God. This wrath, however, is creative and redemptive.

This also allows for a number of metaphorical identifications with traditionally female roles. God, for instance, is a midwife, "Yet you brought me out of the womb; you made me trust in you . . ." (Ps 22:9). In less direct ways, God is likened to the action of women in the Psalms and parables. Psalm 123:2 reads,

> As the eyes of servants
> look to the hand of their master,
> as the eyes of a maid
> to the hand of her mistress,
> so our eyes look to the LORD our God,
> until he has mercy upon us.

This passage uses both male and female analogies with the singular male pronoun. In Jesus' teachings, God is a woman looking for her lost coin:

"Or suppose a woman has ten silver coins and loses one. Does she not light a lamp, sweep the house, and search carefully until she finds it? And when she finds it, she calls her friends and neighbors together and says, 'Rejoice with me; I have found my lost coin.' In the same way, I tell you, there is rejoicing in the presence of the angels of God over one sinner who repents" (Luke 15:8–10). God's kingdom is like a woman baking bread: "Again he asked, 'What shall I compare the kingdom of God to? It is like yeast that a woman took and mixed into a large amount of flour until it worked all through the dough'" (Luke 13:20–21).

If all creation is good, then not only humans but also animals can bear the divine perfections to communicate something of God. God's protection is metaphorically the wings of a bird: "Like an eagle that stirs up its nest, that flutters over its young, spreading out its wings, catching them, bearing them on its pinions, the LORD alone guided him" (Deut 32:11–12). Ruth 2:12 reads: "May you be richly rewarded by the LORD the God of Israel, under whose wings you have come to take refuge." This metaphor is continued in Ps 17:8 and is even used by Jesus himself to describe his love of Jerusalem despite judgment being imminent: "[H]ow often I have longed to gather your children together, as a hen gathers her chicks under her wings" (Matt 23:37b). Similarly, the dove resting on Jesus in baptism draws from this imagery.

The animal images are also interesting in that they are used to communicate God's wrath. God is like a mother bear: "Like a bear robbed of her cubs, I will attack them and rip them open" (Hos 13:8a). The interesting aspect of this analogy is that Israel, while being the child of God's compassion in chapter 11, is the object of wrath here (in other words, Israel is not the cubs).

While there are important metaphors and analogies for God as female and motherly, there are also titles and attributes with feminine connotations. Titles of God, like *El Shaddai*, God Almighty, have been argued to be feminine. *Shaddai* may be derivative from *shadu*, meaning "breasts," suggesting God's power over creation is like human fertility.[47] This is suggested in the fertility blessing of Gen 49:25:

> because of your father's God, who helps you,
> because of the Almighty [*El Shaddai*], who blesses you
> with blessings of the skies above,

---

47. See Gen 17:1; 28:3; 35:11; 43:14; 48:3; 49:25. Several of these coincide with themes of fertility, thus corroborating the connotation. See Biale, "The God with Breasts," 240–56. Also see Mollenkott, *The Divine Feminine*.

blessings of the deep springs below,
blessings of the breasts [*shadayim*] and womb.

Biale notes that the title *El Shaddai* may come out of the culture, as the Yahweh religion fought for supremacy over Asherah religions, but it seems that the title gets appropriated to Yahweh as a way of polemicizing, transforming it into connotations of both fertility and war. Phyllis Trible also notes that one of the Hebrew words for compassion (*rahum*) is a word with womb-like connotations, tender compassion as a mother has for a child due to the strong maternal bond.[48] In Jer 31: 15–22, God comforts "Rachel weeping for her children" (v. 15), children who are crying out in Ramah (the traditional city of Rachel's burial), and God comforts her by describing God's own love of Ephraim using this word:

> "Is not Ephraim my dear son,
> the child in whom I delight?
> Though I often speak against him,
> I still remember him.
> Therefore my heart yearns for him;
> I have great *compassion* for him,"
> declares the LORD. (Jer 31:20)

This passage powerfully uses motherly bonds to reassure Rachel (who is a personification here). Nevertheless, the use of female imagery to speak to the female is noteworthy. God's love is motherly, and this comforts mothers when they think about what their children endure.

Some important insights can be gleaned from this brief survey. First, analogies and metaphors for God very much arise from the cultural experience of Israel. Aquinas is incorrect in asserting that language does not come from convention. Moreover, if they did not arise from the experience of the Israelites, they would be meaningless. The fact that they are used to illustrate God's love very much confirms the analogical and metaphorical theory laid out that God is the goodness of every good, such that the goodness of creation can be used to point to God. However, this brings up the question of projection. As already hinted, the love of God in acts of deliverance shows that God exceeds every attempt to reduce God's being to human convention. God uses human language and convention, but it is God's actions that show no language can contain it.

Second, one should note the existence of "dual" gender references. Deuteronomy 32, for instance, couples father language (v. 6) with

---

48. Trible, "Feminist Hermeneutics and Biblical Studies," 25.

motherly images like birthing (v. 18). This is echoed in a passage like Job 38:28–29. This point is conceded by Donald Bloesch as he vigorously disagrees with female pagan imagery. After a brief survey of some of these aforementioned scriptures, he writes,

> Nevertheless, because feminine as well as masculine imagery for God exists in the Scriptures, it is possible to speak of a divine motherhood as well as a divine fatherhood. Yet the latter is the controlling symbol. Feminine is grounded in masculinity in the Bible (Eve came out of Adam) just as motherhood is grounded in fatherhood. The masculine is the ground of the feminine, but the feminine is the goal and glory of the masculine (1 Cor. 11:7).[49]

However, Bloesch's point is drowned out by the obvious cultural ring the line of reasoning has. For instance, the references to the Father having a womb may be a metonym for the mother, one that is not used today. While there are biological descriptions of women's reproductive organs, it cannot be ignored that there are very few, if any, references to God having male reproductive organs. The imagery of the Bible overlaps and differs in a polymorphous way (for example, God is both parent and lover despite the two being incompatible at the same time). This could mean for these specific passages that the pairing is a merism, symbolizing both genders in God. If this is the case, it combines, from a cultural standpoint, the authority of the father with the power of fertility of the mother. While this concedes much to the culture, on the one hand, where women were objectified for their ability to produce children, on the other hand, it does symbolize the incorporation of femininity into God, a negating of God as purely or straightforwardly male. Is the meaning of these symbols that masculinity grounds femininity or that these cultural lines of reasoning are showing a deeper theology where God is found in both the male and female (and yet beyond both)? If it is the former, it is a conviction that finds no basis in biological history. Thus, Carl Raschke and Susan Doughty Raschke assert that the God of the Bible is often portrayed as having both genders. This is masked, again, to most readers in that God is often portrayed with the male pronoun (with the exception of Lady Wisdom, see chapter 5), but the fixation on the male pronoun does not properly reflect Gen 1:27's insistence that both male and female are in the

---

49. Bloesch, *The Battle for the Trinity*, 34–35.

image of God, nor does it really explain the complex portraits where the biblical writers use strong female characteristics with male pronouns.[50]

Based on this, God is Father but has breasts and a womb (the cultural-biological marks of femininity), and thus, contains both genders. These images have important moments of recognition in Christian theological tradition. This language was even taken up in the description of the Trinity in the eleventh council of Toledo in AD 675, which describes the Son as begotten from the "womb of the Father." Aquinas does not draw this implication when he discusses the Trinity, but other writers do. Clement of Alexandria (ca. AD 150–ca. AD 215) writes concerning the Son, "The Word is everything to his little ones, both father and mother and tutor and nurse."[51] Clement goes on to speak of the breasts of the Father, Son, and Spirit that nourish the church: ". . . little ones who seek the Word, the craved for milk is given from the Father's breasts of love for man."[52] Teresa of Avila speaks a similar way: "For from those divine breasts where it seems God is always sustaining the soul, there flow streams of milk bringing comfort to all people."[53] Similarly, John Chrysostom hails God as, "Thou art my Father, thou art my Mother, thou my Brother, thou art Friend, thou art Servant, thou art House-keeper; thou art the All, and the All is in thee; thou art Being, and there is nothing that is, except thou."[54] Writers such as John Calvin did not miss these references but failed to integrate them into their theology and liturgical practices. For instance, in commenting on the Isaiah passages, Calvin writes, responding to arguments that "Father" is a more appropriate title for God, "that no figures of speech can describe God's extraordinary affection towards us; for it is infinite and various." However, in regards to Isa 46:3, he writes God "has manifested himself to be both . . . Father and Mother."[55] Calvin, in Isaiah 49:15, writes,

> *Shall a woman forget her child!* In order to correct that distrust, he adds to the remonstrance an exhortation full of the sweetest consolation. By an appropriate comparison, he shews how strong is his anxiety about his people, comparing himself to a

50. See Raschke and Doughty Raschke, *The Engendering God*.
51. Clement of Alexandria in *Christ the Educator*, 1:6.
52. Clement, *Christ the Educator*, 1:6.
53. Teresa of Avila, *Interior Castle*, 179–80. See also Haddad, "Evidence for and Significance of Feminine God Language."
54. Chrysostom, "Homilies on the Gospel of Saint Matthew," 447.
55. Calvin, *Commentary on Isaiah*, vol. 3, sect. 46:3.

> mother, whose love toward her offspring is so strong and ardent, as to leave far behind it a father's love. Thus, he did not satisfy himself with proposing the example of a father, (which on other occasions he very frequently employs,) but in order to express his very strong affection, he chose to liken himself to a mother, and calls them not merely "children," but *the fruit of the womb*, towards which there is usually a warmer affection. What amazing affection does a mother feel toward her offspring, which she cherishes in her bosom, suckles on her breast, and watches over with tender care, so that she passes sleepless nights, wears herself out by continued anxiety, and forgets herself! And this carefulness is manifested, not only among men, but even among savage beasts, which, though they are by nature cruel, yet in this respect are gentle.[56]

More of these instances will be explored later, but their existence is important. They cannot be overemphasized, however, as to make it seem that the history of the church is impeccable. It is far from that. These moments are few, and they were not well integrated into the rest of the respective thinkers' theology. However, they are there in a kind of latent form for theology today to consider.

Third, the accusation against feminine imagery is that femininity is associated with paganism, pantheism, and polytheism. In fact, while God is virtually never described by the reproductive organs of a male in the Bible, it is vastly more common that God is described with the reproductive organs of women: breasts that nurse and a womb that delivers. The accusations are stunningly neglectful of the above passages, which make it abundantly clear that female anatomy and motherly descriptions do not imply paganism. Feminine analogies and metaphors do not negate the biblical text with something outside the Bible but negate a proof text by appealing to a fuller canonical sense. The fact that they are criticized as such could be indicative of deep-seated unconscious prejudice, associating femininity with these things or, in turn, fuelling such prejudice. On the other hand, contemplating and emphasizing these passages can be used to negate patriarchal images that have dominated many people's thinking. Ironically, the very accusations against female imagery, given the biblical passages, actually offer an appropriate warrant for emphasizing them today.

---

56. Calvin, *Commentary on Isaiah*, vol. 4, sect. 49:15.

Furthermore, there seems to be a kind of double standard in this discussion. Mother and feminine language are inherently sexualized in the view of some, whereas Father language is not. Divine Fatherhood does not indicate gender, the defense goes, but nevertheless, male pronouns for this symbol are the only ones permitted. It seems odd to say that the Father symbol and the accompanying pronoun "he" are not about maleness and then to insist that we use only them, and not use female imagery. These assertions smack of literalism. To pretend that masculine imagery does not in some way correspond to masculine analogies in the human sphere, even to overturn patriarchal usages, drains the symbol of rhetorical power. It would make more sense to say that the male pronoun does speak of masculinity in that God is imminent to all the good of creation, and this particular way of speaking has an important cultural-rhetorical significance, but this does not limit God to the masculine. God uses the masculine to challenge the masculine. God uses female language as well, but God is beyond all language and gender, ultimately.

Fourth, the characteristics associated with these feminine and motherly metaphors also do not conform entirely to gender stereotypes. God's creative power, providential strength, and wrath, which, according to common stereotypes, are predominantly male traits, are actually imaged according to female metaphors and analogies in places. While there are, of course, the nurturing qualities of the mother, this does not form a binary that suggests a harsh father image. As it will be seen shortly, God as Father is the gentle Father. Also, if the Father symbol was used to uphold transcendence, as some argue, that would imply that the imminence of God, whether in the presence of God or the incarnation of God, ought to necessarily be female. Neither is strictly the case, and thus, the use of gender binaries is often highly problematic. Elizabeth Johnson has suggested that motherly traits can fill out the portrayal of God's suffering love (which, as shown, is utilized in Scripture).[57] To say that God suffers with creation as a mother in labor is a biblically meaningful analogy. However, some caution is appropriate here. Sarah Coakley warns that the creation of gender binaries can further reiterate stereotypes.[58] Painting the Father as oppressive and powerful and the Mother as oppressed and nurturing can further reinforce patriarchy in the very act of abolishing Father language. Furthermore, one should not say that motherhood is

---

57. Johnson, *She Who Is*, 254.
58. Coakley, *God, Sexuality, and the Self*, 326–27.

the definitive expression of femininity. Gender is a vastly more complicated and multifaceted phenomenon than any one set of attributes. All gender is a cultural construction by which a person or community interprets their physical sex, resulting in different roles that the body is expressed through. While there is an appeal to common social experiences and roles that are cherished (e.g., an expecting woman's bodily connection to their unborn child, the experience of birth, the nursing mother's connection with her baby), they need to be employed carefully not to reduce femininity to one role nor exclude the other gender from positive qualities. As Isaiah wisely employed, an experience like birth, while it is a time of pain, vulnerability, and joy, can also be a display of great strength and anger. Thus, one should proceed with care in using the gendered traits of God but also know that there is great meaning in these common experiences.

THE NATURE OF NARRATIVE

The rules for analogy and metaphor have been sufficiently clarified, but questions remain: if both analogy and metaphors of God as Mother and Father, masculine imagery and female imagery, are possible, how are they employed appropriately? For example, Hos 11:10 says that God will "roar like a lion." However, 1 Pet 5:8 also likens the devil to a "roaring lion." If God is a Father, how is God understood differently from abusive fathers? How does analogy resist projection? The answer to this, as Soskice reminds us, is that these figures of speech always find their fuller meaning in larger linguistic units. For Scripture, this is primarily narrative, but what this means for the historicity of the Bible, the Bible as canon, its interpretation, and human experience needs clarifying.

The meaning of narrative is, in part, the question of whether it refers to historic events or merely the expression of perennial human experiences. The last century has seen vigorous debates concerning the history of Scripture, particularly the rise of historical-critical methods. This has impacted the debates, as already noted, since, for instance, some have judged that the biblical narrative has very little or no historicity (or if it does, such historicity does not appear essential to its function as a faith document) and thus, its narrative functions like pure poetry, offering expressive symbols of human experience, which can be supplemented and correlated based on contemporary needs.

ANALOGY AND NARRATIVE

Are the narratives of the Bible primarily allegories? As Hans Frei argues, the narrative means what it says in regard to the character it renders. It offers realistic narratives even when it is not rendering precise history or a narrative that is not intentionally historical. They are not firstly allegories of something other than themselves (and this is particularly the case with the Gospels' rendering of God in Jesus, Frei's main focus). They have a primary particularity to them that finds its meaning firstly in the rendering of the character. This does not bar historical-critical insights or force the narrative to be treated as historically pristine but rather admits there is an inherent particularity to the narratives. George Lindbeck comments on this dynamic:

> We now can make a distinction (unavailable before the development of modern science and historical studies) between realistic narrative and historical or scientific descriptions. The Bible is often "history-like" even when it is not "likely history." It can, therefore, be taken seriously in the first respect as a delineator of the character of the divine and human agents, even when its history or science is challenged. As parables such as that of the prodigal son remind us, the rendering of God's character is not in every instance logically dependent on the facticity of the story.[59]

However, this does not mean the narrative is ambivalent to historicity. While the Bible contains mythological material and even its narratives, which do claim to report history, are not infallible or unquestionable (and still further, it must be noted that much of the Bible's narrative simply fall beyond the scope of historical verification); nevertheless, there is a consensus of scholars that see a historical core, particularly with the life of Christ, and there are events (such as the crucifixion and the resurrection) whose truth is bound up with whether they did occur in history. More will be said about this matter in the next chapter, but to read the Bible as a realistic narrative, the way it is intended, is to see it pointing with its narratives to the event of Jesus, who is the ultimate truth of the Bible. The truth of the text is not firstly found in its contemporary relevance (although it is important); it is found firstly in its realistic depiction that prefigures Christ, who is the culmination of the Bible's story, the risen one who continues to encounter the church today. Only through Christ then does this narrative speak to the present.

---

59. Lindbeck, *The Nature of Doctrine*, 122.

However, it must be cautioned that the category "realistic narrative" is by no means a way of rendering the text in an oversimplified manner. When one comes across a passage that could seem ethically problematic at face value, one must keep in mind that the narratives of Scripture have both vertical depth and horizontal breadth in meaning. As the literary critic Erich Auerbach noted, the terse nature of the Hebrew narrative is that it is "fraught with background."[60] It invites questions and curiosities. It has rich layers of meaning. For instance, a narrative like the sacrifice of Isaac, which at face value it might seem like God's approval of child sacrifice, actually, in the sweep of the narrative, displays a complex subversion of sacrifice by God's generosity. One must discern this as it is subtly spelled out. Similarly, the treatment of Hagar by Abraham and Sarah, a gruesome story like the death of the Levite's concubine, or tragic tales like the fate of Jephthah's daughter are not told to praise the moral character of the Israelites. As Phyllis Trible points out, these narratives must be read to disturb and disrupt, remembering the fatal consequences of patriarchy. She says, "If art imitates life, scripture likewise reflects it in both holiness and horror."[61] As singular texts are read through the whole sweep of the Bible, the canon allows for an expansive "polysemous" meaning, the meaning of a single passage getting richer and deeper as the text expands to include the whole range and scope of the Bible.[62] Northrop Frye points out how the narratives, while referring outside themselves (like a "centrifuge," he says), also acquire a "centripetal" meaning as the narrative elements refer back and forth to each other, revolving around its central typologies.[63] This forms a single unified narrative within the canon, which Frye describes:

> What matters is that "the Bible" has traditionally been read as a unity and has influenced Western imagination as a unity.... It has a beginning and an end and some traces of a total structure. It begins where time begins, with the creation of the world; it ends where times ends, with the Apocalypse, and it surveys human history in between.[64]

---

60. Auerbach, *Mimesis*, 12.
61. Trible, *Texts of Terror*, 2.
62. Frye, *The Great Code*, 220.
63. Frye, *The Great Code*, 57.
64. Frye, *The Great Code*, xiii.

The priority of a unified story allows for important counter-oppressive possibilities of interpretation. Reading the text through its central narratives of the exodus and resurrection places liberation as the apex of both the story and God's character and intention, and therefore, an important pragmatic criterion of how the story is retold well. Robert Alter notes that interpretation is a process of continual revision, where there is an essential "indeterminacy of meaning" in the text, a richness to the text that resists simplistic univocity of meaning that can be invoked in an authoritarian manner: "Meaning, perhaps for the first time in narrative literature, was conceived as a *process*, requiring continual revision—both in the ordinary sense and in the etymological sense of seeing-again—continual suspension of judgment, weighing of multiple possibilities, brooding over gaps in the information."[65] This allows for the interplay of listening, interpreting, imagining, and weighing different possibilities. Thus, while the narrative is realistic, this does not create an unquestionable literalism or dogmatism.

Thus, Scripture presents this unified story, a story of many stories, and this collection is the canon that regulates Christian thought. Now, one should note that the Bible, as a collection bound together as a canon, is not as obvious as we would assume it. It is the work of the traditions of the synagogue and the church, which show a complicated history of canonization over several centuries. As Craig Allert notes, there were many documents considered revelatory, inspired, the word of God, and Scripture in the early church that were not included as part of the New Testament canon.[66] Thus, none of these categories succeed in themselves in saying why the canon is authoritative. The claims of revelation and prophecy had to be discerned. They were discerned in the community using the Old Testament and the oral tradition passed on from the apostles. Thus, the canon is not the exclusive revelation, but since it records the person of Jesus, it came to be what regulates all other claims of revelation.

There are variations in what limits the canon between Roman Catholics, Greek Orthodox, Protestants, and others. Fiorenza suspects anti-female prejudice influenced the formation of the canon we have today. She notes that Tertullian objected to the *Acts of Paul and Thecla* being included because they promoted female leadership.[67] Nevertheless, this book was never considered in the main group of documents. Fiorenza is

---

65. See Alter, *The Art of Biblical Narrative*, 12.
66. See Allert, *A High View of Scripture?*
67. Fiorenza, *In Memory of Her*, 53–56.

right to suspect that patriarchalization affected the church, but her suspicion regarding the canon is overstated. It is more accurate to say that patriarchalization probably affected the transmission of a large body of secondary documents; some of these were destroyed because they were spurious, and others fell out of usage for unclear reasons. One of these reasons very likely was an anti-female prejudice growing in the church. While an early "closed" canon is not really accurate to the travail of debate regarding a number of documents, there was a core list of books that the consensus of the church regarded as trustworthy early on, which are recorded in the Muratorian Fragment, the earliest canonical list. This is to say that when the unified story of Scripture is presented to the church through the contemporary canon today, this is neither to regard it as impeccable nor unreliable. The canon is the vehicle for the story, and in that regard, it presents the center of the narrative despite questions concerning the circumference.

What does this mean for human experience and the interpretation of the Bible? One does not merely come to the Bible and impose categories upon the narrative. Remember that George Lindbeck warns that to see Scripture as offering a cultural-linguistic system means that through the process of interpretation, the text absorbs the world, not vice versa. In other words, the figures and narrative of the Bible are not made into some other story or transferred into some other kind of reference point than its reference to the story of Jesus Christ. This does not forbid criticism, revision, contextualization, etc., but it does mean the center of Scripture has a regulative and interpretive capacity over all other things brought into conversation with it. The narrative of the Bible takes priority, and it is through this that all other narratives are understood.

What this means, then, is that the Bible as a canon can be taken as a realistic narrative, revealing God, and this opens up the possibility for the incorporation of other figures, not the exclusion of them.

NARRATIVE AND THE FATHER SYMBOL IN THE OLD TESTAMENT

The canonical story presents a single character, acting from beginning to end: God. It is within this narrative context that the Father symbol is best understood.

ANALOGY AND NARRATIVE

As Paul Ricoeur argues, "The naming of God is thus, first of all, a narrative naming. The theology of traditions names God in accord with a historical drama that recounts itself as a narrative of liberation. . . . It is these events that name God."[68] The analogical and metaphorical ways are susceptible to projection and confusion that make them dependent on being understood through God's acts in history as concrete descriptors for Israel's worship.[69] Here, the revelation of God as "I am who I am" cannot be forgotten (a detail we have commented on in the previous chapter). The central confession of Israel was based on God's forgiveness of Israel after the idolatry of the golden calf, where Moses beholds God's identity as "the LORD" and, therefore, "compassionate and gracious God, slow to anger, abounding in love and faithfulness" (Exod 34:6–7). As Brueggemann notes, this "credo of adjectives" runs through the whole Old Testament.[70] It is these loving attributes that often get communicated with parental imagery. This suggests that fundamental to the divine essence is not gender (as there are no specific gender references in the divine name or central attributes), but this ineffable character of agapeic love is illustrated with gender. In this regard, the metaphors of God as a father of Israel will be explored here to show how these metaphors are not only used to communicate God's redemptive acts but also are used in the Old Testament in a way that resists absorption into the patriarchal culture from which the analogies are often taken.

As Ricoeur writes, "The revelation of the name is the dissolution of all anthropomorphisms, of all figures and figurations, including that of the father. The name against the idol."[71] God is a rock, but God is not found in idols. Aquinas is more than aware of these kinds of confusions, and so, his own way of analogically understanding God moves from affirmation and negation to what he calls the way of eminence, where a purer referring is possible.[72] An isolated metaphor for God must be understood within the narrative patterns of God's action, whether the actions of God as Father and Mother are truly understood. What this shows is that the characteristic behavior of God is described with a diversity of

---

68. Ricoeur, "Naming God," in *Figuring the Sacred*, 225.

69. See Wright, *God Who Acts*.

70. See Brueggemann, *Old Testament Theology*, ch. 5.

71. Ricoeur, "Fatherhood: From Phantasm to Symbol," in *Conflict of Interpretations*, 486.

72. Aquinas, *Summa Contra Gentiles*, 1:30.4. See Long, *Speaking of God*, 149–215, for an account of these ways of language in Aquinas.

descriptions and that these descriptions, whether fatherly or motherly, are not referring to God's gender but rather to God's goodness and love. We see this with the metaphor of God as Father.

The title "Father" is given a concrete description in the narratives of Israel and reflected in the doxology of the Psalms. This is shown in the following passages: the Song of Moses (Deut 32:6), the vision of Nathan (2 Sam 7:12–14; cf. 1 Chr 17:13; 22:10; 28:6), several in the Psalms and wisdom books (Pss 68:5; 89:27; 103:11–14; Prov 3:11–12; Job 38:28), as well as in the prophets (Isa 63:16; 64:7; Jer 3:4–20; 31:7–9; Mal 1:6; 2:10).[73] This metaphor is important (though not exclusive, given what we saw of female imagery) to how God communicates to an ancient patriarchal culture that worshiped the "father of the gods" and whose families were ruled by a patriarch. Because God is powerful and because men were powerful in the ancient culture, one sees the analogical reference of God as the Father. Feminists are correct to criticize this. Women did have a low worth in this culture, which factors into this prioritization, but the biblical narrative shows a characteristic surmounting of patriarchy in and through this accommodation.[74] God was like these supreme gods in authority, and God was like a father: creating, providing, protecting, promising, blessing, etc. However, this becomes a pathway of saying that when one looks at the narrative actions God does to define God's self, God is shown to be so much more than these. There is both metaphorical employment and narrative subversion of patriarchal images similar to Aquinas's affirmation and negation.

God was not merely the central God of the ancient pantheon, but rather, called Abraham out of this belief, out of his father's household, into a new reality of God's loving care, one that surmounts the regionalization of deity or the brutality of child sacrifice, etc. Similarly, God's fatherliness is central to God delivering his "firstborn" Israel out of Egypt (Exod 4:23). As this Father God is the God that made promises to the fathers of Israel, so also, God delivers his oppressed children, protecting them and giving them a new inheritance (Exod 6:6–8). Thus, the fatherly quality of God is, in many ways, a way of countering oppression and reiterating that God is unlike any other.

---

73. For an extended treatment on some of these passages, see Tasker, "The Fatherhood of God."

74. For a good analysis of how the Bible has been both repressive as well as the means of redemption, and how to understand these in interpretation, see Webb, *Slaves, Women, and Homosexuals*.

This forms the background for the Song of Moses in Deuteronomy 32. We have already noted the motherly metaphors here, but the fatherly qualities, based in part on the social roles of the patriarch of the culture, still show characteristic subversions. The traits ascribed to God are as follows: "The Rock, his work is perfect / and all his ways are just. / A faithful God, without deceit / just and upright is he" (Deut 32:4). The passage notes the rebellion of God's children, Israel, and then recounts the actions of God in sustaining (v. 10), protecting, caring, and guiding (v. 11), as well as feeding and nursing (v. 13). The passage warns of the jealousy of God, who is coming to punish Israel for their rebellion (vv. 15–28). After which, God speaks about how the nations defeated Israel, but God is the true source of vengeance (v. 35). Because of this, God will vindicate and have compassion on Israel (v. 36). This then leads into the declaration "See now that I, even I, am he; there is no god besides me" (v. 39). Set within the context of the covenant, this song speaks of the patriarch's role in providing, protecting, and punishing, but it exceeds the expectations of fatherly love as God pledges still, despite the people's rebellion, to vindicate and have compassion. The contractual nature of the covenant is infused with God's character, transforming a covenant between sovereign and people into the relationship between child and parent, but not only that, a parent that is trustworthy and committed to compassion unlike any other.

While this will be taken up further in the explanation of God as Father in the New Testament, a significant employment of the title Father is in the covenant with David and his line. The covenant reads,

> When your days are fulfilled, and you lie down with your ancestors, I will raise up your offspring after you, who shall come forth from your body, and I will establish his kingdom. He shall build a house for my name, and I will establish the throne of his kingdom forever. I will be a father to him, and he shall be a son to me. When he commits iniquity, I will punish him with a rod such as mortals use, with blows inflicted by human beings. (2 Sam 7:12–14)

This passage is alluded to in 1 Chr 17:13; 22:10; 28:6, but also in Ps 2:7 and more explicitly in Ps 89:27. This claim of the king as the son of the Father God mirrors Israel as the child of God. Nathan's vision seems to carefully specify that David will produce the descendants of David; they are not directly fathered by God. Kings of the time typically claimed parentage from the gods to secure divine status. This is not the case here.

Solomon will build the temple, but he will not be above the law. It seems that the king will be disciplined for wrongdoing in the same way as Israel, suggesting a much higher degree of accountability for the king than in surrounding cultures. Nevertheless, this comes with the promise of a throne and kingdom that will last forever. This, again, is accommodated to the patriarchy of the time, where queens were rare. It is very much based on the convention of the familial bond combined with the pledge of God to the king and the subsequent kings.

With the messianic theme in Ps 2, fatherhood is implied throughout the Psalms despite rarely being stated explicitly. Nonetheless, Ps 68 praises God and calls him "Father of orphans and protector of widows" (v. 5). In the preceding verses, there are clear allusions to the deliverance and presence of God from the Exodus narrative (vv. 1–4), implying that the character of God as Father to orphans and protector of widows is consistent with God's liberating presence to Israel. Psalm 103 displays the Fatherhood of God in particular redemptive beauty. The beginning of the Psalm recounts God's works:

> Bless the LORD, O my soul,
> and do not forget all his benefits—
> who forgives all your iniquity,
> who heals all your diseases,
> who redeems your life from the Pit,
> who crowns you with steadfast love and mercy,
> who satisfies you with good as long as you live
> so that your youth is renewed like the eagle's.
> The LORD works vindication
> and justice for all who are oppressed. (Ps 103:2–6)

Then the psalm recites the credo of attributes (v. 8). However, while the first credo of attributes in Exod 34 mentioned that God would punish to the third and fourth generation (Exod 34:7), this characteristic seems to disappear as descriptions of God's overwhelming forgiveness are stressed.

> He will not always accuse,
> nor will he keep his anger forever.
> He does not deal with us according to our sins,
> nor repay us according to our iniquities. (Ps 103:9–10)

This forms the context for the Psalmist's invocation of the title Father:

> For as the heavens are high above the earth,
> so great is his steadfast love toward those who fear him;

> as far as the east is from the west,
> so far he removes our transgressions from us.
> As a father has compassion for his children,
> so the LORD has compassion for those who fear him.
> (Ps 103:11–13)

The flow of this psalm is paradigmatic for understanding the Father symbol. It begins with God's name, the LORD (YHWH), coupled with the credo of attributes. It is only then that the title Father gets invoked as an illustration of these attributes. The impression it gives is clear: God loves like a father, but this only pertains to good fathers, and even so, God is unfathomably more loving.

There are moments that surmount patriarchy as fatherly metaphors were used to speak of God's care in light of Israel's waywardness, and so, in other words, the coldness of an unloving patriarch is transformed into a symbol of God's incomparable love: the father that never stops loving his children, unlike any other father. The Proverbs speaks of this relationship. As the reader often goes the way of foolishness, God speaks like a wise father trying to guide his son back:

> My child, do not despise the LORD's discipline
> or be weary of his reproof,
> for the LORD reproves the one he loves,
> as a father the son in whom he delights. (Prov 3:11–12)

Similarly, Isaiah invokes Father language as a means of mercy: "Yet, O LORD, you are our Father. We are the clay, you are the potter; we are all the work of your hand. Do not be angry beyond measure, O LORD; do not remember our sins forever" (Isa 64:7–9). Jeremiah sees God's fatherliness as incomparable love in the midst of Israel's rebellion: "They will come with weeping; they will pray as I bring them back. I will lead them beside streams of water on a level path where they will not stumble, because I am Israel's father, and Ephraim is my firstborn son" (Jer 31:9, cf. 3:19).

So strong is this metaphor that it forms the basis of a complaint to God by Isaiah. The writer of Isa 63 couples the power of God with the compassion of God the Father to charge God with causing the people to stumble:

> Where are your zeal and your might?
> The yearning of your heart and your compassion?
> They are withheld from me.
> For you are our father,

> though Abraham does not know us
> and Israel does not acknowledge us;
> you, O LORD, are our father;
> our Redeemer from of old is your name.
> Why, O LORD, do you make us stray from your ways
> and harden our heart, so that we do not fear you?
> Turn back for the sake of your servants,
> for the sake of the tribes that are your heritage. (Isa 63:15–17)

Like many of the Psalms, the prophet uses the promises and power of God as a basis for lament and even accusation. So strong is the insistence on God's providence that no event is outside the scope of God's action, and thus, these events form the basis of charges against God. While the primary testimony of Scripture is one that insists God is holy and good, this does not prevent a kind of counter-testimony where the people bring these laments before God. They are permitted and welcomed in prayer as the ambiguity of God's character is clarified in the process of history. In other words, what is perceived as God forsaking the people in the short term is eventually overshadowed by God's faithfulness in the long term. Nevertheless, the fatherly relation for Israel opens up a space of honesty and authenticity that is unmatched by the authoritarian nature of other deities to their subjects.

Finally, in Malachi, the fatherhood of God is reiterated. Interestingly enough, the analogy of the earthly father is again appealed to as a basis for understanding God:

> A son honors his father, and servants as their master. If then I am a father, where is the honor due me? And if I am a master, where is the respect due me? says the LORD of hosts to you, O priests, who despise my name. You say, "How have we despised your name?" (Mal 1:6)

If human fathers and masters deserve honor, how much more does God? This is stated in response to the corruption of the priesthood, who obviously would have appealed to conventions of honor to uphold their position. In the next chapter, the Father symbol is appealed to again:

> Have we not all one father? Has not one God created us? Why then are we faithless to one another, profaning the covenant of our ancestors? Judah has been faithless, and abomination has been committed in Israel and in Jerusalem; for Judah has profaned the sanctuary of the LORD, which he loves, and has married the daughter of a foreign god. (Mal 2:10–11)

As it will be shown in a later chapter, the Father symbol uses the love of the father as the leader of the household to expand the ethical duties of the members to one another by identifying them as all in the Father's household.

Thus, the Father symbol very much does arise out of human experience as an analogy, similar to Mother language previously sketched out, but the acts of God in the narratives of Scripture provide a reorientation point (whether the prophetic messages of God's incomparable love or the covenant with David) where this notion of fatherly love exceeds human projection. It should not be overlooked that while fatherly language is prioritized in this patriarchal society, the language also counters patriarchy, and there is an employment of gendered metaphors that shows awareness that such language does not fully grasp the narratives of God's faithful love. It seems that both sets of language are employed *not to make a statement of God's gender but in order to describe the incomparable love God has for Israel.* Thus, there is a kind of narrative travail of God with humanity, where symbols are not merely taken from the culture, nor are they revealed from on high untouched by history. They begin with analogies taken from the good experiences of the family, but in the process of narration, the character of God's forgiveness and love is shown to be faithful and incomparable to any human analogy. Robert Hamerton-Kelly comments on this dynamic:

> Among the prophets, God is called father directly, in order to emphasize his care for his people, as a foil to their sin—sin as an expression of ingratitude. Throughout the prophetic stage, whether the symbolization is direct or indirect, explicit or implied, there is a tendency to move back and forth between "father" and "mother" imagery. The symbol is described as that of a "parent," with a preponderance of the "father" element.[75]

Fatherliness (and motherly language) becomes less about the social order of power and more about "a symbol of free relationship and divine kindness."[76] This narrative clarification of metaphors and analogies anticipates the further clarification of both male imagery (coming to an apex in the biblical narrative with the Gospels of Jesus Christ) and the meaning of the Father (as Jesus uses it in trinitarian fashion).

---

75. Hamerton-Kelly, *God the Father*, 51.
76. Hamerton-Kelly, *God the Father*, 51.

The Father and the Feminine

REFLECTING THE IMAGE OF GOD

What follows is only a brief sketch of what these reflections can mean for human identity. It should be clear now that the goodness of creation and the events of its redemption in the story of Scripture offer the conditions and context of meaning by which one can refer to God with analogies and metaphors: God births and nurses like a mother, comforting her children, but as the narratives show, as the perfect Mother; God blesses as fathers did in that culture, only this God is the perfect Father to all humanity, never ceasing in inviting God's children to return to him. Yet, God is beyond every pattern of gender, calling humanity into transformation through union with God's ineffable nature. Becoming aware through one's thoughts and speech of this dynamic of God's being—where God is the being of all beings and the good of every goodness, where language for God has a characteristic "is and is not" or similarity and dissimilarity—opens up pathways for the healing of gender as one situates oneself in the narrative journey from recognizing the goodness of creation to embracing God's redemptive transformation.

As it will be shown in the concluding personal postscript of the concluding chapter, analogical contemplation does not merely get suggested by one's experience; rather, it is the means to experience further. To think of God in only male terms effectively often translates into a refusal to see the goodness of the feminine, denying the goodness of a facet of creation. In contemplating God as female, one is prompted to see in a fuller way how all that is feminine (as well as masculine) is something created good, receiving its goodness from the goodness of God, thus participating and reflecting God to those who are open to seeing it.[77] All metaphors and similes of Scripture aid in this kind of awareness and contemplation of God's omnipresence in the created order. God is like a rock, wind, fire, water, light, and dark; God is like a tree, lion, eagle, bear, mountain, etc. All of these are ways of communicating God and also a way of saying God is present here; this person bears God's presence and fingerprint as a creature; this role has goodness one must recognize. As the Quaker saying states, "There is that of God in everyone."

While the title "Father" is not explicitly mentioned in Genesis, the actions and designations are implied in the nature of the image of God.

---

77. While this book focuses on the more often denied presence of God in women and how these affect men, there are works that rebuke patriarchal tendencies that strive for healthy contemplation of masculinity. See Fox, *The Hidden Spirituality of Men*.

Humans are made in God's image and likeness, male and female (Gen 1:27), and Genesis 1 suggests several things: that humans reflect God as gendered creatures; male and female reproduce in a way that continues something of the creative generosity of God in producing life on earth; humans play a role in stewarding creation as God's representatives, etc. To be made in the "image and likeness of God" (Gen 1:27) is an ancient way of declaring children as Adam uses that same language to talk about his son (e.g., Seth in Gen 5:3). Thus, it appears to be a way of identifying parenthood, which is used in the New Testament for Jesus.[78] Thus, one meaning of the image of God is that humans are God's children and are made to resemble God in God's character of love. Furthermore, as children, humans have a bestowed worth that does not depend on performance. Thus, the image of God forms the basis of humane treatment, rights, and dignity.[79]

This has significant implications for how humans construe themselves as gendered creatures. Currently, there is a debate in feminism and gender studies concerning the degree to which gender has an essence versus being something culturally constructed. Essentialists look for an enduring and universal nature to gender, a robust correspondence between bodily sex and culturally expressed gender, while constructivists see these descriptions too often as products of patriarchal discourses, resulting in binaries and expectations of normalcy that are even harder to question. Gender is fundamentally not equivalent to one's physical body. Judith Butler has argued that the body is overdetermined by linguistic practices and discourses such that what is "female" or "male" is constructed, and Butler pointedly demonstrates that what is "female" often is constructed vis-à-vis the male as normative and dominant.[80] Butler's reflections are powerful reminders that gender has been culturally constructed and corrupted with discourses framed by patriarchy. However, Butler's own refusal to see the body beyond what is absorbed

---

78. This notion of image as a parental-child relationship cannot be dismissed, as it is appropriated by Paul to describe how Christ is the Son of God: "The Son is the image of the invisible God, the firstborn over all creation" (Col 1:15). Jesus is the "Son" and "firstborn" as he is the "image" of the invisible God, the three imply each other. Similarly, Hebrews draws this close connection between sonship and image: "The Son is the radiance of God's glory and the exact representation of his being" (Heb 1:3). Only children are in the image of their parents.

79. See Gushee, *Sacredness of Human Life*, sect. 2.1.

80. Butler, *Gender Trouble*, particularly part 2.

by these discourses,[81] while resolute in compelling readers to scrutinize all the ways bodily perceptions are through certain lenses, undermines the possibility of a kind of critical realism of the body, where authentic self-knowledge of the body's limits and potential can break through patriarchal discourses, albeit sometimes only in glimmers. While gender and physical sex are not the same, there is an interplay of influence. Serene Jones has offered what to my mind is the most sensible proposal, called "strategic essentialism,"[82] where the goodness of the body as typically male and female (although this should not be used to suppress the experiences of intersex, transgender, and other individuals that do not fit into a gender binary) is upheld, admitting a generous pluralism of possibilities. What this means socially is worked out with a set of pragmatic criteria as to whether an ascription to one's sex and gender indeed corresponds to available personal and sociological data. These descriptions create deeper possibilities of human authenticity and flourishing as a movement within a discourse where the body is seen as created good (with one's dignity grounded in being in God's image), but is also in a process of transformation toward God's redemption.

Thus, a Christian engagement with Butler might begin by looking at these analogical and narrative discourses. To be human with sexuality and gender is firstly to understand that in whatever way one is gendered, however one interprets one's physical sex and gender identity, God sees the person as having inherent dignity. Yet the person is a process. All humans are tasked with searching for their authentic selves, not merely seeking to discover a static self within. As suggested in the previous chapter, the self is marred by the effects of patriarchy. So often, it is hard to know what we are as gendered creatures apart from these distorting forces (and sadly, there are versions of Christian theology that perpetuate these distortions). Nevertheless, the travail toward authenticity in one's identity is undergirded by a nonnegotiable presumption of dignity God has for all God's children, and this allows a person to work out the

---

81. Butler, "Bodies that Matter" (accessed online, no page numbers). Butler writes, "To 'concede' the undeniability of 'sex' or its 'materiality' is always to concede some version of 'sex,' some formation of 'materiality.' Is the discourse in and through which that concession occurs—and, yes, that concession invariably does occur—not itself formative of the very phenomenon that it concedes?"

82. Jones, *Feminist Theory and Christian Theology*, 42–48. Jones situates strategic essentialism in a similar way to what I have spelled out here (a discernment of the goodness of the body and possibilities of authenticity against inaccuracies and distortions), but she uses the Protestant discourses of justification and sanctification.

meaning of their bodies and identity toward the ends of loving, healthy authenticity, as they see God desires for them.

As gender constructions are analyzed, deconstructed, and renegotiated, the various ways the body is interpreted and expressed are also guided by the promptings that humans were made in and for the divine likeness, that is to say, made to resemble God in a similar love. Human gender is intended to reflect and deepen the relationality that produces kinship bonds, intimacy, care, as well as honesty, acceptance, justice, and flourishing. This, along with how one refers to God using gendered language, will differ from culture to culture with different understandings of the divine and human social roles[83] (the criteria of which will be taken up in chapter 5). So, while the travail to interpret one's body, the task of finding authentic ways of being gendered people, is plagued with obscurity in culture (not to mention also church cultures) with such toxic ways of expressing gender, overwritten by dehumanizing forces of objectivization, consumerism, domination, etc., Scripture suggests that if gender is part of what it means to be created by God, it is good and is meant to reflect God's own character of grace, faithfulness, and love toward all others (including oneself). Coupled with the notions of apophatic negation (spelled out in the previous chapter), Beverly Lanzetta has noted that the contemplation of female images and voices is a part of negating patriarchy's particular configuration of male and female.[84] Thus, all people are tasked with discerning their bodies, social roles, and identities, sometimes called to act in ways that are perceived to be "un-masculine" or "un-feminine" by the corrupted discourses humans inhabit in order to be faithful to the transformation God desires.

Furthermore, humans live in and live out stories, and so to find authenticity means reflecting on one's past, present, and future in ways congruent with God's actions of redemption. In that regard, McClendon has rightly intuited that human experience, while not unimportant, also requires interpretation. Moments of human experience are meaningful when they come together in a larger narrative, but a human story is only truly meaningful when seen in the light of a larger narrative than any one person. McClendon comments on this:

---

83. For an article that reflects on female language for God in other, non-Western cultures and its implications for Christian language, see Barron, "My God Is *enkAi*."

84. See Lanzetta, *Radical Wisdom*, 16.

> My story is inadequate, taken alone, and is hungry for a wider story to complete it.... My story must be linked with the story of a people.... Our story is inadequate as well: The story of each and all is itself hungry for a greater story that overcomes our persistent self-deceit, redeems our common life, and provides a way for us to be a people among all earth's peoplehood, their own stories, their own lives.[85]

McClendon continues on to insist that because of the narrative character of people's lives, truth entails character, and the qualities of an individual's character find their fuller meaning in a community that is, in turn, story-shaped. This, however, should not be taken to undermine feminist critiques. Rather, it invites a form of feminist interpretation as something that flows from the narrative itself. The stories people have as gendered individuals are part of the creational goodness of the world, and how people have harmed one another is a part of the fallenness of a sinful world. Stories of liberation and redemption find a home in the figures of exodus and resurrection, where they flesh out what these can mean as the full implications of salvation are discerned. Rather than using a certain scheme of experience imposed on the text to critically evaluate it before it can be believed, as the African American theologian James Evans notes, the central proclamation of liberation, its resonance with all who are suffering, invites an imaginative interplay with the interpreter's social location in order to be faithful to it.[86] Rather than seeing the biblical narrative shutting out "outside" perspectives, Rowan Williams sees the narrative as opening the church up to these stories:

> Revelation, from this perspective, is nothing to do with absolute knowledge. It both is and is not completed, "over"; *what* we are interpreting is unquestionably this historical narrative and not another; we are not waiting for a more comprehensive or adequate story, because precisely of the comprehensiveness of the questioning provoked by this story. Yet this is not to say that there is an end to the questioning or unclarity. The claims of our foundational story to universal relevance and significance mean that it must constantly be *shown* to be "at home" with all the varying enterprises of giving meaning to the human condition. Thus, the "hermeneutical spiral" never reaches a plateau. For the event of Christ to be authentically revelatory, it must be capable of both "fitting" and "extending" any human circumstance; it

---

85. McClendon, *Ethics*, 351.
86. Evans, *We Have Been Believers*, 52–53.

must be re-presentable, and the form and character of its re-presentation are not necessarily describable in advance. The work continues, for the theologian and the Church at large, for discerning and naming the Christlike events of liberation and humanization in the world *as* Christlike, and at the level of action, expressing this hermeneutical engagement in terms of concrete, practical solidarity.[87]

Thus, feminist insights and other perspectives can be a natural extension of the biblical narrative and its logic, a welcomed challenge for those who seek to live the story to its fullest extent.

Thus, reflecting in an analogical way admits that God has acted as the creator of all things and, in particular, the creator of humanity in God's image and likeness. However, it also means looking to God as a redeemer, the one who liberates from sin with acts of forgiveness, calling all people into a repentance that opens them up to the breaking in of God's kingdom. Scripture is the story that enfolds and configures all other's stories. It is the story by which all other stories find their significance. To know that all our stories are bound up together with each other in this narrative of creation moving toward eschaton necessitates the need to listen to other people's stories. Without these other stories, one never fully understands the wounds one has inflicted on others, nor does one understand the full scope of the mission of this kingdom story. Thus, the narrative of Scripture is aided by an intersectional approach, acts of listening to the stories of people from different social locations, understanding that harm, neglect, and oppression look very different based on race, gender, sex, bodily ability, class, geopolitics, etc.[88] Against Jean-Francois Lyotard's accusation that Christianity is a tyrannical metanarrative,[89] it is the story of a particular people that welcomes other stories, not because it is a universal story, but because of its central character.

The self, made in God's image, is only completed as it looks to Christ, the true image of the invisible God (Col 1:15), and to the love that Christ shows on his cross. To interpret oneself situated in a larger narrative entails living in a community formed by this story. The church, as the "body of Christ" (Rom 12:5; 1 Cor 12:12–27; Eph 3:6; 4:15–16; 5:23; Col 1:18, 24), is to live and reflect to the world around it this kind of love with its bodily and communal resources. Stanley Grenz calls this the "ecclesial

---

87. Williams, *On Christian Theology*, 142–43.
88. See Kim and Shaw, *Intersectional Theology*.
89. Lyotard, *The Postmodern Condition*, xxiv.

self."[90] In so doing, in creating a space of other-directed care, a community of loving patience, reflecting the kind of grace God is, the church ought to be a place where the true self is realized in a fuller degree, where one's gender is nursed to come to the full manifestation of the fruitful love God has designed humanity for in all the various expressions and roles it can live out. (Sadly, many churches fail at this.)

The way of analogy finds its context of meaning in Scripture's story as the narrative of Scripture finds its center point in the incarnation, cross, and resurrection of Jesus and asserts, "God is like this." Thus, the human search for an authentic self finds its configuring rhythm in the life of Christ: finding God's presence in the goodness of creation, the call to a loving expression of bodily practice, and hope that God has resurrection for their life. McClendon sees Christ as the pattern of transformation-recognizing presence, acting in virtue, and embracing further gifts of newness.[91] Thus, Scripture says, "Beloved, we are God's children now; what we will be has not yet been revealed. What we do know is this: when he is revealed, we will be like him, for we will see him as he is. And all who have this hope in him purify themselves, just as he is pure" (1 John 3:2–3).

Thus, the way of analogy, situated in the biblical narrative, places all people on a journey from creation to redemption, seeing their goodness and longing for transformation beyond what sin has distorted. The way of analogy comes into focus in the image of God in humans and thus is fulfilled in Jesus Christ, the visible image of the invisible God. Jesus Christ is, admittedly, a male symbol in its history, an issue for feminists such as Butler, who would see the male as still the symbolic control over gender, which raises new questions for speaking about God and us, leading us into the next chapter. However, as this work has been contending, Christian grammar does have male symbols based on historical revelation, but when the grammar is understood, it shows an opening up of possibility (as we will see, a kenosis of male privilege), making space for the other.

CONCLUSION

This chapter has charted again the middle ground territory between a literalistic view of God as male and a view that employs metaphor in a

---

90. Grenz, *The Social God and the Relational Self*, 312–13.
91. McClendon, *Ethics*, 149–60.

way that downplays the reality of revelation. In discussing metaphors, the notion that religious language is inherently metaphorical is problematic. Figures of speech are contextual, and whether a statement about God is metaphorical says nothing as to whether it is or is not realistic purely based on the fact that it is a metaphor, and so, these patterns of language must be situated in the larger narrative of the Bible in order for them to be fully meaningful. In this regard, McFague's proposal is problematic. However, Aquinas's own way of analogy is unclear regarding why the title Father is privileged over female analogies. If God is the goodness of every good and the being of all beings, then God can be a mother. As the biblical narrative shows, such language is more than permitted. On the other hand, the charge of patriarchy against the title Father is unjustified as the title has an important history where God's love goes *beyond* human fatherly love. Thus, in contemplating God with these different analogies and metaphors, it is suggested that this opens up a stronger realization of God's presence in others, inviting the person to reconceive the meaning of their gender from the standpoint of inherent dignity and toward the purposes of resembling divine love.

4

Christ and the Cross

IN THIS EXAMINATION OF the rules that guide Christian speech, there is one rule that stands above the rest, summed up in three words: *Christ is Lord*. Discourse about God must be in conformity with Jesus Christ, the very Word of God made flesh. Already noted last chapter, gender can be clarified along analogical lines, seeing its created goodness in the image of God and intended transformation in grace from the distortion of sin through the biblical narrative. The way of analogy finds its focus in Jesus, as gender is then interpreted and transformed through the incarnation's presence, the cross's loving example of virtue, and the resurrection's potential for transforming newness. However, the fact that the historical Jesus is male has been a point of contention: Does the maleness of Jesus reify God as male? Can one bypass Jesus as a historically male figure to a female symbol? Furthermore, objections are brought against the cross of Jesus: Does the cross suppress women and victims? Is the cross not applicable to women when it depicts a man dying? Again, our task is to navigate past two extremes to understand how Jesus' gender does not secure patriarchy. Like the title Father, when one looks at the narrative of the cross and resurrection, one sees a subversive meaning to Jesus' maleness, and that, if the dynamic of the incarnation is properly understood, does not prevent feminine imagery either. Congruent with the multiple grammars explored previously, it will be shown how male language opens up a space for the female, and while reiterating the historical is important, it can be supplemented to fill out and correct distortions.

COMPETING VIEWS OF CHRISTOLOGY

In regard to Christology, there are divergent assumptions about the historicity of Christ, which, in turn, motivates two sensibilities. Some on the male-exclusive side argue that the maleness of Christ prevents female images. Still further, some argue that it motivates male-only leadership. On the other hand, some feminist arguments see the historical maleness of Jesus as inherently reinforcing patriarchy, and furthermore, the cross as reinforcing submission to abuse.

When it comes to the possibility of female representations of God, proponents of exclusively male language often see Christology as where the proverbial buck stops. Ray Anderson writes, "One can call God 'Mother' by switching metaphors, but one cannot make Jesus into a female."[1] For many, the historical Jesus becomes a bulwark against female imagery. The question is whether a positive conviction about Jesus' historicity (and therefore maleness) must necessarily rule out depictions of Christ as female.

While there are many who hold to exclusively male language for Christ while being egalitarians, there are instances where Jesus' maleness has been used to delegitimize women. Orthodox theologian Maximos Aghiorgoussis and others have argued against women in the priesthood because Jesus was a man. For instance, he states,

> The ordination of women to the Holy Priesthood is untenable since it would disregard the symbolic and iconic value of male priesthood, both representing Christ's malehood and the fatherly role of the Father in the Trinity, by allowing female persons to interchange with male persons a role which cannot be interchanged.[2]

In Protestant theology, the argument is more likely to be made by looking at "headship" and the theological analogy between the relationship between men and women, on the one hand, and Christ and the church,

---

1. Anderson, "The Incarnation of God in Feminist Christology," 288. One should note that Anderson does permit "mother" metaphors, as the above quotation shows, but these are of a different sort to the language of Jesus' maleness and therefore God's fatherliness.

2. Aghiorgoussis, *Women Priests?*, 3, 5. Also see Hopko, "On the Male Character of Christian Priesthood."

on the other: men lead over women as Christ leads with authority over the church.[3]

Meanwhile, there are some in feminist theology that have built their representations of Christ on denying or bypassing his historicity. Sallie McFague has stated, "I have not found it possible as a contemporary Christian to support an incarnational Christology or a canonical Scripture; nevertheless, I have found it possible to support a 'parabolic' Christology and Scripture as the Christian classic."[4] For her, Scripture is not an authority so much as a beginning point and holding to Christ as merely a "parable" suggests an inability to incorporate historicity with Jesus' identity. The "Christ" here is a linguistic and metaphorical phenomenon, not a historically realistic one.[5] The narratives of Christ do not pertain to the historical person of Jesus but are allegories of something else, namely human liberation in general. For McFague, the resurrection is a triumphalist mythology and, by implication, a delusional one.[6] Similarly, Carter Heyward has abstracted Christology from its fuller sense in the Gospels to claim that their portrayal of Jesus was merely about his moral aspect: "The Jesus story is about a person who knew and loved a God of justice. This is its particular message. This is its creative power."[7] Carter's is an attempt to glean a redemptive piece from the biblical and traditional portraits, leaving behind the rest as patriarchal chaff.

Ruether has some of the most developed objections. She asserts that Jesus' messianic status has been conflated with a reification of God as male. While Judaism had a symbol of femininity in God in Lady Wisdom, a figure who emerges from Proverbs and finds fuller expression in the Wisdom of Solomon, this character is depicted as the Logos or Son of God in Christianity, and so, Ruether writes,

> Because Christianity chooses the male symbol for this idea, however, the unwarranted idea develops that there is a necessary ontological connection between the maleness of Jesus' historical

---

3. For example, see Poythress, "The Church as Family." For a popular example, see Matthis, "Why Jesus Was Not a Woman."

4. McFague, *Metaphorical Theology*, viii.

5. For a survey on approaches to the historical Jesus, see Powell, *Jesus as a Figure in History*. More nuanced approaches to the historical Jesus that describe a narrative approach are assumed here, see Frei, *The Identity of Jesus Christ*, and Johnson, *The Real Jesus*.

6. McFague, *Models of God*, 56.

7. Heyward, *Our Passion for Justice*, 220–21.

person and the maleness of the *Logos* as the male offspring and disclosure of a male God.[8]

Ruether states further,

> Today, a Christology which elevates Jesus' maleness to ontological necessary significance suggests that Jesus' humanity does not represent women at all. Incarnation does not include women, therefore women cannot be redeemed. That is to say, if women cannot represent Christ, then Christ does not represent women.[9]

This reification becomes increasingly politically problematic, she argues, as the symbol is coupled with the emergence of a male-only-led church, where Christ as a man leads the church, so also, men lead in the church.[10] Thus, as the church becomes imperialized, in Christendom, "Christology becomes the apex of a system of control over all those who in one way or another are 'other' than this new Christian order."[11] Furthermore, by linking the Logos with masculinity, the subjectivity of women is downplayed. "Christ represents the male as the normative human being," she says.[12] Due to this, coupled with misappropriated scriptural proof texts, female voices are often downplayed and dismissed.

Ruether continues on to say that the particularity of Jesus' humanity is problematic, "Jesus' maleness as essential to his ongoing representation not only is not compatible but is contradictory to the essence of his message as good news to the marginalized *qua* women."[13] Ruether's solution is to treat the historical maleness of Jesus as having "no ultimate significance."[14] Rather, she sees it as having a social significance that symbolizes the "kenosis of patriarchy, the announcement of the new humanity through a lifestyle that discards hierarchal caste privilege and speaks on behalf of the lowly." However, one reason she is able to separate masculinity and Logos so easily is because she is convinced of a disparity between the Christ symbol and Jesus of Nazareth. She writes,

> The sayings of Jesus in the Gospels are basically the work of Christian prophets. They are not originally preserved by a

8. Ruether, *Sexism and God-Talk*, 117.
9. Ruether, "The Liberation of Christology from Patriarchy," 140.
10. Ruether, *Sexism and God-Talk*, 124.
11. Ruether, *Sexism and God-Talk*, 125.
12. Ruether, *Sexism and God-Talk*, 128.
13. Ruether, "The Liberation of Christology from Patriarchy," 147.
14. Ruether, *Sexism and God-Talk*, 137.

process of historical memory in which the prophets wrote down what they remember Jesus to have said. This does not mean that they preserved nothing similar to what the historical Jesus actually said. Rather, it means that what is preserved is the "spirit," the iconoclastic and prophetic vision of Jesus.[15]

For Ruether, then, Christ is the event of the Spirit in the present, a symbol for a present prophetic experience, and so, this allows for a female representation in the place of Jesus of Nazareth in iconoclastic fashion. Ruether names an important problem in representation, one that certainly has a history of misuse, namely, that the maleness of the historical Jesus has been used to prop up men and subjugate women. Thus, we see a characteristic criticism of the maleness of Jesus and an accompanying concern to bypass it. However, the question is whether affirming the historical Jesus necessarily means reiterating patriarchy or even ignoring female representations.

Next, the cross is another contested aspect of the identity of Christ, and the cross similarly is bound up with the question of maleness. There are clear examples where the cross has been used by some to form an ethic where the victim has been encouraged to submit to the abuser. It must be confessed that concern about an ethic of the cross as valorizing suffering to keep women trapped in abuse is not unfounded. In fact, such an error is not merely the fault of a "popular" unreflective Christianity; these tendencies are displayed in one of the most influential ethicists of the late twentieth century: the Anabaptist theologian John Howard Yoder (1927–97).[16] While the ethic in his most famous work, *The Politics of Jesus*, recommends a broad ethic of submission to evil, most disconcerting, there is a correlation between his theology and his personal life.[17] Yoder committed multiple improprieties against women before (very minimal) disciplinary action was taken by denominational authorities. Most problematic was that his ethic of submission was invoked by those

---

15. Ruether, *Sexism and God-Talk*, 123.

16. While there are many theologians one could chose for this section, Yoder has a particular importance for me as a Baptist, whose convictions have been shaped by the Anabaptist tradition, and, more particular, as one who read Yoder's work, both his theology of non-violent discipleship and ecclesiology, and found it profoundly persuasive. It was not until my own colleague Anna Robbins—theologian and ethicist, and now president of Acadia Divinity College—offered astute criticisms about his life and theology that I made the connections that I will be delineating more fully here.

17. For a discussion on the history of Yoder's abuse, see Goossen, "A Failure to Bind and Loose."

in the community and institutions he served to silence the women he harmed, suggesting they ought to respond with "Christlike" passivity to abuse.

Yoder's theology exposes how the cross, while it is certainly central, can nevertheless get misconstrued and misapplied. Yoder did this, as many Christians do, by overemphasizing the nature of submission. While Yoder was convinced against patriarchy, hierarchy, slavery, violence, etc., his reading of the ethic of the cross saw the transformation of these fallen realities entirely through the work of God by intervention with very little emphasis on human agency. His reading of the submission passages (such as Col 3:18—4:1; Eph 5:21—6:9; 1 Pet 2:13—3:7) saw them as the new reality of Christ giving the person strength to endure submitting to these unjust structures, doing good to one's oppressors, hoping that God would change the perpetrator's heart or some other kind of divine intervention. This he saw as the most faithful way Christians are to emulate the cross. He writes,

> His [Jesus'] motto of revolutionary subordination, of willing servanthood in the place of domination, enables the person in a subordinate position in society to accept and live within that status without resentment, at the same time that it calls upon the person in the superordinate position to forsake or renounce all domineering use of that status. This call is then precisely not a simple ratification of the stratified society in which the gospel has come. The subordinate person becomes a free ethical agent in the act of voluntarily acceding to subordination in the power of Christ instead of bowing to it either fatalistically or resentfully. The claim is not that there is immediately a new world regime which violently replaces the old; rather, the old and new order exist concurrently on different levels. It is because she knows that in Christ, there is no male or female that the Christian wife can freely accept that subordination to her unbelieving husband, which is her present lot. It is because Christ has freed us all, and slave and free are equal before God that their relationship may continue as a humane and honest one within the framework of the present economy, the structure of which is passing away (1 Cor. 7:31).[18]

Yoder saw the New Testament's prescription of subordination as derived from the cross, but if these are timeless principles, they would seem to preclude the possibility today of a victimized person under an authority

---

18. Yoder, *The Politics of Jesus*, 186.

ever acting in a way that insists on their freedom and equality in a material way against the will of the authority (whether the one in power is a husband, employer, government leader, or military oppressor). Instead, the sanctioned path is to only verbally witness to them and wait on the intervention of God. While faithfulness to God takes priority over the will of the human authority, particularly over who is ascribed worship (believing wives and slaves ought to refuse to worship their husband and master's gods, for instance), the reality of grace is relegated to matters of piety while the rest of the person's material situation remains unconnected to redemption, existing "concurrently" to it.

Thus, feminists have seen the ethic of the cross as a barrier to liberation. Daly was one of the first to voice this objection:

> The qualities that Christianity idealizes, especially for women, are also those of the victim: sacrificial love, passive acceptance of suffering, humility, meekness, etc. Since these are the qualities idealized in Jesus, "who died for our sins," his functioning as a model reinforces the scapegoat syndrome for women.[19]

Similarly, Joanne Carlson Brown and Rebecca Parker's important feminist essay, "For God So Loved the World?," proposes a significant criticism of the theology of the cross: that the symbol itself of the cross has caused women to accept abuse. In their own words, their intention is as follows:

> Christianity has been a primary—in many women's lives *the primary*—force in shaping our acceptance of abuse. The central image of Christ on the cross as the savior of the world communicates the message that suffering is redemptive. If the best person who ever lived gave his life for others, then, to be of value, we should likewise sacrifice ourselves. Any sense that we have a right to care for our own needs is in conflict with being a faithful follower of Jesus.[20]

They continue with a forceful ultimatum: "The only legitimate reason for women to remain in the church will be if the church were to condemn as anathema the glorification of suffering.... In order for us to become whole, we must reject the culture that shapes our abuse and disassociate ourselves from the institutions that glorify our suffering."[21] In other words, their critique not only criticizes Christology as a source that

---

19. Daly, *Beyond God the Father*, 77.
20. Brown and Parker, "For God So Loved the World," 2.
21. Brown and Parker, "For God So Loved the World," 3, 4.

promotes abuse, they go so far as to say the symbol of the cross inherently enables the abuse of women and this requires us to call into question the very notion of redemptive suffering entirely. Anything short of its complete purging from Christian belief warrants leaving the religion.[22] They assert, "The symbol itself is a form of abuse."[23]

Parker and Brown conclude by making heavy-handed corrections to Christian doctrine, which they believe are necessary if Christianity is to be viable. (Among these are, for instance, that Jesus is only one—and not the unique—manifestation of a greater reality of God, Immanuel.) Theologians must, according to them, refuse any characterization that Jesus, in his opposition to injustice, *chose* the cross. Also, Jesus was not a sacrifice for sin, for God did not need appeasing. In fact, "no one was saved by the death of Jesus."[24] The cross can only be understood as a tragedy, as suffering is never redemptive. To be a Christian is to live in opposition to injustice, refusing the threat of death. The resurrection, then, is "radical courage" that "death is overcome in those precise instances when human beings choose life."[25]

Is the maleness of Christ essential to the incarnation? Is Jesus' history essential to the incarnation as well? If so, does it mean men are prioritized over women? Does the cross recommend women staying in abuse? As already stated, to speak as a Christian means all our speech is intending conformity to who Jesus is, and thus, in order to speak about Jesus well, these questions need to be clarified.

THE HISTORIC MALENESS OF JESUS

God has been revealed in the man Jesus of Nazareth; this is as insurmountable as it is essential to Christian theology. However, what is the meaning of this history and this man? In this regard, at the suggestion of some feminist writers, I would claim that the maleness of Jesus, properly understood, is the very kenosis of patriarchy.

First, it must be insisted that the dismissal of any relevant link between the Gospels' Logos and Jesus of Nazareth is unsound. One could simply say that such a dismissal is unsound doctrinally, but it is more a

22. Brown and Parker, "For God So Loved the World," 4.
23. Brown and Parker, "For God So Loved the World," 11.
24. Brown and Parker, "For God So Loved the World," 27.
25. Brown and Parker, "For God So Loved the World," 27.

matter of the very fabric of the narrative itself. The Gospels' narratives are the primary means of their significance, and in this regard, the Gospel narratives are about Jesus. The Gospels are not firstly about a contemporary existential experience, political liberation in general, or anything other than Jesus Christ. While the Gospels surely are relevant to all of human life and reality, they are relevant firstly because of the meaning of the narrative of Jesus, his cross, and resurrection, not vice versa. All Gospel portraits of Christ, while they are indeed different, claim congruence with who this historic person was. This does not mean that the narratives are historically pristine in their recollection of memory or even at all points intending pure history as modern thinking sees it. However, in these cases, these narratives are not referring back to a purely mythical figure divorced from history or to a figure that has meaning separate from Jesus of Nazareth. They ground themselves in the kind of person the historical Jesus was as the community of eyewitnesses remembered him.[26] As Craig Kenner notes, the Gospels are ancient biographies,[27] and while these biographies were written with ancient conventions that were far looser than today's, this does not detract from the overall intention of rendering faithfully a historical person for a community attempting to follow the essence of that person's teaching. Thus, it is problematic to dismiss the historical references of the Gospels or bypass these references in order to interpret Gospel narratives as meaningful primarily in and through present experiences. In seeking Christ, one cannot sidestep history.[28] The historical Christ was a man, and for that very reason, language for Christ has been and continues to be male.

However, it is often observed (and criticized) that the Bible is a deeply androcentric text, and one could say this about the Gospels as well, where the majority of the characters are male, Jesus included.[29] To enter into the biblical world is to occupy a predominantly male subjectivity. Luce Irigaray has noted the ways language affects agency, specifically

---

26. Two examples where studies on memory and oral communities of recitation and what they mean for the range of historical reliability of the Gospels are Dunn, *The Oral Gospel Tradition*, and Bauckham, *Jesus and the Eyewitnesses*.

27. See Keener, *Christobiography*.

28. Although this should not be taken as to mean all historical problems are solved or that one can verify that all the passages of the Gospels are historical. See, for instance, Allison, *The Historical Christ and the Theological Jesus*.

29. In regard to the Gospel of Mark, Joanna Dewey makes this point, see Dewey, "Gospel of Mark," 470.

male language and female agency.[30] However, a part of the question of whether the maleness of Jesus reifies maleness as God incarnate or whether a male savior dying on the cross can really save women is also whether God's revelation can accommodate itself to a cultural circumstance or discourse, ones that bear the distortion of sin, while still being able to communicate the enduring truths of the gospel for those not in that social location. In other words, just as Jesus was found in the "likeness of sinful flesh" (Rom 8:3)—that is to say, resembling fallen humanity (not as a man qua male as a creature created good but as a man in a society that privileges men due to the effects of sin)—it is possible to recognize the biblical discourses articulate themselves within a culture of patriarchy while also offering the content by which patriarchy is overcome. This is a dual insistence: particularity (like Jesus' maleness) can communicate something universal just as something fallen (like the patriarchal culture the Bible articulates itself within) can communicate redemption.

It is worth noting this accommodational yet subversive rhetoric in the Gospels works in other examples. The Gospels use imperial and war metaphors to communicate the victory over the dark powers in a non-violent way. The very name Jesus ("Yēshu" is most accurate to the Aramaic) is a direct allusion back to the biblical story of Joshua (Yēshu being a variant form of Yehoshua, Joshua). Jesus bears the name (Luke 1:31) of a man who slaughtered the Canaanites in the conquest of the land. There are lots of facets to interpreting the book of Joshua as Christian Scripture, but suffice it to say the violence of the book is in stark contrast to Jesus' treatment of his enemies. Jesus, typologically, as the New Joshua, conquers and has victory in the war against sin, death, and the devil, but this violence viewed as a metaphor for a decidedly non-military reality. For instance, when Jesus went to Jericho (alluding back to the story of Jericho, a stronghold of the Canaanites), he had an exchange with Zacchaeus, a tax collector who was a collaborator with the Roman occupation, extorting people's money to fund their own oppression. Yet, Jesus graciously eats with this man, and Zacchaeus is so moved by Jesus' kindness that he resolves to give half his possessions to the poor and pay back fourfold to those whom he had wronged. The passage ends with the proclamation, taken from military terminology, "Salvation has come to this household" (Luke 19:9). Similarly, at the end of Matthew, as Kenton Sparks notes, Jesus promises to be with his disciples even onto the end

---

30. This is demonstrated in Irigaray, *I Love to You*.

of the age (Matt 28:20), alluding back to the commissioning of Joshua where "the LORD your God is with you wherever you go" (Josh 1:9), thus employing terminology from Joshua's conquest in a non-militant way.[31] Yet, the disciples "conquer" through discipleship, not violence. Thus, violent terminology is used to speak of non-violence. War imagery is used to undo war.

Also, Jesus is the "Son of God," a term that alludes back to God's covenant with David, primarily, but also is a title of the emperor, who claimed divinity for himself.[32] Monarchy in Israel began, as the text says, because Israel wanted to "be like the nations" (1 Sam 8:5), and so, the installation of Saul is depicted as a *concession* by God. A number of reasons have been suggested in church history why Jesus was born male, but the covenant with David seems like the most direct reason in the biblical narrative.[33] He must be a son of David if he is to be the king. But does this merely uphold the authority of human (male) kings? It has been used this way, just as Father language has been used to uphold patriarchy. However, this is a misunderstanding based on the narrative grammar. Jesus' particular way of being the messianic king shown in the story is *very different* to the way earthly kings operate. Jesus was a king without wealth, military might, or earthly splendor, and he ruled by becoming a servant. Thus, Jesus is the "Son of God" in part because of this line of accommodation to a patriarchal line of kings, which he fulfills, but in doing so, Jesus is set up as the king who overturns earthly power.

Through this dynamic, the maleness of Jesus has a historic importance in his portrayal as the messianic king for countering patriarchy. Catherine LaCugna writes, "The total identification of God with Jesus the Son, even unto death on a cross, makes it impossible to think of God as a distant, omnipotent monarch who rules the world just as any patriarch rules over his family and possessions."[34] Elizabeth Johnson makes the case that the maleness of Jesus offers the "kenosis of patriarchy . . . for

---

31. Sparks, "Gospel as Conquest," 651–63.

32. See Myers, *Binding the Strong Man*.

33. Gibson, "Could Christ Have Been Born a Woman?" Some reason are based on complementarity (e.g., Peter Lombard and Thomas Aquinas): Jesus was born of a woman, and so by him (male) and Mary (female) redemption came to men and woman. Others are for symmetry (Albert the Great): as Adam as a man was the one in whom death came (cf. Rom 5), so redemption was though Jesus as a man. Still others are more problematic, such as Albert's other arguments: introducing the Aristotelean notion that since women were defective males, Christ could not come as a female and still be perfect.

34. See LaCugna, "Baptismal Formula," 243.

a man to live and die in this way in a world of male privilege is to challenge the patriarchal ideal of the dominating male at its root."[35] There is something particularly important about the servant Messiah being male for feminist thought. The fact that Jesus, despite his claim to messianic status, becomes a servant, taking on the lowest possible status as one on an execution cross (cf. Phil 2), allows him to represent anyone of any status, regardless of gender. This is a part of the larger work of Jesus as a mortal human dying on the cross as a sign of God's solidarity with sinful humanity in order to overturn sin itself.

The cross has important implications for masculinity. As Carolyn Custis James notes, the masculinity of Jesus demonstrates humility and compassion, teaching his disciples to refuse selfish status-seeking and power.[36] The kenosis of the cross suggests that true masculinity is found in vulnerability, self-sacrifice, and service to the other, all in commending oneself to God in faith. In feminist theory, bell hooks argues that for men to heal the wounds of patriarchy, all people, men and women, must engage in accepting love in vulnerability, combating the ways power and control have infected the masculine identity, distorting relationships with women, children, oneself, and other men.[37] Thus, looking at the God who dies for humanity at the cross, the messianic man who lowers himself to be a servant, Christ reveals a vision of masculinity that refuses these toxic reductions of a man's worth to the performance of work and power over others.

The resurrection, by Paul's own description, is the definitive truth claim of the Christian faith: "If Christ has not been raised, then our proclamation has been in vain, and your faith has been in vain" (1 Cor 15:14). There are various apologetics for the historical resurrection that need not be summarized here.[38] All that is being insisted upon here is that the narrative portrays a historical and bodily resurrection. Like the rest of the Gospel narratives, despite their obvious differences and developments, their intention is to render faithfully a historical event and figure. Whether one thinks the resurrection of Jesus is true or ridiculous, one must accept that this is what the narratives mean. Frei comments on this:

---

35. Johnson, *Consider Jesus*, 111.
36. James, *Malestrom*, ch. 8.
37. bell hooks, *The Will to Change*.
38. For a methodical apologetic for the historicity of the resurrection, see Craig, *The Son Rises*.

> The true fact of the Christian story, the center of the Christian story, is the passage in which Jesus is most truly who he is, crucified and resurrected. The resurrection is not an ordinary historical fact in an empirical sense. Is it therefore only a symbol? I believe that it's not the Christian vision, nor the Christian witness. The resurrection is a fact the truth of which Christians affirm even though they have to say that the nature of it is not such that we are in a position to verify it, because even though we affirm it, we do not think of it under that category of an ordinary empirical datum; it is a fact rendered effective to us thought the story and we cannot have it without the story in which it is given to us.[39]

Rowan Williams comments on the traditional reading: "I find it the least difficult interpretation of the New Testament record. Other options are more easily defensible on other grounds, but all seem unduly to shrink the range and complexity of our narratives."[40] At the very least, again, it must be insisted that the resurrection narratives be read realistically: the narrative offers the meaning and not a reconstruction behind it or a contemporary schema of experience imposed on it.

As patriarchy in the biblical narrative is portrayed as the result of sin, resurrection is the possibility of its overturning. Eve's curse is that "your desire will be for your husband, but he will rule over you" (Gen 3:16), a part of the death of sin entering the world. However, Jesus' resurrection shows the victory over this and all sin. The Father raises the Son further, implying that this language is counter-oppressive in the possibilities of hope it opens up. Johnson further comments,

> The significance of this event for all of humanity cannot be overestimated, for Jesus' resurrection is the beginning of the resurrection of all the dead. Indeed, we are dealing here with an event of the future that has arrived in advance of the last day.... This is a deep encouragement for men and women who face the reality of their own death. But in a particular way, it is profoundly good news for persons who are poor, denigrated, oppressed, struggling, victimized, falsely accused, disappeared, questing for life and the fullness of life. The crucified victim of state injustice is not abandoned forever. God's pure, beneficent, people-loving Spirit seals him in unimaginable life as pledge of a future for all the violated and the dead. Henceforth, his cross

---

39. Frei, "On Interpreting the Christian Story," in *Reading Faithfully*, 1:79–80.
40. Williams, *Resurrection*, 110.

becomes the flashpoint that discloses how God participates in the suffering of the world in order to save it.[41]

As the resurrection is seen as the apex of the Gospel narrative, demonstrating the faithfulness of God to liberate humanity of sin, vindicating Christ by the Spirit, which is poured out at Pentecost, this realistic reading allows for the imaginative possibilities that think about the world in non-patriarchal ways. Perhaps put another way, any feminism that seeks the liberation of women from the forces of domination that flow from the drive of death must stand on the resurrection as an event that has occurred in history.

Thus, the concern for history is vital to the redemption proclaimed in the Christian faith, which includes the liberation of humanity from sin (including the sin of patriarchy) through Jesus' incarnation, cross, and resurrection. While the specifics of historical inquiry are complicated, Christianity is a response to the present reality of Christ, the risen Jesus, who leads the church further into the new creation.

THE INCARNATION INTO ALL FLESH

Thus, the maleness of Christ does not reify patriarchy. And while regard for the importance of history means we continue to affirm Jesus as a male, this affirmation should not be taken as refusing all alternative depictions of Jesus if they communicate the point the historic cross makes. Rather, one (the historical Jesus) leads into the other (imaginative portraits), allowing for artistic depictions that can comment and tease out implications often missed. One often missed dimension is that the incarnation includes femininity.

The maleness of the historical Jesus does not necessarily prevent female representations of Christ if the representation is not an attempt to rewrite history. Can Jesus' identity ever be pictured in a non-historical way without contradicting his history? To understand this, it must be stated that Jesus is not *merely* a historical figure. It was just stressed that Jesus must be *at least* historical, but that does not mean Christ is *only* a figure in the past. As Luke Timothy Johnson points out, the "real" Jesus of the New Testament is not merely the historical Jesus as an object left in the past to be discovered by historians, but rather, Jesus is the living,

---

41. Johnson, "Resurrection: Promise of the Future," in *Abounding in Kindness*, 192–93.

resurrected Jesus, whose Spirit is present to believers in the church.[42] In other words, the way a believer "knows" Jesus, who walks with them and talks with them, is essentially different to how one "knows" a figure like Abraham Lincoln or Julius Caesar. This does not mean that the Christ figure is independent of the historical Jesus. Johnson defends a historical core to the Gospels, noting a congruence of the portrayals of Christ's character in the Gospels. This living Christ is not at loggerheads with the historical Christ but rather is in continuity. Yet this continuity allows for the development and expansion of reflection on Jesus, which is something we can see in the New Testament itself. For instance, while Jesus in the Synoptic Gospels is nowhere portrayed as a formal priest, the writer of Hebrews applies the typological imagery of Melchizedek to Jesus. This flows from Jesus' claims to fulfill the sacrificial system with his body and blood, and thus, is an imaginative figural expansion of Jesus' identity within the Christian canon. Thus, there is a continuance and compounding of imagery that the historical Jesus permits.

In Matt 24:37, Jesus, after denouncing the Pharisees, looks at Jerusalem and laments its sin: "Jerusalem, Jerusalem, the city that kills the prophets and stones those who are sent to it! How often have I desired to gather your children together as a hen gathers her brood under her wings, and you were not willing!" Here, Jesus expresses his love of Jerusalem using the metaphor of a mother hen. The fact that a male person has used female metaphors to describe loving action did not go unnoticed in theological reflection throughout the ages. Now, we have stressed that we must be firm in insisting that Jesus, as portrayed by the Gospels, was a historical person, and that insofar as we speak about this historical person, Jesus is male. Nonetheless, in church history there exist imaginative reflections on moments like this one in Matthew that portray Jesus as feminine and motherly, not as a corrective or contradiction to the historical narrative but as a way of accentuating and underscoring its logic. The title "Mother Christ" is used by several writers. Anselm of Canterbury (1033–1109) once prayed, "And you, Jesus, are you not also a mother? Are you not the mother who, like a hen, gathers her chickens under her wings?"[43] Similarly, Bernard of Clairvaux (1090–1153), in one of his letters, like Anselm, prayed this: "Do not let the roughness of our life frighten your tender years. If you feel the stings of temptation . . . suck

---

42. Johnson, *The Real Jesus*, 167.

43. Anselm in "Prayers to Saint Paul," in *The Prayers and Meditations of Saint Anselm with the Proslogion*, lines 396–98 on p. 153.

not so much the wounds as the breasts of the Crucified. He will be your mother, and you will be his son."⁴⁴ Others like Julian of Norwich used the title "Mother Christ,"⁴⁵ and while these mentions are by no means the majority in church history, much like other female imagery, they remain a kind of minority report that cannot be ignored either.

Such language in the tradition suggests that while masculine language for Jesus is conventional, because the historical Jesus was male, it is not exclusive. Importantly, none of these thinkers dismissed Jesus's historical life. In fact, their reflections flow *from* the narrative. Thus, when one understands the purpose and portrayal of Jesus' person, the reason why Jesus' maleness works for all humanity is the very reason it permits femininity: Jesus' incarnation is into all flesh, showing God's love for all. This is particularly important as one thinks about the Pentecost reality, the Spirit of Christ on all flesh, and the formation of the church, the bride and body of Christ. While the church is not Jesus, it does show a becoming one of the two where the image of God in humanity, both male and female, is re-dignified in salvation. This reality shows the inclusion of all races, classes, and genders into Christ. The image of Christ is being impressed upon all flesh, and all flesh reflects Christ as all believers are priests to one another (1 Pet 2:5). Thus, while the historical Jesus is male, the *exalted* Jesus, by the Spirit, takes *all* flesh into the body of Christ (contra Ruether, the later must be understood through the former).⁴⁶ Understanding the Spirit as the Spirit of Christ and the church as the bride of Christ and the body of Christ showcases how Scripture has multifaceted overlapping imagery of all gender identities in God.

Nevertheless, it is through this line of reasoning that femininity and Christology can be reconciled. As Gerald O'Collins advocates, the concern for historicity should not stop believers from seeing Christ as possessing female presence in a way that fully fleshes out the incarnation in pastorally beneficial ways.⁴⁷ In fact, an early writer like Clement of Alexandria (ca. AD 150–ca. AD 215) mentions this dynamic, seeing it as faithful with the concerns of the biblical grammar, arguing that Christ has both a male and female nature, indeed all human nature. He writes,

---

44. Bernard of Clairvaux in "Letter 322 PL 182: col. 303B–C," as quoted in Bynum, *Jesus as Mother*, 117.

45. Julian of Norwich, *Julian of Norwich: Showings*, ch. 59.

46. This is laid out in Johnson, "Redeeming the Name of Christ: Christology," in *Freeing Theology*, 129.

47. O'Collins, *Christology*, 352–57.

The Father and the Feminine

> For what further need has God of the mysteries of love? And then you shall look into the bosom of the Father, whom God the only-begotten Son alone has declared. And God Himself is love, and out of love to us became feminine. In His ineffable essence, He is Father; in His compassion to us, He became Mother. The Father by loving became feminine: and the great proof of this is He whom He begot of Himself; and the fruit brought forth by love is love.[48]

The fact that Clement was one of the first theologians of the church and was concerned about gender representation in the incarnation is quite remarkable: the issue of gender inclusion is not the invention of modern feminism. Now, Clement characterizes the masculine and feminine with a problematic binary (masculine = ineffable essence and feminine = becoming love); nevertheless, Clement is one of several writers that see Jesus, while historically male, nevertheless, is fully reconciled with femininity and even as incarnated into femininity as one aspect of the greater reality of Jesus incarnating into all flesh.

This dynamic of the incarnation explains why the church has not been limited to one contextual portrait of Jesus. Jesus has been portrayed as resembling particular groups of people and their concerns, reiterating the truth that God is with humanity, God Immanuel. For instance, Matthias Grunewald's famous Isenheim altarpiece in 1512–16 has Jesus depicted on the cross as suffering from a plague the local people experienced, called St. Anthony's Fire. Obviously, Jesus did not suffer from this plague, historically, but the truth of the incarnation permits an imaginative rendering that reiterates God's loving solidarity with those suffering in this situation. Thus, Christian thought has historically been comfortable with a diversity of artistic portrayals of the cross that communicate the truth of what the history of Jesus was about.

On the other hand, certain portrayals get bundled together with social concerns, and thus, in the case of Jesus being depicted as White, often, whether intentionally or unintentionally, an image can reinforce the notion that Jesus is only like this and only with that particular group of people, reinforcing their privilege at the expense of another. For instance, leading up to World War II in Germany, as Susanna Heschel documents, a full-scale theological project was undertaken to divorce Jesus from his Jewishness and to argue for an Aryan Jesus in order to

---

48. Clement of Alexandria, "Who Is the Rich Man That Shall Be Saved?"

legitimate German cultural superiority and military expansion.[49] Or, more recently, one need only recall the portrayal of Jesus as White in the notebooks of Dylann Roof, the gunman who fired upon a prayer meeting at Emanuel African Methodist Episcopal Church on June 17, 2015, killing nine people. For him, Jesus is exclusively White, and God is on the side of White supremacy. This does not mean that every picture of Jesus where he is depicted as White is racist (to think so would be to throw out many beautiful depictions of Jesus in the Western tradition), but it does indicate that there has been a consistent portrayal of Jesus as White or European, which has functioned problematically in contexts that are not monoethnic. Pictures are often more ambiguous in intention, and some have clearly been reappropriated beyond their original intentions. Some have implied that Christians then ought to defend a deeply Westernized portrayal of Jesus (and Christianity) as universal rather than recognizing these depictions as belonging to a certain context.

Countering problematic appropriations of Jesus as White, there are ways Jesus has been portrayed as Black that female depictions could operate with. As Kelly Brown Douglas notes, Jesus came to be understood as Black in the theology and spirituality of enslaved African American believers. Robert Alexander Young first asserted Christ as Black in 1829 as a negation of the ways slave-owners' churches were co-opting Jesus.[50] Furthermore, as James Cone elaborates, the depiction of the cross as the lynching tree in the Black imagination fostered the powerful hope that God was on their side: "If the God of Jesus' cross is found among the least, the crucified people of the world, then God is also found among those lynched in American history."[51] To see Christ as Black, as Cone explains, is not to ignore the historical Jesus, who was Jewish, but to see this historical particularity (a Jew under Roman occupation) as communicating God's love for the least of this world, whoever they may be.[52] In the spirituals and writings, this depiction functioned to reiterate that Jesus was with the slaves rather than the slave-owners, that the oppression done to them was also being done to Jesus, that Jesus was suffering alongside them, and in this knowledge of divine companionship, they had hope of freedom.[53]

49. See Heschel, *The Aryan Jesus*.
50. Douglas, *The Black Christ*, 28.
51. Cone, *The Cross and the Lynching Tree*, 23.
52. See Cone, *God of the Oppressed*, ch. 6.
53. Also see Copeland, *Knowing Christ Crucified*.

Any depiction of Jesus in intention ought to be for the purpose of communicating Jesus' solidarity with others, the truth of God Immanuel, God for us, particularly the forgotten of this world (rather than representing those in power). In so far as Jesus has taken on all flesh in the incarnation, the Jewish and male flesh signifies this truth for all people, all who are born under the curse of sin, all who are treated last in this world, and thus, contextual representations, including female portrayals, communicate the truth that the gospel proclaims in its historical location.

THE CROSS AGAINST PATRIARCHY: REFLECTING ON CHRISTA

However, does the cross, the center of Jesus' work and identity, reinforce submission to abuse? As already noted, the cross of Christ suggests a form of masculinity against patriarchy. The New Testament considers this pattern for all people, male and female, but often, in church cultures, the application is lopsided. As we have been pursuing, there are multiple grammars in play in how one talks about God: one where the male symbol seeks to undermine patriarchy (and thus is not offensive), but also, this symbol opens up space for female symbols to be permitted, and this is particularly relevant when the male symbols are literalized and distorted. By the grammar of the incarnation into all flesh, it is possible to artistically render Christ in feminine ways. Using the example of the sculpture *Christa*, it might be suggested that in picturing Christ's cross in feminine ways, the meaning of the historic cross is restated and distortions corrected.

In London in 1975, at the United Nations' International Decade for Women, a large bronze sculpture weighing about 250 pounds and measuring 4' by 5' was hung on a glassy Lucite cross: the figure was of a woman. The art piece by Edwina Sandys is called *Christa*. As to be expected, there was an outcry. When it was displayed at the Cathedral of St. John the Divine in New York, it drew the most pointed criticism from the suffragan bishop of the Diocese of New York, Walter Dennis, who described the pieces as "desecrating our symbols" and as "theologically and historically indefensible."[54] However, Sandys's own rationale for the project is illuminating. In a 2011 interview for the *New York Social Diary*, she was asked about the rationale for the sculpture. She responded,

---

54. Barron, "An 'Evolving' Episcopal Church Invites Back a Controversial Sculpture."

> When I did "Christa," it was using the idea of Christ and turning it into a woman and feeling that women should be included in the most important image, in a way, Jesus on the cross. I did it very, very quickly. It just came out. I was working in a studio in London and there were other people working in the studio. One woman came out and said, "Hmm, there's a lot of women like that,"—suffering women. It was to show the suffering of women as well.[55]

In 2015, she was interviewed on the significance of the sculpture thirty years later.

> I didn't make *Christa* as a campaign for women's rights or Women's Lib as such but I have always believed in equality and I am glad that *Christa* is just as relevant today as it was in 1975. I didn't make *Christa* just for women. Men also suffer and that is one of the meanings of Jesus on the Cross. (Over the years I have received many letters from men, many of them priests of all denominations.) In the past there were matriarchs in many societies and religions, and gender was not always a factor. Today women are finding their way to take their place in the Christian church and in society in general. Most women of my generation have been stamped with the idea of Man's superiority over Woman which is hard to throw off without seeming aggressive. I hope that *Christa* continues to reveal the journey of suffering that we all have in common.[56]

In an interview with Edwina Sandys, the interviewer, Nettie Reynolds, spoke about seeing *Christa* in seminary: "Seeing the picture of *Christa* during our class was a sacred moment for me. It echoed my journey and pain and yet also uplifted the beauty inherent in human suffering and our daily gift of grace and promise of resurrection."[57] The art piece created a profound connection for Reynolds to Christ, one that was lacking in how conventional images of the cross were portrayed. This image reiterated the truth that God understood her and was with her. It would seem that this is exactly what a portrayal of the cross ought to do and why female language has a place in confronting patriarchy in the church. In so far as this sculpture coincides with the grammar we have been thinking about, *Christa* is a provocative and powerful reflection on the incarnation and cross.

---

55. Ballen, Hauge, and Hirsch, "Interview with Edwina Sandys."
56. Reynolds, "Christa Interview."
57. Reynolds, "Christa Interview."

The church does not possess a photograph of Jesus, and the church has historically not been iconoclastic. What the church does possess is rich traditions of iconography and other materials that imaginatively depict the theological truths of the Gospels, some emphasizing different points from others. Yet, so often, the crucifixion is portrayed in deeply sanitized ways that make the cross seem banal. For instance, Jesus, in most depictions, is inaccurately portrayed as clothed, his body clean, and usually unmarred by torture or beatings. Roman crucifixion practice would have insisted on the person being naked to humiliate and expose the person to all the vulnerability of the elements. Ironically, it seems that implicitly, a historically accurate cross would be too scandalous to show in most churches. In a way, *Christa*, in its brave depiction of vulnerability, is more accurate than many mainstream male depictions.

This artistic depiction may open up possibilities to remind believers about what the cross is about. One aspect of oppression (or simply ways some are treated "last" in society) that makes it so difficult to combat is that it is also so easy to justify. It so often is covert, concealed, or conveyed in a way that allows it to be perpetuated. It is hard to imagine that the death of Christ was seen as justifiable by some. It is just about as hard as imaging that there are folk who do not want liberation for all. However, as Caiaphas said in John 11:50, "You do not realize that it is better for you that one man die for the people than that the whole nation perish." In John's account, the plot to execute Jesus was rationalized as a means of protecting the power of the religious establishment. Jesus was scapegoated in order to legitimize violence against him. The implicit statement of the sculpture *Christa* is that women have been crucified and that this violence has been legitimated for religious purposes, similar to why Jesus was killed. As Jennifer Garcia Bashaw writes, women in North America are suppressed, and that suppression is rationalized with religious scapegoating. She writes,

> The most recent attempt at relaying the foundations for the scapegoating process in America can be the founding the Christian movement known as complementarianism. . . . [T]his system relegates women to traditional roles in society and maintains a power imbalance within the family and the church. Complementarian Christians base their theology on a few verses taken out of context from the letters of Paul and on an interpretation of Genesis. . . . They argue that God created men to rule—to lead society and family. Conversely, God created

women to obey—to support men and raise children. The complementarian model of "Biblical manhood and womanhood" claims to value equality between the genders, but in practice, it prescribes inflexible gender roles that lead to a consolidation of authority and power in males.[58]

Citing Sally Gallagher's research, she continues, "The majority of evangelicals cling tightly to the delineation of men and women's roles not for biblical or theological convictions but for political and social reasons,"[59] which she continues on to describe as the agenda of many right-wing political groups, who campaign in defense of "family values," claiming to champion the Christian way of life. She writes, "The political commitment to the 'traditional family' has led to the limitation of women's power through strict gender roles, levied economy penalties on working mothers, and promoted antifeminist sentiment."[60] In other words, female agency is blamed for social ills. Bashaw argues that this results in two lines of scapegoating: economic and sexual. Economically, she notes the "feminization of poverty,"[61] where mothers, especially single mothers, are penalized and obstructed in the workforce due to childcare in a way men are not, and this is exacerbated by a religious-political agenda that idealizes a view of the household where the man is the sole breadwinner. Second, female victims of sexual abuse have been ignored and even undermined and blamed. Male perpetrators of abuse among church leaders, as in the case of the Southern Baptist Convention, have often been defended and protected, while their victims have been told to forgive their perpetrators and stay silent, all in an effort to protect the reputation of the (male-led) religious establishment.[62] As René Girard states concerning scapegoating: "Persecutors always believe in the excellence of their cause, but in reality, *they hate without a cause.*"[63] In defense of family values, there are Christians who are actively undermining the care and flourishing of the members of God's family. For Jesus to be the victim of scapegoating, tried and executed as a blasphemous rebel for proclaiming the kingdom of God, to have this person bear the divine identity as God's Son, vindicated in the resurrection, serves as a constant

58. Bashaw, *Scapegoats*, 81.
59. Bashaw, *Scapegoats*, 82.
60. Bashaw, *Scapegoats*, 84.
61. Bashaw, *Scapegoats*, 88.
62. Bashaw, *Scapegoats*, 90.
63. Girard, *The Scapegoat*, 103 (italics original).

challenge to the church to end practices that suppress and blame in order to preserve power. It is a call to be present to the marginalized of society, and however humans interpret their gender, these expressions cannot be built on practices that suppress and scapegoat others.

Christa and art like it can be an impetus to meditate on the language and meaning of the cross in our context, addressing criticism from some feminist theologians, clarifying the nature of contextualized representations of the cross, and challenging distorted ways the cross has been understood, ways that promote passivity against patriarchy. As it has been argued, an artistic depiction of a female Christ on the cross need not be at loggerheads with the historical depiction of Jesus the man from Nazareth. Rather, it can be used to reiterate important theological truths implicit in the classic Christian doctrines of incarnation and atonement that the church has neglected. By picturing women's suffering as Christ's suffering, those who contemplate this image, men and women, are reminded that God is with all people, not just male flesh. As Girard said, "We have learned to identify our innocent victims only by putting them in Christ's place."[64]

In fact, certain narratives and icons have functioned to picture the cross through suffering individuals. In the *Acts of the Martyrs of Lyons and Vienne*, Blandina, who is killed for her faith, is suspended on a stake, and animals are set loose on her. The writer records the moment as those who looked upon her saw "in the form of their sister the One who was crucified for them."[65] When Scripture is read from the position of solidarity with the crucified, Christ, and those whom Christ identifies with, Scripture reads fundamentally better. In the case of Blandina and other early church martyrs, their suffering drained support for the Roman Empire and its idols of power.

Today, this optic aids in reading passages that are often used to justify suppression. For instance, reading the household codes and their submission ethic as immediately applicable today or as absolute ignores important details of the first-century context. The submission and subordination ethic of the New Testament is an application of the cross, but it is a *contextual* application as it also reflects the plight of slavery and patriarchy as a cultural given that was not within the apostle's power to overthrow in their time.[66] Steps to overtly overthrow this social order

---

64. Girard, *The Scapegoat*, 202.
65. Quoted in Musurillo, *The Acts of the Christian Martyrs*, 75.
66. See Snodgrass, *Ephesians*, 303–5.

would have resulted in further maligning of the Christian reputation and very possibly violence, particularly because it was the obligation of wives, children, and slaves to worship the same god as the paterfamilias. If Christians were perceived as insurrectionists, lethal force would have been used to protect the household order. In light of this, it seems that the apostles chose a subtle ethic that sought to minimize negative perceptions of the gospel (1 Pet 2:12: "Conduct yourselves honorably among the gentiles, so that, though they malign you as evildoers, they may see your honorable deeds and glorify God when he comes to judge"), while still spreading its message. When the New Testament household codes are compared to the Greek and Roman household codes, while the New Testament codes command submission similar to their cultural counterparts, they also recommend mutual submission in Christian families, introducing accountability to husbands and masters, dignifying slaves as family and insisting on treating wives as a husband would treat their own body (more will be said about this in chapter 6 in regards to the Trinity and "headship").[67] What the household codes represent, then, is the greatest possible resistance *in a given situation* where any greater resistance would have provoked violence and disrepute on the gospel. To embrace this ethic completely for today after the development of human rights, movements of emancipation, woman's suffrage, racial desegregation, or other social reforms (which Christians had a hand in leading) would be to reallocate oppressors with power again. For example, it would suggest that an employee could not quit their job in a toxic work environment, or a battered wife leave her husband and go to a shelter, etc. Placed in our context, it seems most persuasive that the enduring principle in these texts is peaceability, mutuality, reciprocity, and accountability, not unopposable and inescapable subordination.

Thus, as a vital correction to an absolutized submission ethic, like that of Yoder's, the cross must be read with the resurrection, the culmination of Jesus' proclamation of the kingdom of God, where the church

---

67. For several helpful articles on the household codes, see Keener, "Mutual Submission Frames the Household Codes." However, I would register that I do not think they go far enough in arguing that these passages have cultural assumptions that necessitate dynamic applications for today beyond their concrete sense. For instance, the principle of mutual submission leaves little prescription for abuse, where submission may be singular in direction. For a woman to leave an abusive marriage in today's cultural context does not present an offense to the social order that could hamper the gospel and incur further violence the way it could in the Greco-Roman world. See Fee, "The Cultural Context of Ephesians 5:18—6:9," who builds the case for dissimilarity.

seeks to live out this as an inbreaking reality. This does not bypass taking up the cross but rather reads it as hope for those who find themselves in a form of crucifixion already: oppression, hardship, and the sacrifice of resisting evil without compromise. For instance, Howard Thurman (1899–1981) saw so many Blacks of his day criticize Christianity as a religion that preached platitudes of love and forgiveness that spiritualized oppression, excused the oppressors, and sought to pacify resistance. As a corrective, Thurman interpreted the virtues of Jesus as the means of survival toward liberation, not merely accepting subordination:

> The basic fact is that Christianity, as it was born in the mind of this Jewish teacher and thinker, appears as a technique of survival for the oppressed. That it became, through the intervening years, a religion of the powerful and the dominant, used sometimes as an instrument of oppression, must not tempt us to believe that it was thus in the mind and life of Jesus. "In him was life; and the light was the light of all men." Wherever his spirit appears, the oppressed gather fresh courage; for he announces the good news that fear, hypocrisy, and hatred, the three hounds of hell that track the trail of the disinherited, need have no domination over them.[68]

Thurman is correct to say that the situation of Jesus was one where people "had their backs against the wall" and had to live out the kingdom, its dignity, truth, and justice as much as they could while navigating living in a system of fear, deception, and hatred, which they did not have the immediate means to change.

Similarly, the New Testament scholar and activist Walter Wink (1935–2021) summarized the ethic of the cross as resistance to evil without resorting to evil: "Jesus, in short, abhors both passivity and violence. He articulates, out of the history of his own people's struggles, a way by which evil can be opposed without being mirrored, the oppressor resisted without being emulated, and the enemy neutralized without being destroyed."[69] In his work, Wink offers the important insight that seeking greater agency and having deeper material aspiration is not wrong, nor is having power and status per se; these things are only wrong when they are used against others and refused to others.[70] For Wink, opposing evil still could entail

---

68. Thurman, *Jesus and the Disinherited*, 18–19. Thurman, it should be noted, uses this Jesus-centered ethic to counter what he sees in the writings of Paul.

69. Wink, *Engaging the Powers*, 189.

70. Wink, *Engaging the Powers*, 111.

giving up one's life in martyrdom, as was the case for Jesus, but this kind of sacrifice is not valorized to the point of fatalistic passivity. It is Thurman and Wink's positive place for increasing human agency by actively resisting oppression without resorting to evil that better applies the way of the cross and resurrection for the present day for men and women.

To return then to Parker and Brown's criticisms, one gets the sense their resistance to evil is an impossible task since, in their estimate, to resist evil one ought not to sacrifice. This leaves one with questions: Is the only way to resist evil at a safe distance? How can evil be resisted without choices that may bring a lament-filled awareness of what evil has done? Can evil be defeated without any personal cost? Since all human life ends in death, there is no space available for Parker and Brown that affirms life without the suffering part of human mortality (which God in Christ has chosen to enter into). In so far as all life is touched by sin, all life has elements of suffering. Sarah Coakley correctly notes a kind of allergic reaction to vulnerability in feminist theology, which, while understandable, also undermines the feminist quest for transformation.[71] In Christ's choosing the cross, something states most pointedly in John's Gospel ("For this reason, the Father loves me, because I lay down my life in order to take it up again. No one takes it from me, but I lay it down of my own accord" says John 10:17), there is a refusal of God to leave humanity without redemption. This encourages an ethic where humanity is called out of its egoism to a love of others, not one that destroys the self but completes it, not one that valorizes suffering but chooses the travail of solidarity and compassion as a refusal to have liberation at the expense or neglect of another. To continue the question of authenticity discussed in the previous two chapters, it is in the narrative center of the cross and resurrection, a living in love, hope, and justice, that one finds one's true self. This does not mean an abused person must confront evil when they are merely struggling to survive. It is a call to the community, where all people are interconnected, to confront evil together, especially when the community sees individuals weary from their own struggles.

Thus, one need not abandon a classic reading of the cross in order to advance liberation. One flows from the other. This is seen in the synoptic portrait of the cross as a ransom, which displays the above dynamic of voluntary service for the other with the end goal of exodus-like liberation.

---

71. Coakley, *Powers and Submissions*, 3–40.

When the disciples argue about who is the greatest, Jesus responds in Mark 10:42–45 by saying,

> You know that among the gentiles those whom they recognize as their rulers lord it over them, and their great ones are tyrants over them. But it is not so among you; but whoever wishes to become great among you must be your servant, and whoever wishes to be first among you must be slave of all. For the Son of Man came not to be served but to serve, and to give his life a ransom for many.

Jesus refers to himself as the Son of Man. It is Jesus' preferred title, and it is an allusion to Dan 7, where "one like a son of man" comes to the Ancient of Days, overthrowing the beasts that oppress God's people in order that the Son of Man reigns over the nations. Jesus then is the Son of Man, who ushers in the kingdom as he comes in the clouds to the Ancient of Days at his crucifixion. The cross is an apocalyptic disclosure of God's kingdom and the coming new age. How does the Son of Man accomplish this? Jesus rebukes domination and selfish status-seeking and emphasizes his call "to serve." The fundamental driving force of the cross is Christ's act of service, giving up his prerogative of high status for others. In the Gospel of Mark, Jesus states the kingdom axiom that the "first will be last, and the last will be first" (Mark 10:31, cf. 9:35). This is the central rhythm of the cross and resurrection: the cross is a ransoming sacrifice, an act of service and humility, displaying Christ "becoming last" for humanity, even on to death on a cross. In the resurrection, Jesus, with all who look to him, is then elevated to first in glory. This act then is understood as a "ransom," an allusion back to Exod 6:6, which says, "Say therefore to the Israelites, 'I am the LORD, and I will free you from the burdens of the Egyptians and deliver you from slavery to them. I will ransom you, with an outstretched arm and with mighty acts of judgment.'" "Ransom" translates the Greek word in the LXX, *lytroomai*, which is what Mark uses (*lytron*), alluding back to Exodus.[72] The cross and resurrection is an exodus-like ransom out of slavery, where Christ has chosen to be the sacrifice to overturn the forces of sin and death.[73]

Read in this way, the cross is part of Jesus' ministry of solidarity (those already found in the position of last in status) in order to bring

---

72. See Baker and Green, *Recovering the Scandal of the Cross*, 58.
73. While this essay has used the ransom theme from Mark, that does not dismiss other classic motifs. See Rutledge, *Crucifixion*.

hope. In the Synoptics, Jesus heals a woman who has been bleeding for twelve years (Mark 5:24–34; Matt 9:20–22; Luke 8:43–48). Notice her insistence on defying cultural expectations of female subordination as well as laws of defilement that would have prevented her from approaching. Yet she was healed and Jesus congratulated her bold faith. Matthew situates this story with a set of healing narratives that Matthew argues shows the fulfillment of Isa 53:4: "This was to fulfill what had been spoken through the prophet Isaiah, 'He took our infirmities and bore our diseases'" (Matt 8:17). Implicit then in the text is that Jesus bore her pain and suffering. This is a preview of the cross, where Jesus bears the full measure of the effects of sin in a humiliating execution to show the full scope of healing for all in the resurrection.

When Jesus cries out, "My God, my God, why have you forsaken me?" (Mark 15:34; Matt 27:46), this is an allusion to Ps 22, a psalm of David found on the lips of Jesus at the cross. Psalm 22 expresses lament, wondering where God is, who has promised to protect the anointed one in the midst of persecution, and it is this psalm that was prayed as the words of the entire people of God, lamenting the state of oppression they were in, wondering when God would come to establish his kingdom. For Jesus to speak these words at the cross indicates, as Richard Bauckham argues, that Jesus stands in solidarity with those who feel forsaken by God, all to reassure them with the hope of the resurrection.[74] Jesus uttering the cry of dereliction on the cross symbolizes the voice of the forsaken, as Jesus' cry to God, but also as God, and thus is a sign that the presence and promises of God are for people who feel God is absent. As Elizabeth Gerhardt states, "The suffering, living Christ is present among the suffering of millions of women and girls who are oppressed because of their gender. God is found among those millions of women and girls who continue to suffer because God is always found among 'the least of these.'"[75]

Thus, the cross inspires an ethic that implores those who have power and status to sacrifice in order to lift others up (the first becoming last) and is a promise made to those marginalized that hope is possible (the last will be first). While redemption is willing to wait (or flee) if no godly way is available to overthrow evil, to insist that subordination is absolute is to deny the inbreaking reality of Jesus' proclamation: "The time is fulfilled, and the kingdom of God has come near" (Mark 1:15). In

---

74. Bauckham, *Jesus and the God of Israel*, 254–68.
75. Gerhardt, *The Cross and Gendercide*, 141.

order to apply the cross better, believers must read with the forsaken of this world with eyes toward the resurrection.

As it has been suggested, to find one's true self and heal the wounds of sin, a person must take on Christ, that us, dwell in God's movement of incarnational presence (affirming all that is good in oneself), cruciform love of others (giving up egoism, which holds onto privilege and power over others), and welcoming resurrection newness (liberation rather than absolute submission).

Thus, it might actually be that a female representation of Jesus on the cross, like *Christa*, might aid Christians in better following what the historical cross of Jesus Christ is all about, one that shows solidarity with the marginalized, seeking liberation, not endless submission.

CONCLUSION

This chapter has argued between two polarized positions: one that uses the maleness of the historical Jesus to close down female interpretation and the other that emphasizes femininity to the point of undermining the historical Jesus. As an alternative, through affirming realistic revelation, the incarnation of Christ, while historically male, is able to incorporate and encourage female figures. By having a more traditional understanding of the incarnation, cross, and resurrection, one is able to see the revealed presence of God on all flesh, the counter-patriarchal movement of the Gospels, and the hope of victory over sin and patriarchy in the resurrection. Far from Christology and femininity being opposed, one opens up the possibility of the other. As several church thinkers have pointed out, it is possible to think about Christ as a mother in order to imaginatively emphasize the meaning of the incarnation. In reflecting on *Christa*, a sculpture of a feminine Christ on the cross, it is argued that this might remind the church that the cross, rather than reinforcing patriarchy, stands against it. Now, it should be noted that nothing has been said here about a more complicated figure by which Christ is spoken of in feminine ways, one that overlaps with the Spirit: the figure of Sophia, both the subjects of our next chapter.

5

Spirit and Sophia

REVELATION OF GOD IS possible through the action of the Holy Spirit, but is the Holy Spirit male or female? If the Spirit can be spoken of in feminine ways, what implications does this have for believers? Last chapter, a case was made for the centrality of Christ, who was historically male, as the site by which redemption came, and it is through the historical sending of the Spirit of Christ at Pentecost that the incarnation came to *all* flesh, thus allowing the incorporation of femininity into Christ's body. As we will see, however, consideration of the imagery for the Spirit forms the most consistently appealed to avenue for female language for God and this imagery is consistently downplayed today by some in order to preserve male-only depictions. Also, there is a kind of appropriation of Lady Wisdom (or Sophia) beyond the Christ-centred particularity of the biblical narrative in some feminist theology. This leaves questions as to what the rules of appropriate discourse are for speaking about the Holy Spirit, as it is the Spirit that is understood to be Sophia primarily in intertestamental books like the Wisdom of Solomon but later in the New Testament, Sophia is primarily portrayed as fulfilled in Christ. Understanding Lady Wisdom, for instance, as the complementary figure of the incarnate Christ demonstrates the argument that we have been exploring this whole project: there are biblical and historical ways these sets of imagery can be used that are not at loggerheads. Perhaps the locus of the most complicated sets of images and references, the Holy Spirit takes on rich metaphors like wind (as well as fire and water) but also complex figures like the Shekinah presence and Lady Wisdom, images that overlap with Christ's fulfillment of them. Here it will be argued that the Spirit as the breath of life and as the Shekinah presence of God further prompts the Christian to understand all of human experience, including gendered experience, as meaningful, further encouraging believers to read the Bible through the Spirit's liberating love. Also, as the Spirit (as well as Christ) comes to be understood as the figure of Sophia, this figure not only opens up another important avenue for female language for God, but also the criteria by which Christians can discern truth and goodness in the inter-cultural milieu we live in.

COMPETING VIEWS OF THE SPIRIT AND SOPHIA

The Spirit, throughout the biblical narrative, is often identified with God and Christ. Often, the question of "femininity" of the Spirit is dismissed with a reiteration that the Spirit in the Bible is the Spirit of God, the Father, and the Spirit of Jesus Christ, and so, the Spirit is only to be spoken of in male terms, even though most would insist that this does not make God male per se. Nevertheless, in Scripture, the Spirit is a "he," not a "she" or an "it." However, in modern theology, there has been debate about the use of gendered imagery for the Spirit, with notable feminists using female imagery, especially Lady Wisdom, to propose revisions.

Some have argued that *ruach* (spirit) in Hebrew is grammatically feminine; however, as Anthony Thiselton states, the arguments that a word is feminine are moot as similar words like the Greek *pneuma* (spirit) in the New Testament are grammatically neuter. Disappointingly, Thiselton's massive five-hundred-page book, *The Holy Spirit* (2013), which catalogs the history of the theology of the Holy Spirit from the Old Testament to today, does not mention a single feminist writer or offer any sustained engagement with feminine pneumatological themes.

While there are not many female reference to the Spirit in the canonical Scriptures, it seems that there have been moves in church tradition to appropriate feminine implications and connotations. While, for instance, the grammatically feminine nature of *ruach* is not an exegetically convincing ground for the Spirit being portrayed as female, the fact that Christians have constantly looked to this as an avenue to express the femininity of God is at the very least significant.

Other theologians who do emphasize the "femininity" of the Spirit often do so with only brief arguments. Clark Pinnock, in his *Flame of*

Love, merely notes that the Spirit is female in some Syriac theology without developing the argument in detail and without employing much female language for God in the actual body of the work.[1] Jürgen Moltmann argues for female God-language and, in particular, for the Spirit to be understood in female and motherly terms. However, it is a fairly minimal argument. He appeals to the Shekinah of God being feminine and notes the motherly actions of the Spirit in producing spiritual birth.[2] Leonardo Boff's short work displays a brief argument for the figure of wisdom as legitimate female language for God, but also thinks this overlaps with how Mary and the church are talked about. The question would be to what extent can Mary be used to talk about the Spirit? Can Mary be used as a figure of the Spirit's femininity?[3] And there are others too,[4] but again, most offer relatively brief arguments.

While one can grant the link between pneumatology and Christology, the real point of controversy is concerning the figure of Sophia. For instance, a central controversy over feminine language occurred at a World Council of Churches initiative, the Re-imagining Conference, held in Minneapolis in 1993. There, the image of Sophia was used in worship, and it drew widespread condemnation from conservatives who regarded the image as an imposition into and against the biblical depiction of God. Tina Ostrander wrote in criticism,

> Who is "Sophia"? For an increasing number of feminist theologians and probably for a great many of the Re-Imagining participants, Sophia is a unique and divine person. How she relates to God is a matter of varying interpretations. It has been argued that Sophia is superior to God, that she is equal to God, that she is God, or that she is inferior to God, yet still divine. The biblical understanding of Sophia which is most true to the scriptural context is that Sophia is none of these things. Sophia is nothing more than a Greek noun describing an important attribute of God. . . . As we continue the search for an inclusive understanding of God, it is imperative that we remain within the bounds of Scripture.[5]

---

1. Pinnock, *Flame of Love*, 15–17.
2. Moltmann, *Spirit of Life*, 27.
3. Boff, *Come Holy Spirit*, 119–25.
4. Some of the other pneumatologies that argue for "femininity" of the Spirit include the following: Congar, *I Believe in the Holy Spirit*, 3:155–64; O'Donnell, *The Mystery of the Triune God*, 151–57; Durrell, *Holy Spirit of God*, 151–57; Gelpi, *The Divine Mother*, 215–39.
5. Ostrander, "Who Is Sophia?" It can only be said that this is an odd critique.

Conservatives consistently downplay the legitimacy of uses for the figure of Lady Wisdom, arguing the image is merely metaphorical.[6] While the figure of Lady Wisdom is portrayed as the Spirit in some intertestamental books, as will be shown, the fact that Christ is the fulfillment of much of this imagery in the Gospels is seen as de-legitimizing the feminine imagery, whether for Christ or the Spirit. This is coupled with the insistence that in the New Testament, the grammar of the Holy Spirit is that the Spirit is a "he," because the Spirit is the Spirit of Christ (e.g., John 14:15–17; Rom 8:26).

Some theologians have suggested that Sophia imagery can be used to speak of Christ as a feminine character. For instance, Elizabeth Johnson argued for a Wisdom Christology that develops Ruether's contention.[7] Grace Ji-Sun Kim has argued for a Sophia-Christology that directly portrays Christ as overcoming the sin and oppression colonized women face (specifically, Korean North American women).[8] Jann Aldredge-Clanton has argued that if the resurrected Christ through the Spirit has come into all flesh, femininity, which she sees as biblically symbolized in the figure of Sophia, can be used to image Christ.[9] Clanton, as well as Sally Douglas, have both used the Wisdom figure as she appears in the New Testament to emphasize the social justice teachings of Jesus for today.[10] As noted, there is always a concern for safeguarding the historical revelation of Jesus, and this also explains why Wisdom imagery is absorbed into Christology in most places in the New Testament and the early church (although not all places). Christ typically fulfills the figure of Wisdom. All of these authors (Johnson, Kim, Douglas, Aldredge-Clanton) superimpose the female figure onto the acts of Jesus in the biblical narrative. Ruether, also appealing to the risen Christ in the Spirit, notes that there have been mystics and prophetic voices outside the mainstream of Christianity who have experienced Christ as female. Notably, the Montanist prophetess

---

Ostrander cites Fiorenza and Bulgakov's works (which this chapter will explore), who, while two very different Christian scholars, both offer scriptural quotations and rationales for their Sophia theologies. However, Ostrander does not interact with their arguments.

6. Frye, "Language for God," 34.
7. Johnson, *She Who Is*, ch. 8.
8. Kim, *The Grace of Sophia*.
9. Aldredge-Clanton, *In Search of Christ-Sophia*.
10. Douglas, *Jesus Sophia*.

Priscilla and some Shakers saw Christ as feminine, and these were vital to understanding the full measure of the incarnation.[11]

Meanwhile, Lady Wisdom is interpreted in problematic ways in some radical feminist revisions. Feminists such as Reuther seek to make Lady Wisdom a figure of universal female empowerment that surmounts the particularity of the biblical narrative to become a trans-religious figure greater than Christianity or any of the world religions. Ruether sees Lady Wisdom as a female figure that was merged into Judaism, possibly from the Asherah, and thus, she is a figure born in the biblical thinking of a monotheist patriarchal polemic repressing and absorbing a female.[12] This clandestine religion of femininity, rooted in the ancient fertility cults, is something Ruether pulls together from strands of different religions, sects, and philosophies all over history.[13] In her later work, she is more skeptical about a unified pre-historic religion of femininity, but nevertheless, in these strands and fragments, she sees parts that can be woven together now to form a new Goddess ecofeminist spirituality. She comments,

> I regard all these paths as equally legitimate. There are difficulties but also rich creativity to be found in each of these paths of the feminist religious quest. I personally am more inspired by the first path. That we are not likely to clearly identify feminist goddesses and cultures from pre-patriarchal histories means that reclaiming goddesses from the ancient Near East, such as Inanna, Isis, or Demeter, or Kali and Durga from India, is also a work of feminist reinterpretation for today, not a ready-made feminist spirituality that we can lay hold of literally and reproclaim in its ancient historical form. This means taking responsibility for our own work of reinterpretation and new myth-making today.[14]

As we will see, the association of Sophia with a generalized notion of wisdom separated from Christ is one contributing factor to the mainstream church distancing itself from Sophia language. However, this does not warrant a complete dismissal. Sophia imagery offers important insight for inter-religious engagement that does not sacrifice the particularity of the Christian faith.

11. Ruether, *Sexism and God-Talk*, 131–33.
12. Ruether, *Sexism and God-Talk*, 54.
13. Ruether, *Goddesses and the Divine Feminine*, 4.
14. Ruether, *Goddesses and the Divine Feminine*, 307.

Meanwhile, two early sustained arguments for female language for the Spirit are found in the work of Alwyn Marriage and Elizabeth Johnson, and both seek a more robust, trinitarian account of the Holy Spirit. Marriage's book *Life Giving Spirit*[15] is a multifaceted argument for using female imagery, seeing the Holy Spirit as the identity most consistently presented in feminine ways and thus most apt for supplementing male imagery. In other words, while she grants the place of Father language and the historical maleness of Jesus Christ, the Spirit is understood as female through the motherly imagery of the breath of God, the femininity of the Shekinah presence, and, most substantively, the figure of Lady Wisdom. Johnson, in her book *She Who Is* (1992), offers a defense for Shekinah-Sophia language along similar lines[16] and in a small set of lectures published as *Women, Earth, and Creator Spirit* (1993) focuses on pneumatology, the experience of women, and applies these insights to the environmental crisis.[17] These are commendable works that this investigation will supplement and argue further. One important avenue of supplementation is from the often-missed tradition of the Russian Sophiologists, which will be explored further shortly.

What is the gender of the Spirit? What is the nature of Sophia imagery? What does it mean for the gender of God, particularly in how this points to Christ? What is the relevance of this image being taken from sources outside the Hebrew religion? These are some of the questions that need clarification.

SPIRIT AS THE BREATH OF LIFE

The first image is the Spirit as the breath of life. At the beginning of the Old Testament, the wind of God (Heb. *ruach*) hovers upon the waters of chaos to initiate creation (Gen 1:2), much like a mother bird hovers over a nest, suggesting a combination of masculine and feminine images for God in the very first chapter of the Bible. This is similar to previous discussions that show God (typically male), nevertheless, possesses female traits, whether nursing, bearing, or here, nesting. In the second creation story, it is the breath of God, "the breath of life," that animates the first human as a "living being" (Gen 2:7). This description occurs elsewhere,

---

15. Marriage, *Life-Giving Spirit*, particularly 63–76, 84–87.
16. Johnson, *She Who Is*, 82–94.
17. Johnson, *Women, Earth, and Creator Spirit*, 51–57.

like in Job and Isaiah: "The Spirit of God made me, and the breath of the Almighty has given me life" (Job 33:4). It is God that "gives breath to the people upon it [the earth], and spirit to those who walk on it" (Isa 42:5). The Spirit of God is the Spirit of life. The wind of God is also a way of speaking of God's action, as it was the wind that blew the path through the Red Sea (Exod 14:21).[18]

While gender cannot be inferred from these descriptions, what is relevant is that the Spirit is the basis of life, and therefore, the experience of life cannot be separated from our experience of God. The wind of God sets the scene for the wind the blows on Pentecost, as it is the same wind that liberates Israel from slavery that also liberates men and women from patriarchy.

SPIRIT AS SHEKINAH

Another early image is that of God's Shekinah, from the Hebrew *shakan*, which literally means "to dwell." It is a descriptor for God's dwelling in the tabernacle or simply with God's people:[19] "And have them make me a sanctuary, so that I may dwell among them" (Exod 25:8). Similarly, it comes to dwell in Solomon's temple (1 Kgs 8:10–11; 2 Chr 5:13–14). The Shekinah is also the site of the name of God "dwelling" with God's people (Deut 12:11; 14:23; 16:6, 11; 26:2; Neh 1:9). Thus, because of the connection with the temple and other manifestations of God, Shekinah becomes synonymous with the beauty and splendor of God (Exod 24:16–18; 33:18–23), and thus, in the New Testament, uses the term "glory" or *doxa*. Isaiah particularly picks up this theme of God dwelling in Zion (Isa 8:18) and speaks of further presence from the messianic figure: "On that day the root of Jesse shall stand as a signal to the peoples; the nations shall inquire of him, and his dwelling shall be glorious" (Isa 11:10). It is later in Isaiah that this Shekinah presence, the Spirit, and the messianic converge. "The Spirit of the LORD is upon me" (Isa 61:1; cf. 59:21) says one of the servant songs that speaks of this anointed figure who will bring about the kingdom of God, which is described in terms of liberation, hope, comfort, and joy (Isa 61:1–3). With the presence of the Spirit on the servant, who will

---

18. On the nature of the earliest depictions of the Spirit, see Montague, *The Holy Spirit*, 3–17.

19. Also Exod 29:45–46; Num 5:3; 35:34; 1 Kgs 6:13; Ezek 43:9; Zech 2:14.

suffer for the people (Isa 53), Jürgen Moltmann notes that the Shekinah is the empathy and solidarity of God with the suffering righteous.[20]

Thus, after the New Testament times, as Leore Sachs-Shmueli notes, Shekinah imagery is consistently understood as a female personality in Jewish tradition.[21] As Abelson argues in his classic study, Judaism always had a category for God's imminence. This is an answer to the polemic Christians have sometimes argued against Judaism to bolster the incarnation.[22] While the mere notion of the grammatical feminine or later Jewish employments of Shekinah imagery as female is not definitive and while all the ways Shekinah imagery is taken up in the New Testament goes beyond the limits of this study, it is relevant to see how Shekinah imagery provides an important model for the incarnation, God's presence in all things coming to a particular intensity in Christ (a difference in degree rather than kind). This is just one more way Christians can reflect on God's presence in creation and, thus, in the phenomena of male and female.

SPIRIT AND MOTHER FIGURES

While the Spirit as breath or Shekinah is not directly female, the actions of this identity in the Bible is often portrayed in motherly ways, thus warranting later imagery in the tradition. However, as we will see, this has also meant the conflation of the Spirit with Mary.

The Spirit and Mary

One reason why the Spirit is often portrayed as a mother is because of a conflation with the figure of Mary, the reasons for which need to be understood. Luke alludes to the Shekinah presence coming upon Mary: "The Holy Spirit will come upon you, and the power of the Most High will overshadow you; therefore the child to be born will be holy; he will be called Son of God" (Luke 1:35). As Mollenkott notes, "overshadow" (Gk. *episkaisei* from the root *skene*, meaning "tent" or "dwelling," which is also used in John 1:14: "the word became flesh and dwelt [Gk. *eskenosen*]

---

20. Moltmann, *Spirit of Life*, 48–51.

21. See Sachs-Shmueli, "Shekinah and the Revival of Feminine God Language," 347–69. Also see Lodahl, *Shekinah/Spirit*. For a more popular level work, see Novick, *On the Wings of Shekinah*.

22. See Abelson, *The Immanence of God in Rabbinical Literature*.

among us") may be an allusion to the Hebrew Shekinah "dwelling" with the people.[23]

Thus, this coinciding of the Spirit and Mary seems to inspire the use of Mary as a figure for the Holy Spirit in church tradition. While this is problematic for Protestants, one cannot deny the imagery is related and has been used this way in Christianity. The veneration of Mary has a long and intricate history,[24] where the historical figure of Mary in the Gospels plays a modest role.[25] However, her identity blossoms in the early church, particularly around her title *Theotokos* ("God-bearer"), and its relationship with defending and clarifying the two natures of Christ. Another contributing factor to this is the figure of the woman in Revelation (Rev 12:1–6), who escapes the dragon with the child. She has a "starred crown," thus Mary, who is often seen as the reference of this figure, is crowned "queen" in several icons (notably fig. 5.2, where she is crowned with the Spirit or as the Spirit). Catholic commentators identify this figure as both Mary and God's people, the church.[26] This, coupled with the birth narratives that have Mary coinciding with the Holy Spirit as the mother of Jesus, forms the seeds for a set of images that emerge in the church, ones that Protestants regularly miss. However, few can dispute the ubiquitous nature of the mother and child image in Christian iconography. Notice how in Konrad Witz's piece, "Man of Sorrows and Mary" from 1450 (fig. 5.3), Mary stands with Christ before the Father. There is no Holy Spirit, yet Mary has the halo of divinity that the Son and the Father share. By implication, Witz saw Mary as a figure to conceptualize the Holy Spirit. As imagery for God grew more patriarchal, Mary seemed to be the site of sacred female imagery. Similarly, in fig. 5.4, Mary is a statue, which opens us to reveal the Father and the cross of the Son. By implication, the Marian figure is a pathway

---

23. Mollenkott, *The Divine Feminine*, 35.

24. A full charting of this imagery would be too much for this book, but it has been analyzed elsewhere. See Pelican, *Mary through the Centuries*, esp. chs. 12, 13, and 15. This has also been examined in Ruether, *Mary—The Feminine Face of the Church*; Boff, *The Maternal Face of God*. However, it should be noted that there is important critical discussion on the portrayal of Mary. For instance, her virginity has been used to shame women's sexuality and the way Mary is idealized as a female image of God is also portrayed in subservience to the male imagery.

25. However, the recent work of Peeler, *Women and the Gender of God*, shows that reflecting on Mary generates a rebuke of patriarchy and the reification of God as male. Her work is superb in refuting a masculinized vision of God as "blasphemy" (106).

26. See, for example, Balthasar, *Mary for Today*, 9–14.

of revelation representing the Spirit. Thus, Yves Congar observes, "the maternal function of the Holy Spirit has often been replaced in recent Catholic devotion by the Virgin Mary."[27] This is a move that he, as a Catholic theologian, approves. Again, while this imagery is lost in Protestantism, it seems that throughout much of church history, Mary has served as a figure of the church and the Spirit. While no person should be elevated to divine status (to this Protestant theology has rightly objected), nor should Mary as a historical individual be reduced to symbol, one also cannot dispute the use of symbolism as evidence that the church has throughout history found ways to express femininity in God.

This explains in part why Marian devotion is prevalent in Roman Catholicism. For Protestants who find this elevation of Mary to be beyond what the Bible permits (as I certainly do), the fact that Mary seems to stand as a way of expressing both the Spirit's maternal intimacy with believers and a desired connection of femininity in God in general (similar to how writers have looked to the grammatical femininity of the Spirit and Shekinah as an avenue) must be understood and appreciated.

Fig. 5.2

27. Congar, *I Believe in the Holy Spirit*, 3:162.

Fig. 5.3

Fig. 5.4

The Spirit as Mother

However, as distinct from Mary, the Spirit is described with motherly qualities, which provides a more biblically grammared pathway for speech about the Spirit: if the Spirit acts in motherly ways, the title is warranted, despite the Spirit being beyond gender. We have already noted how the Spirit is the Spirit of *life* at creation, hovering over creation as a mother bird over a nest. This is reiterated in the book of Job: "The spirit of God has made me, and the breath of the Almighty gives me life" (Job 33:4). Elihu continues on to say of God, "If he should take back his spirit to himself and gather to himself his breath, all flesh would perish together, and all mortals return to dust" (Job 34:14–15). It is in the speeches of God out of the whirlwind asks, "Does the rain have a father? Who fathers the drops of dew? From whose womb comes the ice? Who gives birth to the frost from the heavens?" (Job 38:28–29), which speaks of God both as Father but also as possessing motherly qualities (a point made in an earlier chapter). One sees the Spirit of God as the basis of life, and this source of life is womb-like, birthing creation sustaining it.

Paul uses birthing imagery to speak of the work of the Spirit. Romans 8 uses the metaphor of the travail of labor to speak of cosmic redemption where the Spirit reveals the children of God (Rom 8:1–15, but notably vv. 22–24). Paul combines birth imagery with harvest imagery as he speaks about the labor of redemption leading to the "first fruits" and "bearing fruits" (Rom 8:23),[28] which forms a connection where the Spirit causes the adoption of people as children of God (Gal 4:6), "born of the Spirit" (Gal 4:29), and in them, the Spirit bears fruit (Gal 5:22–23, cf. Eph 5:9).

The Spirit in John's Gospel takes on important motherly qualities, namely that of birthing and nursing. John 3 speaks of being "born again" and "born from above." Jesus says to Nicodemus, "Very truly, I tell you, no one can enter the kingdom of God without being born of water and Spirit" (John 3:5). This points back to the beginning of John where the author reports, "But to all who received him, who believed in his name, he gave power to become children of God, who were born, not of blood or of the will of the flesh or of the will of man, but of God" (John 1:12–13). The Spirit implicitly is the mother of Jesus and the disciples as she performs the function of birthing the children of God.

---

28. Also see Rom 7:4, 5; 8:23; 11:16; 1 Cor 15:20, 23; Col 1:6, 10; 2 Thess 2:13.

SPIRIT AND SOPHIA

Important motherly imagery appears later in the New Testament, which early church theologians picking up feminine pneumatic language. Hebrews mentions that disciples grow through the "milk" of the "word of righteousness" (Heb 5:13), and 1 Peter similarly states, "Like newborn infants, long for the pure, spiritual milk, so that by it you may grow into salvation" (1 Pet 2:2).

The Spirit as a mother appears in several early documents. The Odes of Solomon date from the second century CE and perhaps earlier. They are a Christian collection of worship songs used in the early church. In them, several descriptions of the Holy Spirit as a mother are referenced, along with other general references. For instance, Christ is described as Mother (Odes 8:14). Ode 35 speaks similarly to Isaiah of God being motherlike in care:

> And I was carried like a child by its mother;
> And He gave me milk, the dew of the Lord.
> And I grew strong in His favor,
> And rested in His perfection. (Odes 35:5–6)

However, it is most commonly the Spirit who takes on these characteristics in the Odes:

> As the wings of doves over their nestlings, and the mouths of their nestlings towards their mouths,
> So are the wings of the Spirit over my heart. My heart continually refreshes itself and leaps for joy, like the babe who leaps for joy in his mother's womb. (Odes 28:1–2)

This Ode displays a creative synthesis of imagery. It draws together the images of God protecting like a mother bird (cf. Deut 32:11–12; Ps 57:1) and applies them to the Spirit (who is depicted as a dove at Jesus' baptism), but also, the language of this Ode reflects Luke 1:41, where Elizabeth's baby in the womb leaps for joy.

> A cup of milk was offered to me, and I drank it in the sweetness of the Lord's kindness.
> The Son is the cup, and the Father is He who was milked; and the Holy Spirit is She who milked Him;
> Because His breasts were full, and it was undesirable that His milk should be ineffectually released.
> The Holy Spirit opened Her bosom, and mixed the milk of the two breasts of the Father.

> Then She gave the mixture to the generation without their knowing, and those who have received it are in the perfection of the right hand.
> The womb of the Virgin took it, and she received conception and gave birth.
> So the Virgin became a mother with great mercies.
> And she labored and bore the Son but without pain, because it did not occur without purpose.
> And she did not require a midwife, because He caused her to give life.
> She brought forth like a strong man with desire, and she bore according to the manifestation, and she acquired according to the Great Power.
> And she loved with redemption, and guarded with kindness, and declared with grandeur.
> Hallelujah. (Odes 19:1–11)

As one can see, the trinitarian theology displays Father, Son, and Spirit, and the Father (reminiscent of the dual-gendered "Father with a womb" in Job and Deuteronomy) is displayed as having breasts, and the Spirit milks them. Alluding perhaps to 1 Pet 2:2 and Heb 5:4–5, the Trinity dispenses spiritual milk for knowledge. This milk, in particular, comes upon the virgin by which Jesus is born, oddly without pain or midwife. In Ode 33, the figure called "the Perfect Virgin" claims she will instruct the believer, similar to how Lady Wisdom will in Proverbs, leading them from destruction to truth (Odes 33:8). Ode 36 offers a theosis-like depiction of a believer being baptized and thus born again from the Spirit's womb-like waters:

> I rested on the Spirit of the Lord,
> And She lifted me up on high.
> And caused me to stand on my feet in the high place of the Lord,
> In the presence of His perfection and His glory,
> where I glorified [Him] with the composition of His hymns.
> [The Spirit] gave birth to me before the Lord's face, and although I was a man I was named a brilliant son of God. . . .
> For according to the greatness of the Most High, so did She make me; and according to His renewing He renewed me.
> (Odes 36:1–3, 5)

The Odes of Solomon are a significant early example as they are a liturgical document indicating that female imagery was incorporated into the worship of the early church. In fact, other than the doxological material in the New Testament itself, these stand as some of the earliest recorded examples of the church's worship.

For the first few hundred years of the church there was a host of literature that was considered authoritative in some way or another as the canon, as we now know it, took shape. In these, we see important examples that prominent theologians reflected upon. One is the Gospel of Hebrews. This work is only known today in fragments, but it seems to be a document dating to the early second century. It is a retelling of Jesus' life and teachings from a Jewish-Christian community. It was quoted as a supplementary authority to the four Gospels by Clement, Origen, Didymus, and Jerome. Its fall from usage is not entirely certain but may have been due to the fact that it was written in Hebrew and used by some later Ebionites.[29] Nevertheless, in the document, Christ is described as saying, "Even so did my mother, the Holy Spirit, take me by one of my hairs and carry me away onto the great mountain, Tabor."[30] Along with references in the Gospel of Philip, it seems that there were Christian communities that assumed the Spirit could be spoken of using female imagery and pronouns, despite Christ being male (and the two were not at loggerheads).[31] Origen cites the Gospel of Hebrews regarding the femininity of the Spirit:

---

29. So notes Metzger, *Canon of the New Testament*, 170: "From these several [known] quotations, the *Gospel of the Hebrews* differed considerably in substance and in character from the gospels that were ultimately regarded as the only canonical Gospels. For this reason, as well as the fact that the Gospel of the Hebrews was written in a Semitic language, we can understand why its use was limited, chiefly among Jewish Christians (some of whom were regarded as heretical), and passed over by the Great Church in the period when the canon was closed." Despite Metzger's insistence, Clement and Origen did not see its differences apparently as too divergent. Cyril of Jerusalem cites an Ebionite opponent quoting it in one of his sermons, which may indicate the book was associated with Ebionitism. However, the fact that Jerome defends the work two centuries after its date of writing is intriguing.

30. Gospel of the Hebrews, Frag. 3., in *New Testament Apocrypha*, vol. I, 158–65.

31. Gospel of Philip is of lesser importance, since it was a spurious gospel (the Gospel of Hebrews has more credibility). Nevertheless, its assumption and observation is relevant to our argument: "Some said that Mary conceived by the holy spirit: they are mistaken, they do not realize what they say. When did a female ever conceive by a female? Mary is the virgin whom the forces did not defile." Again, while the Gospel itself is spurious and it fell out of use due to association with gnostic thinking, the argument of this passage is telling: it assumes in these early Christian communities that the Spirit's gender is obviously and indisputably female. See Gospel of Philip 55:23ff., in *The Gnostic Scriptures*, 325–53, specifically pp. 331–32. There are a number of minor references that are dependent on or continuity with the Odes of Solomon, such as the cosmology of the Bardaisanites and the Acts of Thomas Judas, and these are explored further in Harvey, "Feminine Imagery for the Divine," 111–39.

> If anyone should lend credence to the Gospel according to the Hebrews, where the Saviour Himself says, "My Mother (*mētēr*), the Holy Spirit, took me just now by one of my hairs and carried me off to the great Mount Tabor," he will have to face the difficulty of explaining how the Holy Spirit can be the Mother (*mētēr*) of Christ when She was herself brought into existence through the Word. But neither the passage nor this difficulty is hard to explain. For if he who does the will of the Father in heaven [Mt. 12:50] is Christ's brother and sister and mother (*mētēr*), and if the name of the brother of Christ may be applied, not only to the race of men, but to beings of diviner rank than they, then there is nothing absurd in the Holy Spirit's being His Mother (*mētēr*); everyone being His mother who does the will of the Father in heaven.[32]

Jerome concurs with Origen as he seems to comment on a passage from the Gospel to the Hebrews, but then he looks to other biblical passages, noting the femininity of the Spirit as well:

> And also this: (in the text) "like the eyes of a maid look to the hand of her mistress" [Ps 123:2], the maid is the soul and the mistress is the Holy Spirit. For also in that Gospel written according to the Hebrews, which the Nazoreans read, the Lord says: "Just now, my Mother, the Holy Spirit, took me." Nobody should be offended by this, for among the Hebrews the Spirit is said to be of the feminine gender although in our language it is called to be of masculine gender, and in the Greek language, neuter.[33]

Thus, while the Gospel of Hebrews is not definitive for the church today with its canon, what it does demonstrate, according to two towering minds of the church, is that this language is in agreement with the rest of the Scriptures they affirmed.

As reported by Johannes van Oort, other less prominent thinkers display significant references as well.[34] Epiphanius states, "And the Holy Spirit is (said to be) like Christ, too, but She is a female being."[35] Hippolytus says similarly, "The male is the Son of God and the female is

---

32. Origen, *Commentary on the Gospel of John*, 2.12, quoted in van Oort, "The Holy Spirit as Feminine." Cf. Origen, *Homilies on Jeremiah*, 15.

33. Jerome, *Commentary on Isaiah*, 11, 40, 9, quoted in van Oort, "The Holy Spirit as Feminine." Cf. Jerome, *Commentary on Ezekiel*, 4, 16; *Commentary on Micah* 2, 7, 6.

34. van Oort, "The Holy Spirit as Feminine."

35. *Panarion* 19, 4, 1–2, quoted in van Oort, "The Holy Spirit as Feminine."

called the Holy Spirit."[36] In discussing chastity before marriage, Aphrahat states, "As long as a man has not taken a wife, he loves and reveres God his Father and the Holy Spirit his Mother, and he has no other love."[37] Aphrahat then describes the work of the Spirit in baptism like that of a female dove: "From baptism, we receive the Spirit of Christ, and in the same hour that the priests invoke the Spirit, She opens the heavens and descends, and hovers over the waters [cf. Gen 1:2], and those who are baptized put Her on."[38] Similarly, Symeon, in his sermons, praised the Spirit as the "heavenly Mother."[39] Pneumatology is a neglected topic in much early church theology, but as Oort's work shows, when the Spirit was discussed, the references were often female.

Thus, this survey of references in the early church is quite compelling. It seems there is ample documentation that there were feminine references to the Spirit in worship, preaching, and theological treatises. While some of them are influenced by non-canonical works like the Gospel of the Hebrews or the Gospel of Philip, others are more clearly in the mainstream of Christian reflection. Either way, however, the presence of this language suggests a practice in the early church that was well-accepted.

SPIRIT AND/AS LADY WISDOM

Wisdom is undoubtedly the most significant of the images. This constellation of ideas (Spirit, Shekinah, and breath) seems independent from Wisdom at first but they will converge later. Also, as we will see, the image comes from the Old Testament, through the inter-testamental literature, and on into the New Testament in several important ways. The Spirit as Sophia comes to its most explicit convergence in the Wisdom of Solomon where Wisdom imagery in the New Testament predominantly is understood as fulfilled in Christ, except for the interesting case of the Gospel of Luke.

---

36. *Refutatio*, 9, 13, 3, quoted in van Oort, "The Holy Spirit as Feminine."
37. *Demonstrations*, 18, quoted in van Oort, "The Holy Spirit as Feminine."
38. *Demonstrations*, 6, quoted in van Oort, "The Holy Spirit as Feminine."
39. Symeon, *Hom.* 27, 4, cf. *Hom.* 28, 4; *Hom.* 27, 1, quoted in van Oort, "The Holy Spirit as Feminine."

Wisdom in the Old Testament

Wisdom (Heb. *hokmah*) begins to be regarded as an object in the Psalms and the book of Job. For instance, Ps 104 states, "O LORD, how manifold are your works! In wisdom you have made them all; the earth is full of your creatures" (Ps 104:24, cf. 136:5). Wisdom does not seem to be a full-fledged point of reflection in the way it later becomes, but here the attribute of God is praised as central to the act of creation.[40] Job 28 speaks of wisdom but, again, not in personal terms. Wisdom is a thing to find or a place to seek, not a person: "But where shall wisdom be found? And where is the place of understanding?" (28:12). Here, Death and Abaddon are personified, but wisdom is not. Nevertheless, wisdom is seen as essential to the way of God: "Truly, the fear of the LORD, that is wisdom, and to depart from evil is understanding" (Job 28:28). Thus, it seems from there that the notion of wisdom begins to snowball.

Proverbs is a book traditionally attributed to King Solomon (perhaps as an honorary attribution or as a way of noting the Israelite wisdom tradition has its origins in him), though it reached its final editorial form in the sixth century BCE. It is here that one sees the introduction of Wisdom as a figure, particularly in the first several chapters, where she is contrasted with the seductive adulteress. Wisdom is depicted as "calling out" (Prov 1:20) to the reader, imploring the reader to follow her and what she reveals (1:23), as if she has divine authority. The way of Wisdom is life, goodness, and happiness; the way of the adulteress is foolishness, wickedness, exile, and destruction. The text states, "The LORD by wisdom founded the earth" (Prov 3:19), and this description is expanded a few chapters later:

> The LORD created me at the beginning of his work,
> the first of his acts of long ago.
> Ages ago I was set up,
> at the first, before the beginning of the earth.
> When there were no depths I was brought forth . . .
> When he established the heavens, I was there,
> when he drew a circle on the face of the deep,
> when he made firm the skies above,
> when he established the fountains of the deep,
> when he assigned to the sea its limit,
> so that the waters might not transgress his command,

---

40. Also see Perdue, *Wisdom and Creation*.

> when he marked out the foundations of the earth,
> then I was beside him, like a master worker;
> and I was daily his delight,
> rejoicing before him always,
> rejoicing in his inhabited world
> and delighting in the human race. (Prov 8:22–24, 27–31)

This fascinating description is also rather perplexing. Lady Wisdom is described as a "creation" (in the LXX) or "acquired" (in the Hebrew), but whatever the case, she is around before time and creation. Early church thinkers like Origen heard these descriptions as similar to how Christ was eternally "begotten," for while Jesus was the "firstborn" over creation, this did not detract from his eternal divinity.[41] The end of chapter 8 reiterates an important salvific statement about Wisdom: "For whoever finds me finds life" (Prov 8:35). In Wisdom, there is true life.

Interesting to note is that Wisdom is a beautiful woman who woos the reader (a young man, in the case of Proverbs) into following God's ways. Erotic language is used as the reader is to "love her" (Prov 4:6) and "embrace her" (Prov 4:8). Samuel Terrien notes then that through the figure of Wisdom, eros is used to communicate God's love, and in turn, eros is reconfigured in a fundamentally agapic sense.[42]

The question is whether this goddess comes from outside the Hebrew religion. George Montague describes Lady Wisdom in Proverbs as follows:

> [S]he is not being presented as a messenger with an oracle beginning, "Thus says the Lord." Rather she speaks by herself, on her own authority, like a goddess. The wisdom author, therefore, while maintaining clearly his Yahwehistic monotheism, has personified Yahweh's attribute of wisdom with motifs ultimately derived from ancient representations of a goddess of wisdom.[43]

Some have noted parallels to Egyptian wisdom goddesses like Ma'at or Isis. Others have looked to Canaanite and Mesopotamian goddesses like Asherah and Ishtar, as well as other Semitic wisdom books.[44] However, as Claudia Camp notes, while there are resemblances, no direct antecedent

---

41. Origen, *On First Principles*, Bk. 4, ch. 4, sect. 1. However, Origen uses Prov 8 to speak of the Son, not the Spirit here, linking the Wisdom depictions with the Wisdom Christology of the New Testament.
42. Terrien, *Till the Heart Sings*, 104.
43. Montague, *The Holy Spirit*, 94.
44. Day, "Foreign Semitic Influence on the Wisdom of Israel," 68–69.

has been established.[45] However, John Day has noted an early parallel to the international wisdom book, Wisdom of Ahiqar, which reads, "[From] heaven the peoples are [fa]voured; [W]isdom i[s of] the gods. Indeed, she is precious to the gods; Her kingdom is et[er]nal. She has been established in the he[aven]s. Yea, the lord of the holy ones has exalted her."[46] This is a minimal but clear antecedent, which might simply reflect a larger cultural awareness that the Israelites shared. In other words, there are parallels of the female Wisdom figure, which have been absorbed in from the outside, but the figure is not shoe-horned in. She is not out of place in biblical faith. Beyond that, the development of Lady Wisdom in the following Deuterocanonical literature is unique to Israel.

Nevertheless, Proverbs does intentionally incorporate material from outside Israel. This must be stressed. Proverbs 22:17—24:22 gleans heavily from the Egyptian wisdom book, *The Instruction of Amenemope*.[47] Proverbs 30 and 31 include proverbs by Agur, Son of Jakeh, and King Lemuel's mother, and both are figures from Massa, a kingdom in North West Arabia.[48] This gleaning from non-Hebrew sources suggests that the particularly Hebrew way of wisdom, reflecting on God's ways from observing creation, practical living, and human nature, is open to seeing wisdom at work in general revelation. Thus, wisdom can be found in any culture, philosophy, and even religion, and these axioms, if indeed they are useful to living out what the God of the Scriptures wills, can be borrowed and used.

Wisdom in Intertestamental Literature

The next set of texts comes from between the periods of the Old and New Testaments. In the writings known as Sirach (it has also been called Ecclesiasticus), written around 200–175 BCE by a Jewish sage called Jesus Ben Sirach, the author meditates on the law offering axioms from his studies, and it is here that the Lady Wisdom depiction further develops. Wisdom, as Proverbs suggests, is both created and eternal. Likewise, Sirach states: "Wisdom was created before all other things, and prudent understanding from eternity" (Sir 1:4). Wisdom is described as again being

---

45. Camp, *Wisdom and the Feminine in the Book of Proverbs*, 283–85.
46. Quoted in Day, "Foreign Semitic Influence on the Wisdom of Israel," 70.
47. Day, "Foreign Semitic Influence on the Wisdom of Israel," 55.
48. Day, "Foreign Semitic Influence on the Wisdom of Israel," 55.

a creation of God, but also something that is upon all creation as a gift, particularly those who seek God (Sir 1:9–10, 18–20). This gift of wisdom is the fulfillment of the law: "The whole of wisdom is fear of the Lord, and in all wisdom, there is the fulfillment of the law" (Sir 19:20). This is a subtle but significant expansion of Job and Proverbs. Lady Wisdom also is expanded considerably:

> Wisdom praises herself,
> and tells of her glory in the midst of her people.
> In the assembly of the Most High she opens her mouth,
> and in the presence of his hosts she tells of her glory:
> I came forth from the mouth of the Most High,
> and covered the earth like a mist.
> I dwelt in the highest heavens,
> and my throne was in a pillar of cloud.
> Alone I compassed the vault of heaven
> and traversed the depths of the abyss.
> Over waves of the sea, over all the earth,
> and over every people and nation I have held sway.
> Among all these I sought a resting place;
> in whose territory should I abide?
> Then the Creator of all things gave me a command,
> and my Creator chose the place for my tent. (Sir 24:1–8)

The glory of Wisdom comes from God, like the creating breath of God in Gen 2. She dwells in heaven on a throne, a pillar of cloud—like God's presence in Exodus. This culminates with God commanding Wisdom to dwell with people. One sees here a convergence between Shekinah language and Sophia language.

Baruch, a deuterocanonical book that is pseudonymous, written under the name of Jeremiah's secretary as a letter of consolation and warning, is a much later work than its namesake, compiled somewhere in between 200 BCE and 60 CE. The third chapter of Baruch praises Wisdom personified, and the chapter closes with this description that begins with an allusion to Job 28 with important expansions:

> Who has gone up into heaven, and taken her,
> and brought her down from the clouds?
> Who has gone over the sea, and found her,
> and will buy her for pure gold?
> No one knows the way to her,
> or is concerned about the path to her.
> But the one who knows all things knows her,

> he found her by his understanding.
> The one who prepared the earth for all time
> filled it with four-footed creatures;
> the one who sends forth the light, and it goes;
> he called it, and it obeyed him, trembling;
> the stars shone in their watches, and were glad;
> he called them, and they said, "Here we are!"
> They shone with gladness for him who made them.
> This is our God;
> no other can be compared to him.
> He found the whole way to knowledge,
> and gave her to his servant Jacob
> and to Israel, whom he loved.
> Afterward she appeared on earth
> and lived with humankind. (Bar 3:28–37)

Wisdom here is found by God as if she is more than a creature and more like God's co-equal, and God gives her to Israel as a gift. In doing so, she "appears" on earth and "lives" with humanity. Who is Wisdom? Baruch identifies her as Torah: "She is the book of the commandments of God, the law that endures forever. All who hold her fast will live" (Bar 4:1). One certainly sees the language that would later be applied to the incarnation of Christ here.

Another important book is not a wisdom book per se: the Book of Enoch (sometimes called First Enoch). Its parts were written from 300 to 100 BCE. While it is a composite text, it is predominantly apocalyptic, and the book exercised considerable influence over the early church. In it, there is an important statement regarding Wisdom in the Book of Parables (which most scholars date to 100 BCE):

> Wisdom went forth to make her dwelling among the children of men.
> And found no dwelling-place:
> Wisdom returned to her place. And took her seat among the angels.
> And unrighteousness went forth from her chambers:
> Whom she sought not she found.
> And dwelt with them. As rain in a desert
> And dew on a thirsty land. (1 En. 42:2–3)[49]

---

49. *Book of Enoch*, in *The Apocrypha and Pseudepigrapha of the Old Testament*.

SPIRIT AND SOPHIA

One can see again the themes that John's Gospel will pick up: the themes of dwelling, the rejection, and return to heaven, the actions of solidarity with sinners, etc.

The Wisdom of Solomon dates nearly to the New Testament. Montague writes, "The understanding of the spirit in the wisdom tradition reaches its high point in the book known as the Wisdom of Solomon."[50] It undoubtedly contains the most developed theology of Lady Wisdom. Proposed dates range wide from 250 BCE to 50 CE, but most scholars place it around 38 CE, written in Egypt by Alexandrian Jews who were attacked by rioters. Thus, the book contains a strong polemic against the Egyptians as well as a polemic showing the Hebraic vision of Lady Wisdom as superior to Greek philosophy. Wisdom is introduced briefly at the beginning (Wis 1:6–7), and from there, her identity is expanded. She is described as "radiant and unfading, and she is easily discerned by those who seek her. . . . To fix one's thought on her is perfect understanding" (Wis 6:12, 15). Again, Wisdom is described with salvific qualities:

> The beginning of wisdom is the most sincere desire for instruction,
> and concern for instruction is love of her,
> and love of her is the keeping of her laws,
> and giving heed to her laws is assurance of immortality,
> and immortality brings one near to God;
> so the desire for wisdom leads to a kingdom. (Wis 6:17–20)

The figure of Solomon then begins to describe and praise Wisdom. "I called on God, and the Spirit of Wisdom came to me" (Wis 7:7). She is described as the "mother" of "all good things" (Wis 7:11–12). Solomon's praise of Wisdom leads to a description that is explicitly divine:

> I learned both what is secret and what is manifest
> For wisdom, the fashioner of all things, taught me
> There is in her a spirit that is intelligent, holy,
> unique, manifold, subtle,
> mobile, clear, unpolluted,
> distinct, invulnerable, loving the good, keen,
> irresistible, beneficent, humane,
> steadfast, sure, free from anxiety,
> all-powerful, overseeing all,
> and penetrating through all spirits
> that are intelligent, pure, and altogether subtle.
> For wisdom is more mobile than any motion;

---

50. Montague, *The Holy Spirit*, 100.

because of her pureness she pervades and penetrates all things.
For she is a breath of the power of God,
and a pure emanation of the glory of the Almighty;
therefore nothing defiled gains entrance into her.
For she is a reflection of eternal light,
a spotless mirror of the working of God,
and an image of his goodness.
Although she is but one, she can do all things,
and while remaining in herself, she renews all things;
in every generation she passes into holy souls
and makes them friends of God and prophets. (Wis 7:21–27)

One can see the clear attributions of divinity to Wisdom here, but also allusions to Greek philosophy. The Solomon figure continues to describe Wisdom as next to God on the throne, and they together formed humanity (Wis 9:2–4). She is described in chapters 10–12 as doing all the actions of God in protecting the patriarchs, ransoming Israel out of Egypt, bringing them into the promised land, granting salvation to the righteous, and punishing the wicked. As the figure of Wisdom now has attributes, is praised, and is described as doing the things that God did in the biblical narrative, like liberating people from Egypt, where previous wisdom literature could be argued to be a personification, Wisdom of Solomon seems to move beyond to describe God as Spirit.

The Wisdom of Solomon is clearly influenced by the preceding wisdom books, whether Proverbs or Sirach, but also polemicizes Greek philosophy and mythology. Several of the attributes of Wisdom are similar to the attributes of Isis, as John Kloppenborg suggests.[51] These polemical appropriations of attributes make for an interesting relationship with Wisdom from outside the bounds of the covenant community. It seems that the authors, similar to Proverbs, are fine acknowledging the presence of Wisdom everywhere, but wherever Wisdom is regarded as part of a pagan pantheon, this description is reappropriated to belong to Yahweh, whose identity and superiority is seen in the acts of the biblical narrative. This helps clarify Ruether's claim that there is a trans-religious figure of Lady Wisdom. While there are these resemblances across religions as a classic trope, the biblical writers often used other depictions but narrated them specifically in relationship with Yahweh. Elizabeth Schüssler Fiorenza comments on this:

---

51. Kloppenborg, "Isis and Sophia in the Book of Wisdom," 57–85.

> In contrast to the classical prophets with their harsh polemics against G*ddess worship (see, e.g., Hos. 1–3 or Jer. 44), Wisdom theology, with its inclusive language about the Divine seems intent on using female G*d language for its own theological purposes. The theological discourses on Sophia speak positively about Israel's G*d in the language of their own Egyptian-Hellenistic culture. They use mythological elements from the international G*ddess cults, especially the Isis cult, and integrate them into Jewish monotheistic theology.[52]

She notes, citing Hans Conzelmann, that these Wisdom discourses are "reflective mythology," where Goddess language is used to speak of God's love and care, in which "Wisdom's salvific actions are identified with the actions of YHWH in Israel's salvation history."[53]

At this point, one implication is worth reiterating. Against those that reduce Wisdom to personification and metaphor, von Rad states,

> Nonetheless it is correct to say that wisdom is the form in which Jahweh's will and his accompanying of man (i.e., his salvation) approaches men.... [T]he most important thing is that wisdom does not turn toward man in the shape of an "It," teaching guidance, salvation, or the like, but of a person, a summoning "I." So wisdom is truly the form in which Jahweh makes himself present and in which he wishes to be sought by man.[54]

Now, while these inter-testamental books are not canonical in Protestantism (they, with the exception of the books of Enoch, are included in Catholic and Orthodox Bibles as deuterocanonical), they were read and used by the writers of the New Testament as authorities, and they were read in the early church as Scripture, albeit considered of lesser doctrinal authority than the main canon. The importance of these documents eventually waned, and that begs questions about the nature of the canon, particularly the Protestant list, which cannot be taken up here.[55] As we discuss the New Testament, however, it is important to remember that these works were read by the early church, and we see important allusions to them in the New Testament.

---

52. Fiorenza, *Jesus*, 137.
53. Fiorenza, *Jesus*, 137.
54. Rad, *Old Testament Theology*, 1:444.
55. For a discussion of the formation of the canon, see Goldingay, *Models for Scripture*, ch. 10.

Wisdom in the New Testament

So, the figure of Wisdom expands in the inter-testamental wisdom literature. As it does, there are clear anticipations of Christ who will come and dwell with the people. However, the figure also comes to be identified with the Spirit, the breath of God, particularly in the Wisdom of Solomon.

Wisdom imagery is employed in a number of ways in the New Testament. It is applied to Jesus Christ (which is the primary way it is used, suggesting an important orientation point for the grammar), but also as a distinct figure that witnesses to Christ. This dual way of speaking reappears throughout church history.

The themes of the Old Testament's wisdom literature and deuterocanonical books influence the New Testament heavily, particularly in its Christology and soteriology. Paul is no exception. Montague writes,

> Paul, for example, would never have thought of praying that his readers be filled with the spirit of wisdom and discernment (Phil. 1:9; Col. 1:9–10; Eph. 1:15) had the way not been prepared by the wisdom tradition. At the same time, by exalting wisdom and the spirit to the point of personification, dramatizing poetically these activities toward men with divine traits, the wisdom tradition laid the foundation for the New Testament understanding of God as revealed in the person of his Son, the Word or Wisdom of God, and made real and experiential by the mutual personal gift, the Holy Spirit.[56]

Or, as James Dunn states, "Paul picked up the widespread Wisdom terminology and found it an important tool for asserting the finality of Christ's role in God's purposes for man and creation."[57] Thus, one sees the figure of Wisdom in Jesus Christ and his Spirit. For Paul, the Holy Spirit is the "Spirit of wisdom" (Eph 1:17), and Jesus is "the wisdom of God" (1 Cor 1:24).

This means a certain set of Wisdom qualities are fulfilled in Jesus. Jesus and Wisdom are linked with the act of creation (Prov 3:19; 8:27; Pss 104:24; 136:5; Wis 7:22; 9:9): Wisdom is the "designer of everything" (Wis 8:7) where Jesus is the creator of everything (Col 1:16). Wisdom is the image of God's goodness (Wis 7:26), where Jesus is the "image of the invisible God" (Col 1:15). Wisdom is the first created being (Prov 8:22

---

56. Montague, *The Holy Spirit*, 110.
57. Dunn, *Christology in the Making*, 194.

LXX), where Jesus is the firstborn of all creation (Col 1:15). While Dunn is skeptical about whether the figure of Wisdom is a full hypostasis (and equally skeptical about the figure indicating a belief in preexistence in Paul's thought), nevertheless, Dunn comments,

> The same divine wisdom which was active in creation we believe to have been active in Jesus; that is, the creator God was himself acting in and through Christ. Not only so, but that divine wisdom is now to be recognized as *wholly identified* with Jesus, so totally embodied in Jesus that the distinctive character of divine wisdom is to be read off not from creation or in terms of speculative knowledge (*gnosis*), but from the cross (1 Cor. 1:18–25); that is, what we actually see in Christ's life, death, and resurrection is the very power by which God created and sustains the world (1 Cor. 8:6; Col. 1:16f). That divine concern which shaped the world and established the covenant with Israel, and which had hitherto been seen as expressed most clearly in the Torah, is now to be recognized as most fully and finally manifested in Jesus the crucified and risen one.[58]

Thus, for Paul, the Wisdom imagery is fulfilled in Jesus Christ, the Wisdom of God, whom the church knows through his Spirit.

In the Synoptics, a subtle wisdom identity is present and mentioned as distinct from Jesus (although not necessarily separate). Drawing off of what is called the Q source,[59] Matthew 11:19 states that "Wisdom is vindicated by her deeds," and Lady Wisdom seems to be acting through Jesus and John the Baptist, although uniquely embodied in Jesus. Luke's version keeps Wisdom and Christ more distinct: "Wisdom is vindicated by all her children" (Luke 7:35), referring to Jesus, the Son of Man, and John the Baptist. Wisdom is not Jesus but rather the sender of Jesus. Wisdom is prophetic wisdom connected with Jesus' Spirit-filled proclamation of liberation (Luke 4:18–19, cf. Isa 61:1). Thus, while the figure of Wisdom is not explicitly identified with the Spirit in Luke, the coincidence of Jesus growing and being filled with wisdom (Luke 2:40, 52) and being filled with the Spirit suggests Wisdom is a pneumatic figure. Meanwhile, Matthew keeps Wisdom more closely aligned to Jesus as chapter 11 culminates in vv. 28–30, inviting all who are weary to come to Jesus

---

58. Dunn, *Christology in the Making*, 195.

59. Q or "Quelle" (meaning "source") is a hypothesized source of sayings. While both Matthew and Luke draw heavily from Mark as one source, Q is a body of sayings that are not found in Mark and appear in different versions in both Matthew and Luke, indicating a possible source that both writers are using that is not unique to them.

for his yoke is easy. This is a quotation from Sirach, where the words of Lady Wisdom are cited as Jesus' words:

> Draw near to me, you who are uneducated ...
> Put your neck under her yoke,
> and let your souls receive instruction;
> it is to be found close by. ...
> See with your own eyes that I have labored but little
> and found for myself much serenity. (Sir. 51:23, 26–27)

As Dunn summarizes, "Where Q most presented Jesus as an envoy of Wisdom and most probably as the child of Wisdom, Matthew clearly took the step of identifying Jesus as Wisdom itself."[60]

Later in Luke, Jesus denounces the Pharisees, and in so doing, again cites the words of Lady Wisdom: "Therefore also the Wisdom of God said, 'I will send them prophets and apostles, some of whom they will kill and persecute'" (Luke 11:49). Again, this suggests a link between the Spirit and Wisdom as wisdom and prophecy coincide. This, coupled with the citation in chapter 7, forms an important piece to the Gospels: Wisdom is not merely a figure but a speaking agent, whom Jesus is relaying her message as her prophet. Notice, however, that this text does not cite any Old Testament or Deuterocanonical works. It is a prophecy of Jesus himself. Fiorenza concludes, "It is clear that the Jesus people of Q understand Jesus as a prophet and messenger of Sophia."[61] Matthew's version has Wisdom's words presented as Jesus' own words (Matt 23:34), he speaks as Wisdom, and they are a part of Jesus' prophecy concerning the destruction of the temple (Matt 23:35). One should note the magnitude of this prophecy: the temple was the site of divine Shekinah in the Old Testament, and now, as it was no longer faithful to its task of justice, getting in the way of God, Lady Sophia speaks through (so Luke) or as (so Matthew) Christ, proclaiming its destruction. Thus, while Matthew offers the Christ as Wisdom reading similar to Paul and others, it is particularly Luke's employment of Wisdom that sees the figure as distinct from Jesus, sending Jesus as a prophetic child of Wisdom. If Wisdom is a figure of the Holy Spirit in Luke (or Jesus, in Matthew), then Jesus's claims that Wisdom is vindicated by her children/deeds are the most direct examples of female language for God, and they are found on the lips of Jesus himself.

---

60. Dunn, *Christology in the Making*, 198.
61. Fiorenza, *Jesus*, 141.

The Gospel of John has a definite Wisdom Christology, and this is merged together with his Logos Christology. Jesus is not portrayed as a prophet of Wisdom but as the embodiment of Wisdom. Mollenkott, in her study of female images for God, states, "Not only is Dame Wisdom treated as synonymous with God, with the Old Testament spirit of Yahweh, and with the New Testament Holy Spirit; she is also pictured in terms that link her to Jesus the Christ, the Logos, the Word of God."[62] In John, Christ embodies the qualities of Lady Wisdom. Wisdom was there at the beginning of creation (Prov 8:22) just as "in the beginning was the Word" (John 1:1). Wisdom is the fulfillment of the law of God (Sir 19:20), coming from the mouth of God like his word (Sir 24:3). Thus, Wisdom is the Word of God (Wis 9:1–2), where Jesus is the Word (John 1:1, 14). Wisdom is the means by which creation was made (Ps 104:24; Wis 7:21), while John says, "All things came into being through him [Christ], and without him, not one thing came into being" (John 1:3). Wisdom longs to dwell with humanity (Bar 3:37; 1 En. 42:2), and Jesus as the Word fulfills this: "the Word became flesh and dwelt among us" (John 1:14). However, people rejected Jesus (John 1:11), just like Wisdom (1 En. 42:2). Wisdom is the glory of God (Wis 7:25), just as the Word has been glorified (John 1:14; 2:11; 8:54; 11:4; 17:5). Jesus and Wisdom are linked with salvation and life. John has Jesus say that those that drink of him will thirst no more (John 4:14) just like Wisdom (Sir 24:21). Wisdom is the path, knowledge, and the way (Prov 4:11, 22, 26), and Jesus is "the way, the truth, and the life" (John 14:6). Wisdom is the breath of the power of God (Wis 7:25), and Jesus breathes the Spirit on his disciples (John 20:22).

What does this mean for understanding Sophia imagery? For Paul, John, and Matthew, Christ is Wisdom. To understand the Spirit as fundamentally the Spirit of Christ and Christ as the fulfillment of Wisdom is to refuse any characterization of or appeal to the Spirit (or Sophia) that is not congruent with the way of Jesus Christ. The Spirit is known fully where the good news of God's Yes to sinful humanity is proclaimed, where life exhibits the fruit of the Spirit, where one is committed to Christ's loving way even to the point of martyrdom, where the forces of death and despair are confronted with a persistent hope in solidarity. To speak of the Spirit as a "he" is not to say that God is male. God is Spirit and therefore beyond gender. Yet being the friend and companion of material life, flesh

---

62. Mollenkott, *The Divine Feminine*, 99–100.

in all its frailty, God is revealed through the life of Jesus of Nazareth, the Spirit-filled Messiah. This language refuses literalization but is so often taken that way in the popular mindset. To say the Spirit is a "he" in any other way than as an abbreviation to saying "the Spirit is identified by Christ" is to reduce the Creator again to the creation. For Luke (and the Q source), Jesus is the child of Wisdom, which sets up a distinct identity that witnesses to Christ. This does not separate Wisdom completely from Christ, obviously, as this figure is still pointing to Jesus Christ, but this suggests a way that Christ and Sophia can be used in tandem rather than separate from each other.

This clarification may suggest a pathway forward in those that use a Sophia Christology. There are some that note Jesus as the fulfillment of the figure of Lady Wisdom and use this as the basis for speaking about Jesus as female, reversing the direction of figural fulfillment. In so far as Matthew shows Jesus as the embodied enactment of Wisdom, Sophia is a way of talking about Jesus. Stated precisely, Jesus is the "her" when Matthew says, "Wisdom will be vindicated by *her* deeds" as Jesus goes on to speak the words of Lady Wisdom as his own words. Admittedly, this is a brief reference that pushes the figure to its furthest bounds, which edges on eclipsing the historical figure of Jesus, reversing the direction of typological fulfillment. For many, Luke's usage might be more intelligible for some: Jesus is the child of Wisdom. The Spirit of Wisdom, whose child and prophet is Jesus, offers a way of speaking about both the historical Jesus and Sophia, the later always directing the believer to the former.

Wisdom in Church History

What happens to Wisdom imagery in church history? While books like the Wisdom of Solomon continue to be important to the early church, the figure of Sophia is almost entirely absorbed into Christology, following the strand in the New Testament that was just charted. However, there are notable exceptions. In Western theology, Hildegard of Bingen's use of the figure of Wisdom is notable, and in the East, more pervasively, there is a tradition that looks to the figure that blossoms with the Russian Sophiologists.

As stated, the New Testament saw Sophia primarily as Jesus, with the exception of Luke, who kept them distinct. The early church continued this primary convention. In one of his descriptions of Gnosticism,

Irenaeus mentions that the Gnostics worship many deity personas, one of which is Sophia, the mother of Christ.[63] It is possible that female language was increasingly associated with Gnosticism as time passed, even though it seems likely that Gnostics borrowed these terms from Christians. Irenaeus displays a dual theology of the Father's two hands, Word and Wisdom, but Wisdom, despite various Lady Wisdom texts being cited, is referenced using male language.[64] Similarly, by the time of Basil's *On the Holy Spirit*, which is really one of the first full treatises on the Holy Spirit, the nature of the Spirit as Wisdom is almost entirely grounded in 1 Cor 1:24, where Christ is the "power and wisdom of God." In Augustine's reflections on the Trinity, female imagery for the Spirit is dismissed.[65] Thus, with the use of Sophia language in Gnosticism, the early church writers clung closely to Christ as Sophia, the usage employed from the New Testament.

Yet, Sophia imagery does not disappear. For instance, Hildegard of Bingen (1098–1179) has trinitarian depictions that will be discussed in the next chapter, but here, we must note how these depictions coincide with her understanding of Wisdom. It must be said that one cannot overstate Bingen's intellectual abilities, but neither can one overstate just how badly she has been neglected in subsequent theological history. A German Benedictine Abbess, she was extraordinarily gifted: a philosopher, composer, doctor, biologist, linguist, and theologian. In her theological writings, she reflects on mystical visions she had, and it is here we see female Wisdom imagery. For her, Wisdom is the whole being of the Trinity, and in particular, Wisdom is the Creator:

> She has invoked no one's help and needs no help because she is the First and the Last.... [S]he who is the First has arranged the order of all things. Out of her own being and by herself she has formed all things in love and tenderness.... For she oversaw completely and fully the beginning and end of her deeds because she formed everything completely, just as everything is under her guidance.[66]

---

63. Irenaeus displays important evidence. See Irenaeus, *Against Heresies*, Book 1: ch. 19.

64. Irenaeus, *Against the Heresies*, 4:20.

65. See Augustine, *On the Trinity*, Book XII: sect. 5–6.

66. Hildegard of Bingen, *Book of Divine Works*, 8.2,

Wisdom, following the Old Testament portrayals of the Holy Spirit, is the energy of all life in which all things subsist.[67] Following the imagery in later deuterocanonical books and John, Wisdom is the point at which God and creation dwell together. Wisdom is not merely biblical wisdom, for Hildegard, but all truth in all the sciences, arts, and philosophy (a notion that will get further elaboration shortly).[68]

Lady Wisdom is also bound up with Eve, Mary, and the church. Eve, as the fallen female figure, is restored through Mary, the second Eve. Again, following the Gospel imagery (and echoing the Shepherd of Hermas), Mary then is a figure of the Holy Spirit and the church (which is seen in another illuminated manuscript from the same codex, fig. 5.5, entitled "Wisdom, the Mother Church").

Fig. 5.5

67. Hildegard, *Book of Divine Works*, 2.2.
68. Hildegard, *Book of Divine Works*, 8.2.

SPIRIT AND SOPHIA

In the East, there has been a tradition of personifying Lady Wisdom since the construction of the Hagia Sophia (Holy Wisdom) Cathedral in Constantinople (modern Istanbul). Built between 532 and 537 CE by Justinian I, the church was named after the personification of the virtue of wisdom along with its sister churches, Hagia Irene (Holy Peace) and Hagia Dynamis (Holy Power). As the Hagia Sophia served as the cultural center for the East (standing as the largest cathedral for nearly a millennia), the name took on increasing significance. When sister churches were built in Kyiv, Moscow, Novgorod, and Yaroslavl, each incorporated imagery from the Hagia Sophia, drawing off of the imagery from the Intertestamental books for further inspiration.

Entitled "Holy Wisdom" (fig. 5.1) from the Annunciation Cathedral in Moscow, painted in the fifteenth century, this is one early example of the Sophia icon that is typical in Russian Orthodox iconography. Lady Wisdom is depicted on a throne with seven pillars (cf. Prov 9:1). One sees circular fields engulfing the Father in heaven (symbolized as ineffable with merely a scroll of Scripture and cross) and comes around Jesus and down around Lady Wisdom, an angelic figure with fiery wings. The field itself is star-like in it, which suggests the heavenly glory of the Trinity. Unlike most trinitarian icons that depict the Spirit as a tiny dove, overshadowed by the Father and Son, Lady Wisdom is the most prominent and glorious figure in the icon. She is adorned in gold. The Son stands behind her in approval, along with the Father in heaven. The line of smaller sizes suggests that Lady Wisdom is the one who reveals the Father and the Son. Worshipped by angels, venerated by saints, and witnessed by the Father and the Son, whom she reveals with her glory, this icon brings trinitarian theology and the Spirit's portrayal as Lady Wisdom in the Bible's wisdom literature into compelling beauty.[69]

---

69. Florensky does a fuller treatment on the Sophia themes in Russian iconography in *The Pillar and Ground of Truth*, 268–78.

Fig. 5.1

Three towering figures in modern Russian Orthodoxy, beginning with Vladimir Solovyov (1853–1900), all attest to the reality of Sophia, Lady Wisdom, taking this icon and giving a fuller theology to it. Solovyov spoke of the female Sophia in his theological writings, gleaning from numerous sources, including gnostic and spiritualist sources, which led to accusations of heresy.[70] However, the ideas influenced a younger, brilliant priest named Pavel Florensky (1882–1937), who argued for the validity of Sophia in his defense of the Orthodox faith, *The Pillar and Ground of Truth* (1914). Together with his friend Sergei Bulgakov (1871–1944), the two defended Solovyov's legacy. Bulgakov also had a mystical encounter with Sophia that was essential to his reconversion back to Christianity from atheism, and so, he defended the validity of the doctrine of Sophia in several of his works, but his most sustained treatment is in *Sophia: The Wisdom of God*, which was written in 1937 as a major apologia against the ongoing criticism.

70. See Solovyov, *Lectures on Divine Humanity*.

Solovyov had three visions of Sophia: one in 1862 and two in 1875. He enigmatically describes this encounter in his religious poem "The Three Meetings":

> I saw it all, and all of it was one,
> One image there of beauty feminine....
> The immeasurable was confined within that image.
> Before me, in me, you alone were there.
> O radiant one! I'm not deceived by you.
> I saw all of you there in the desert....
> And in my soul those roses shall not fade
> Wherever it is the billows of life may rush me.[71]

Solovyov wrote about this figure in later works:

> Our ancestors worshipped this mysterious figure, as the Athenians once did the "unknown god," they built Sophia's churches and cathedrals everywhere, and they fixed celebrations and services, in which, in an unknown way, Sophia the Wisdom of God is sometimes close to Christ, sometimes to the Theotokos, thus allowing neither Him, nor Her, to be fully identified with Him.... This Great, royal and feminine Being, who being neither God, nor the eternal Son of God, nor angel, nor holy man, receives veneration both from the finisher of the Old Testament and from the progenitor of the New, who is it but true, pure, and complete humanity itself, the highest and most comprehensive form and living soul of nature and the universe, eternally united and in temporal process united to Deity and uniting with Him all that is. There is no doubt that this is the full meaning of the Great Being, half felt and conscious of Comte, whole felt but not at all conscious of by our ancestors, the pious builders of the Sophia temples.[72]

Solovyov's Sophia is creation, the soul of the world from the Spirit's breath of life, estranged in chaos from Christ at the fall but reunited with Christ in the incarnation to bring humanity into a relationship with God. Sophia is the perfect unity of God with humans and creation, God all in all.

Florensky sought to bring this account into the Orthodox mainstream. He asserted creation *ex nihilo* and, from there, saw Sophia as the coming together of incarnation and creation, thus forming a link of

---

71. Solovyov, *The Religious Poetry of Vladimir Solovyov*, 105.

72. Solovyov, *August Comte's Idea of Humanity*, translated and quoted in Sergey Zolotarev, "Interpretation of Sophia," 174.

being within the whole Trinity. Sophia is the "Great Root by which creation goes into the intra-Trinitarian life and through which it receives Life Eternal from the One Source of Life."[73] Sophia is connected with the church as the bride of Christ and with Mary as a motherly figure. Florensky was also diligent in using the significance of the Sophia iconography of the Orthodox Church, making a case that Sophia is a part of the Orthodox tradition, not novel to it. However, Florensky used the term "fourth hypostasis"[74] to describe Sophia, which again drew accusations of heresy. It sounded like Florensky was positing Sophia as a fourth member of the Trinity. This is not quite accurate, but the language Florensky used made the criticism easy.

On the other hand, Bulgakov, in his mature defense, was much more careful in his language. This was in response to calls in 1935 by the patriarch of Moscow to censure him for his views on Sophia. After an examination of his views, Bulgakov was not censured, but many of the committee members did not approve of his views.[75] He spoke of Sophia as the glory of God and the very being of the Trinity. Each member exists through the other, and so Sophia, as she is identified in the Holy Spirit and Christ (in ways previously sketched out), is not just one member of the Trinity. The Trinity is Sophia in the oneness of their relatedness. Sophia is glory, and glory is ousia.[76] Sophia is the love that binds up the being of God in God's very essence. Bulgakov also made an important distinction between the "creaturely Sophia" and the "heavenly Sophia," which was for him a distinction between the Spirit as the basis of life, even life estranged from God, and the Spirit as poured out in salvation, reunifying creation with God through the incarnation and the church.[77] Moreover, the Spirit, insofar as she is the breath of life and the wisdom that forms creation (Prov 8), is also the sustaining presence in creation at its very root, the very imminence of transcendence to all creation and the transcendence in imminence. Thus, while denying a fourth hypostasis, Bulgakov speaks of the divine and creaturely Sophia as a movement or convergence that brings the being of creation into the being of the

---

73. Florensky, *Pillar and Ground of Truth*, 237.
74. Florensky, *Pillar and Ground of Truth*, 235.
75. See Bamford, foreword, to *Sophia: The Wisdom of God*, xx. Also see Bishops' Council of the Russian Orthodox Church Abroad, "Decision of the Bishops' Council of the Russian Orthodox Church Abroad of the 17/30 October 1935."
76. Bulgakov, *Sophia*, 33.
77. Bulgakov, *Sophia*, ch. 3.

Trinity, uniting source and destination, all becoming one eschatologically in Sophia. This is done in the incarnation (notably for him also in Mary's virginal conception), Pentecost, and through the church, all displaying the figure of Sophia as this point of the divine and human coming together, reconciled and redeemed. Thus, Bulgakov binds together in a masterful trinitarian theology all these figural themes that others mention in a more fragmented or isolated manner.

This tradition of thinkers has inspired others, notably the Catholic spiritual writer Thomas Merton (1915–68), who later had a spiritual revolution contemplating Sophia. For Merton, learning of the Sophia figure in the Russian Sophiologists named and answered a void he perceived in Western spirituality, the inability to contemplate the presence of God in all life, the separating of the sacred from life. Sophia came to name the presence of Christ in life that combatted forces Merton saw the Christian faith as opposing but often failing to stand against in practice: secularization, dehumanization, dogmatism, etc. Thus, in his meditations, he speaks of Wisdom:

> There is in all visible things an invisible fecundity, a dimmed light, a meek namelessness, a hidden wholeness. This mysterious Unity and Integrity is Wisdom, the Mother of all, *Natura naturans*. There is in all things an inexhaustible sweetness and purity, a silence that is a fount of action and joy. It rises up in wordless gentleness and flows out to me from the unseen roots of all created being, welcoming me tenderly, saluting me with indescribable humility. This is at once my own being, my own nature, and the Gift of my Creator's Thought and Art within me, speaking as Hagia Sophia, speaking as my sister, Wisdom.[78]

Merton saw Wisdom as a way of contemplating the presence of God, and his writings are used in new monastic movements as a way of priming spiritual guidance and discernment. Thus, these masters of Russian Orthodox theology offer a surprising manifestation point for female language, ones that have had considerable impact.[79]

Thus, while we see the Sophia figure emerge in intertestamental writings, fulfilled in Christ in the New Testament, the figure does not get fully absorbed into Christology, and so, has continued as both a figure

---

78. Merton, "Hagia Sophia," in an appendix in *Sophia*, 301.

79. The interesting parallels between Orthodox Sophiology and feminist arguments for inclusive language have been noted in Meehan, "Wisdom/Sophia," 149–68.

of contemplation and even direct and powerful religious experience for several Christians, suggesting an ongoing validity to the figure.

LIVING THE SPIRIT AND DISCERNING SOPHIA

So, the Spirit is the breath of life, the Shekinah presence of God, and the Spirit with Christ in different ways comes to be understood through the figure of Sophia. What does this mean for the life of believers? Three things: First is that if the Spirit is the breath of life, all of life and human experience is relevant for reflecting on God. Second, to read Scripture in line with the Spirit is to see the Spirit acting in liberating ways, making possible a community where men and women are equal. Third, the figure of Sophia makes possible not only female references for God, but also a paradigm for discerning the wisdom of God in other cultural and religious traditions.

The first implication, already commented on, is that experience plays an important complementary and coordinating role in faith. There is no faith that is not experienced and no dimension of life that is not meaningful to faith. As the Spirit is the Spirit of life, coinciding with the previous analogical, metaphorical, and incarnational grammars, all of life *qua* life speaks of God. The Spirit is the source of order in creation (Gen 1:1–2), in whom "we live and move and have our being" (Acts 17:28). Creation is good, and knowledge of this goodness is not confined to any ecclesial authority or to even the bounds of the biblical canon, although Scriptures' figures aid in perceiving it more clearly. Wisdom is in creation.[80] The Spirit is what renders life alive (Gen 2:7; Job 33:4; Ps 33:6). With a particular intensity, the breath of life is the root of the soul. God breathed into the first person, and the first human became a "living soul." From the Spirit breathing life at creation to the Spirit's breath in salvation and inspiration, the difference is not one of kind but degree. As Moltmann argues, on the basis of pneumatology, there cannot be an absolute distinction between experience and revelation.[81] Here, the distinction of the "creaturely" and divine Sophia of Bulgakov is useful to name this intersection of God's redemption by the Spirit with the ground of creation that is made possible by the Spirit. Thus, eternal life is setting

---

80. See Perdue, *Wisdom and Creation*, 121.
81. Moltmann, *Spirit of Life*, 7.

creation free from sin, completing creation in the fullness of God, awaiting the final resurrection.

As we discussed in previous chapters, it is the grammar of Scripture that helps us discern our authentic self. To know that the root of the soul is the breath of life, to know that the Spirit is the basis of life and being, is to have the true avenue of authenticity illuminated. One cannot ignore life, rather its joys or pain, and live authentically with God for the grammar of Scripture exposes for us that fact that the experience of God is found in the midst of life.

Second, to read the Bible and listen for the voice of the Spirit is to listen attentively to how Lady Wisdom has acted, where the Shekinah's presence is seen most clearly. Wisdom is the skill of living effectively in relationship with God and the world. This pneumatic aspect of thinking about God shows that the imminence of the Spirit is the presence of salvific life, love, and liberation, such that the feminist pragmatic criterion, when understood through the biblical narrative (not despite it) is valid. Just as there is no experience that is meaningless to God, so also is no domain of life untouched by salvation. Salvation is holistic, and this holism can then be a basis for assessing how one is reading and applying the Bible.[82] A few Pauline examples illustrate this: as Paul identifies the gift of the Spirit upon all people regardless of prejudice, so also the gifts of the Spirit are bestowed in coinciding fashion (Gal 3:28; 1 Cor 12:13). This fulfills Joel 2:28–29's longing for the Spirit to be poured out on all flesh. The curse of sin is defeated to regain the goodness of the mutual image of God. If gentiles are justified by the Spirit to be members of the people of God, so also are women, by this same unprejudiced Spirit, gifted to lead the church, for the Spirit has no criteria of prejudice: all are one in Christ. This forms an important rule: "Where the Spirit is, there is freedom" (2 Cor 3:17). This is not dualistic, spiritualized inner freedom, nor is the freedom of someone who is "equal in value but not in role," but rather, material liberty to respond to God's call in any way that any other person can be called by God, regardless of race, gender, or status. Thus, in the early church there were women apostolic workers and other leaders that the church sadly has often forgotten.[83]

This means that a proper view of the inspiration of the Bible (the precise theology of which need not be spelled out here) is one that at any

---

82. See Comblin, *The Holy Spirit and Liberation*, ch. 2.
83. See, for example, Bellville, "Women Leaders in the Bible."

rate coincides with a liberating reading of the text as an act of the Spirit. The Pauline writer in 2 Timothy describes all Scripture as follows,

> [F]rom infancy you have known the Holy Scriptures, which are able to make you wise for salvation through faith in Christ Jesus. All Scripture is God-breathed and is useful for teaching, rebuking, correcting, and training in righteousness so that the servant of God may be thoroughly equipped for every good work. (2 Tim 3:15–17)

While the writer here understands the Scriptures to be the Scriptures that we now know as the Old Testament, if this statement applies to the current canon of Scripture, it suggests that Scripture must be read for the purpose that Lady Wisdom's breath accomplishes: salvation and right action in relationship with God and others. According to Paul, the Spirit of love is the basis of assessing the law. Based on this, Paul seems to deregulate the requirement of circumcision for gentiles who join the covenant community. Despite it being one of the most important laws in the Old Testament, it was being used to foster ethnic superiority and exclusion in the body of Christ. For Paul, circumcision as a requirement for gentiles did not fulfill its purpose since the only thing that counts is "faith expressing itself through love" (Gal 5:6). The rules that do apply are summarized in the law of love and are discerned by actions that produce the fruit of the Spirit, "against such things there is no law" (Gal 5:23). Similarly, Luke's pneumatology supports a prophetic reading of Scripture where the Spirit of liberation guides interpretation. "Wisdom is vindicated by her children" (Luke 7:35), and the Spirit is on and in Jesus Christ, who proclaims freedom for the oppressed (Luke 4:18–19, cf. Isa 61:1–2). The Spirit is discerned in the effects of applications (a tree is known by its fruit, says Matt 7:16), and the Spirit can then judge between what words are dead letters and living words. Since patriarchy is oppressive and salvation restores the promised dignity God desires for all people, the negative qualities of patriarchy and the positive qualities of liberation form indicators and data to guide a wise interpretation of Scripture. God listens to the voices of the socially marginalized, and so also should the church if it is to read Scripture well. Attending carefully to female voices (especially any that can be identified as victimized, oppressed, and abused) can and must become normative for Christian faithfulness, undoing how patriarchal discourses have suppressed people.

Thus, the third implication is the use of female figures in communicating faith, even if taken from other cultures and religions if they are understood through the biblical narrative. Seeing that these figures draw descriptions from surrounding cultures' mythology and philosophy, the presence of trans-religious and trans-cultural feminine symbolism and experience is not an affront to Christianity's particularity. Actually, it shows the willingness of Christianity to incorporate truths and useful depictions from other cultures, religions, and philosophies in the service of the God of the biblical narrative, whose focal revelation is in Jesus Christ.

As noted previously, female figures have often been associated with paganism, but what the figure of Wisdom suggests dismantles a kind of colonial claim to possess knowledge of the Spirit. While this pattern is suggested in our exploration of the Wisdom images in their borrowing from ancient wisdom and mythology, this pattern is explicitly used in the New Testament in other places, particularly in Acts. The first instance is when Paul and Barnabas are in Lystra. The people there think the apostles have come from heaven. Paul implores them to think otherwise. He says,

> Friends, why are you doing this? We, too, are only human, like you. We are bringing you good news, telling you to turn from these worthless things to the living God, who made the heavens and the earth and the sea and everything in them. In the past, he let all nations go their own way. Yet he has not left himself without testimony: He has shown kindness by giving you rain from heaven and crops in their seasons; he provides you with plenty of food and fills your hearts with joy. (Acts 14:15–17)

Paul's evidence is the display of goodness from nature. The notion that God "has not left himself without a testimony" suggests that God's goodness is discernible outside the assumptions of those with Christian faith.

What Paul may have had in mind can be seen more explicitly in the second instance, where Paul is in Athens. This fascinating encounter begins with Paul debating the "good news of Jesus and the resurrection" with Epicurean and Stoic philosophers, who then move the conversation to the Areopagus (Acts 17:18–19). Paul complements them on their "religious" character and notes they have an altar to an "unknown god" (Acts 17:22–23). Paul then says, "What therefore you worship as unknown, this I proclaim to you" (v. 23), strikingly acknowledging that they are already worshipping the God he is making plain in Jesus Christ, against the claim they make that he is proclaiming a "foreign deity" (v. 18). He continues on,

The Father and the Feminine

> The God who made the world and everything in it, he who is Lord of heaven and earth, does not live in shrines made by human hands, nor is he served by human hands, as though he needed anything, since he himself gives to all mortals life and breath and all things. From one ancestor he made all nations to inhabit the whole earth, and he allotted the times of their existence and the boundaries of the places where they would live so that they would search for God and perhaps grope for him and find him—though indeed he is not far from each one of us. For "In him we live and move and have our being"; as even some of your own poets have said, "For we too are his offspring." Since we are God's offspring, we ought not to think that the deity is like gold, or silver, or stone, an image formed by the art and imagination of mortals. While God has overlooked the times of human ignorance, now he commands all people everywhere to repent because he has fixed a day on which he will have the world judged in righteousness by a man whom he has appointed, and of this he has given assurance to all by raising him from the dead. (Acts 17:24–31)

Paul appeals to a common theology where God is the creator of the world. He speaks in pneumatic terms of the one who gives humans life and breath and even cites their pagan poets, who describe God as one in whom humanity "lives and moves and has its being." He affirms a common theology of ancestry and, again, quotes a pagan poet who indicated all humans are "God's offspring." He even goes so far as to note that they are worshiping the same God as Christ-followers in their religion; they "search for God and perhaps grope for him and find him." From there, however, these truths and the truth about Jesus and the resurrection form the basis of the rejection of idolatry in repentance. This masterful example shows Paul acknowledging the truths of another religion, acknowledging God's work in the other religion, and that religion's (successful, albeit incomplete) quest to find God. Also applicable here is a theology of divine parentage (father in this instance) taken from the culture, using their poets to introduce the definitive revelation of Jesus and the need to reject the false dimensions of their religion: idols. This stands as the most viable biblical paradigm for accepting ideas from other religions and philosophers and using them to point to Jesus Christ.

This is just what others in the church have realized and done. A few brief examples are warranted. Irenaeus and Origen both appealed to Platonism and wider Greek philosophy to illustrate the Logos in their own time. Boethius had visions of Lady Philosophy in his *Consolation of Philosophy*. She is the epitome of all wisdom (but particularly in his case, Greek philosophy), who comes to minister to him in prison and teaches him theological truths, not unlike the Comforter Spirit in John's Gospel.

These can help us understand some non-Western examples. Cicilia Titizano argued that indigenous depictions of the Mother Creator Spirit ("Mama Pacha") could be understood as the presence of God operative before the arrival of colonialist Christianity, which assumed the Spirit was absent there before the gospel's arrival.[84] These examples are important to note as a colonialist and male-exclusivist way of referring to God can coincide. Moving beyond a colonialist paradigm of referring to God will require extending liberty to allow diverse imagery for God to be used. For instance, theologian Steven Charleston speaks about his use of female imagery in thinking about his indigenous Christian faith:

> One of the images of God is that of a Grandmother, the wise old Native woman with gray hair and eyes as ancient as the Earth. She takes my face gently in her hands and holds me in Her gaze as She tells me what She thinks I need to know, forming the worlds slowly so I can remember them and let them sink in.... [L]ike the theologians of ancient Israel, I give the voice a female personification because I experience it in that way.[85]

Robert Johnston states in his work on general revelation, "Christians are called to witness to the fact that God has been and continues to be active throughout creation and history, . . . active apart from Jesus Christ through the Spirit who remains the Spirit of Christ."[86] Discerning this presence is vital to combatting colonialism since often Western Christianity has proclaimed the evils of another culture's experiences. Recognizing Lady Wisdom can be helpful to reminding the church that it does not control the Spirit. Thus, certain feminine ways of relating to God that are more familiar to other cultures are welcomed as they are used to point to the love of Christ.

While we have been concerned about accommodation and projection in previous chapters, these concerns remain, but this cannot detract from a pattern which is displayed in the Bible of identifying materials from surrounding culture as God's truth or images that can be used to

---

84. Titizano, "Mama Pacha," 127–59.
85. Charleston, *The Four Vision Quests of Jesus*, 45.
86. Johnston, *God's Wider Presence*, 214.

communicate God's truth in Christ. Not only this, but Scripture also shows the way to safeguard these from overriding what is central to the Bible. One is situating them within the core narrative of Jesus' life, death, and resurrection. Oscar Garcia-Johnson comments on this dynamic coinciding with the rise of post-colonial thought and global Christianity:

> I perceive fear that the so-called shift of the center of Christianity from the global North to the global South might have adverse consequences after all, leading to a suspicion that global Christianity is not attending to orthodox ways of reflection and practice.... [T]he key to the continuity of the Christian tradition does not rest on an archival-historiographic logic rooted in Western culture, but on the incarnational power of the Spirit of the triune God who reveals truth and gives life to every culture and generation everywhere.[87]

To revisit Ruether's original argument (that there is a trans-religious figure of female emancipation previously repressed but now manifesting), this is an assertion that is not entirely accurate (for the individual traditions and religions are far more diverse than what can be neatly synthesized together) but neither is it entirely objectionable to Christianity, given the dynamic just discussed. Rather than seeing the surmounting of Christ toward a new religion of femininity, the figure of Wisdom, as she witnesses to Christ and is fulfilled in Christ, allows the Spirit to be discerned in patterns of speech and action in other cultures. Given that Sophia is narrated through the biblical text, such as in Proverbs and Wisdom of Solomon, other female figures can be used to communicate faith but in ways that are congruent with the identity of God as revealed in Israel's story. What is true, beautiful, and good in them is the witness God has left in all cultures. This is Sophia's witness.

How are figures discerned as to whether they are the testimonies left by God or whether they are obstacles? Culture has its ambiguities; however, the biblical narrative offers these constant indicators seen in this chapter: life, love, truth, liberation, and whether they are open to the name of Christ. This indicates that the virtues themselves, while they are only fully expressed in a Christlike way, are recognized outside the bounds of the Christian community. For Christians to see the presence of love, truth, goodness, etc., in others is not an affront to the truth of Christ but an expansion. It can also be a challenge as Christ so often

---

87. Garcia-Johnson, "In Search of Indigenous Pneumatologies in the Americas."

chooses those outside the people of God to be exemplars of faith as a critique of the kind of tribalism the people of God are always susceptible to.[88] Using these criteria, for instance, one can understand how the prophet Jeremiah attacked offerings to the "queen of heaven" (cf. Jer 7:18; 44:17–19, 15), which was bound up with idolatrous worship that involved child sacrifice (to the counterpart god, Baal). As we have seen throughout the biblical passages, the Spirit is identified with life to the full, the rule of love, prophetic truth-telling, and liberating action. This means asking whether or not images and concepts are bound up with acts that truly do good to people made in God's image (and thus are permissible) or those that are harmful. Again, while these only find their deepest articulation in the way of Jesus Christ, who is the embodiment of Wisdom, this does not mean the Spirit has not been operative beyond the bounds of God's people.[89] Thus, when speaking about female figures and concerns for liberation, whether experiences are bought to the Bible or flow from the Bible, this interplay of Scripture and experience invites the kind of experiential and pragmatic criteria that is the work of biblical discernment.[90]

This dissolves some of the dichotomies presented at the beginning of this book. Experience, even spiritual experience from other religions and philosophies, is neither ignored nor invalidated on the basis of its source. Rather, it is welcomed into conversation and coalescence with the figures of the Bible, allowing Christ with Lady Wisdom to sift them. On the other hand, the Triune God may be spurring the church to recognize these other figures as the witness of the Spirit in service of drawing all that is into Christ's truth and love.

CONCLUSION

To speak of the Spirit is to realize that there are many ways of speaking, many images and figures of the Spirit in Scripture (and only a few that are pertinent to this discussion are covered here): the breath of life, the Shekinah presence, one who acts in a motherly way, and how the Spirit and Christ are both seen as Sophia. In unpacking them, we are confronted

---

88. For the exclusivity of Christ as a means to open oneself up to truth in other religions, see Williams, "The Finality of Christ," in *On Christian Theology*, 93–106.

89. See the pneumatology of mission in Taylor, *The Go-Between God*, ch. 9.

90. See Yong, *Discerning the Spirit(s)*.

with a vast liberty. However, there are some important rules of grammar. The Spirit is the basis of life, the presence of God over all things, which forces the church to realize that it does not have a monopoly on the Spirit. All of life is meaningful to God because the Spirit envelopes all existence. Wherever there is truth, beauty, and goodness, there is data for the Christian to reflect on. How do Christians discern what these are? Certainly, there must be an openness to wisdom from many sources as the wisdom writers freely borrowed from surrounding wisdom. However, this wisdom comes to fulfillment, a focus on Jesus Christ as Wisdom. Thus, we can understand why the Spirit is portrayed using male pronouns in the NT, for the Spirit is the Spirit of Christ, and so has been consistently portrayed this way in Christian thought, wary of Gnostic attempts to divorce Sophia from Christ. Yet, unless the church commits a kind of reduction of pneumatology to Christology, the church must be open to seeing the figure of Wisdom in how she brings all things to the Lordship of Christ. In this, the Spirit as Sophia can be contemplated in all her richness. In fact, as we saw, the figure Sophia has appeared to some as a female personality, wooing believers into the ways of life and love. In this, the two figures are not at loggerheads: Spirit as Sophia and Christ as Sophia. The relationship perhaps can be illustrated with the following icon.

Entitled "Wisdom hath built her house" (fig. 5.7), this icon dates to the sixteenth century. What house is this? At the top of the icon is the house of the church, with all the saints. The lower part of the icon depicts Jesus with Mary (right) and Lady Wisdom (left). Notice that Lady Wisdom is featured more prominently, both having the circular heavenly fields that are characteristic of Russian iconography, but hers has medallion-like icons in the outer layer, which represents the first order of heavenly beings. She rests on a throne of seven pillars, and in her hand, as well as on the top of the circular fields, is a communion cup. Also, the circles float over and above a feast or communion table. This is where it gets particularly interesting: The feast depicts one group giving another group the chalices of wine. The group without the wine, closest to Jesus, has what appears to be John pointing to Lady Wisdom with his writings. On the other side is King Solomon (representing the wisdom literature), pointing to Jesus with his writings. Thus, this feast is of the Old and New Testament saints coming together, as the Old Testament points to Jesus and the New Testament points back to Lady Wisdom. However, it is the Old Testament saints that are giving the wine to the New Testament believers, as if to say the church cannot forget the much-needed wisdom there. One cannot help but see a kind of anti-Marcionite guard here, showing the goodness of both the Old and New Testaments (which Marcion famously denied), but particularly the dependence of the New on the Old. The Old Testament and its accompanying literature have salvific wisdom that is given to the New Testament from Lady Wisdom through Jesus Christ. What this means for a fully trinitarian theology, hinted at here, is the subject of the next chapter.

Fig. 5.7

6

Trinity and Mutuality

THE EXPERIENCE OF THE early Christians was that of worshiping the one God, the God of their Jewish heritage, but also Jesus Christ, who they understood as not only the Messiah they longed for but also one who claimed the prerogatives of divine lordship. In addition to this, they experienced the intense presence of the Holy Spirit that came through Christ. Their experience necessitated holding in tension that while each of these identities is distinct, they are the one God. This created an integral motif of the Christian relationship with God, as the Pauline benediction says, "May the grace of the Lord Jesus Christ, and the love of God, and the fellowship of the Holy Spirit be with you all" (2 Cor 13:14). How Christians speak of God must conform to the structure where God reveals the oneness of God's being in three persons of eternal loving relationship and unified action, but what this means for gendered language about God is far from clear. Is the Trinity masculine because of the references to Father, Son, and Spirit? Is "Father" the name Jesus gave the first member of the Trinity? Do these persons relate to each other in a way that suggests there is a hierarchy within the being of God that humans are to emulate in their own gendered ways of living? Or are there feminine patterns of referring to God? If so, how does this enrich the Christian understanding of God as triune? Here, it will be argued that "Father" is a profound title, but not a name, and while it should not be taken as offensive (although, sadly, it has been used to reinforce patriarchy), other ways of referring are possible, ones the complement and reinforce the meaning of the Trinity for the Christian life.

COMPETING VIEWS ON THE NATURE OF THE TRINITY

Trinitarian discourse has manifested two extremes. On the one side, the fact that Jesus normatively refers to the first member of the Trinity as "Father" is taken by some to mean this is the exclusive rule for referring. While many do not see this pattern as prescribing hierarchy either in God's being or for human relationships, there are certainly those who do. On the other side, there is an extreme that seeks to dismiss the relevance of the Trinity entirely, reducing the trinitarian personal relationships displayed in the Gospels to more experiential structures.

Safeguarding Father, Son, and Spirit trinitarian discourse is part and parcel of safeguarding the rule of revelation in some conservative estimates. Alvin Kimel writes, "This triune name forms the identity of the Christian church and structures the grammar of catholic belief and practice."[1] Note here that Kimel very much assumes that the Father symbol is a name. Historically, there is precedence for understanding it as a name. This approach has a long history, so it is not without warrant. For instance, Tertullian refused it as an analogical title: "Whereas other analogical terms like Lord and Judge indicate a merely functional relation to the world, the names Father and Son point to an ontological relation of distinct persons within the godhead itself."[2] Twentieth-century theologians like T. F. Torrance argue that the Father symbol is a name to the degree that this reflects who God is eternally. He writes that the names Father, Son, and Holy Spirit are "determined by what God is inherently in himself and are thus no detachable or changeable representations."[3] However, is it necessarily the case that because Father language is realistic, it, therefore, creates an *exclusive* ontological reference? As demonstrated in looking at Dionysius, all the names of God can be negated in order to prevent misunderstanding.

Some have taken the notion that the first member of the Trinity is named Father to the point of suggesting that there is a hierarchical pattern in the Trinity that humans are to emulate. Wayne Grudem writes,

> So, we may say that the role of the Father in creation and redemption has been to plan and direct and send the Son and

---

1. Kimel, "The God Who Likes His Name," 194.
2. Tertullian, *Adversus Praxean*, 9–10, as quoted in Bloesch, *A Theology of Word and Spirit*, 295n77.
3. Torrance, "The Christian Apprehension of God the Father," 140.

Holy Spirit. This is not surprising, for it shows that the Father and the Son relate to one another as a father and son relate to one another in a human family: the father directs and has authority over the son, and the son obeys and is responsive to the directions of the father. The Holy Spirit is obedient to the directives of both the Father and the Son. Thus, while the persons of the Trinity are equal in all their attributes, they nonetheless differ in their relationships to creation. The Son and Holy Spirit are equal in deity to God the Father, but they are subordinate in their roles. Moreover, these differences in role are not temporary but will last forever: Paul tells us that even after the final judgment, when the "last enemy," that is, death, is destroyed and when all things are put under Christ's feet, "then the Son himself will also be subjected to him who put all things under him, that God may be everything to everyone" (1 Cor. 15:28).[4]

Grudem defends the eternal subordination of the Son and Spirit to the Father, believing this is what the Nicene Creed espouses.[5] In turn, he suggests this is the pattern in gender relationships, citing 1 Cor 11:3: "Here just as the Father has authority over the Son in the Trinity, so the husband has authority over the wife in marriage."[6]

Meanwhile, in some feminist theology, the notion of the Trinity as displaying personal relationships between identities is often downplayed and de-particularized. In fact, early works like Mary Daly's *Beyond God the Father* simply ignore the Trinity outright. Others offer de-particularized substitutions. For example, McFague would not see the trinitarian language of Father, Son, and Spirit as "naming" God so much as offering a threefold metaphor of God's mystery, physicality, and mediation.[7] The modalistic implications of this and other revisions, like changing the trinitarian formula to "Creator, Redeemer, Sustainer," has not been lost by her critics.[8] As the early church thinkers warned, this does not do justice to the threefold personal revelation that upholds God's identity as love itself. Again, McFague represents the extreme wing of the approach, and her proclivity for anti-realism has continually been noted. If God's identity as love itself is lost, something vital to liberation is lost with it.

---

4. Grudem, *Systematic Theology*, 249.
5. Grudem, *Systematic Theology*, 251.
6. Grudem, *Systematic Theology*, 257.
7. McFague, *The Body of God*, 193.
8. This criticism is quite common, but one instance is in DiNoia, "Knowing and Naming the Triune God," in *Speaking the Christian God*, 170.

Just as literalism ironically misses key features and intentions of the biblical text, the pragmatic approach can, by having an allergic reaction to biblical authority and realistic revelation, undermine the means within the Christian community whereby liberation can be endorsed. The question really is whether the personal identities of the Trinity can be maintained with other languages for the first member.

Other feminist theologians demonstrate a fair degree of agreement with the concerns of someone like Alvin Kimel Jr. For instance, Janet Soskice, who wrote an essay in Kimel's edited volume, defends the possibility of a feminist using Father language. She also writes that the Trinity is not "an additional conviction, but rather the frame in which central convictions rest. It is a grammar of Christian faith, whose function was to safeguard what the early church took to be the central Christian witness."[9] She continues on to note that the strategy of simple offense and substitution has done little to remedy the complex problems of trinitarian discourse.[10] Soskice rightly intuits the connection of trinitarian discourse to realistic revelation and the rules of incarnation that have been previously sketched out. Feminist theologies, whether radically post-Christian or moderate reformist, move along the fault line of whether Jesus is God incarnate: "If you do not wish to say 'Jesus is God incarnate,' you do not need the Trinity; if you do wish to say this you can scarcely avoid it."[11]

This discussion piggybacks from the other rules, not just the incarnation. In particular, ineffability is a key question. Elizabeth Johnson argues, "The Trinity is not a blueprint to the inner workings of the Godhead, not an offering of esoteric information about God. In no sense is it a literal description of God's 'being *in se*.'"[12] This has concerned some conservative theologians who worry that not having real knowledge of God's being *in se* undermines God's presence fully with us, Immanuel.

The question these positions bring up is what *does* the Father symbol do for trinitarian doctrine? Is it fully enmeshed in the patriarchy of the time, or does it have an ongoing redemptive function that is still meaningful today? Are other patterns possible? These are the necessary clarifications to the Christian trinitarian grammar we must explore.

---

9. Soskice, "Trinity and Feminism," 136.
10. Soskice, "Trinity and Feminism," 137.
11. Soskice, "Trinity and Feminism," 137.
12. Johnson, *She Who Is*, 204.

THE MEANING OF FATHER IN THE NEW TESTAMENT

Jesus and Yahweh function as proper names, although that is not to say they also do not have their own cultural histories. Can the same be said for the words "Father" or "*Abba*"? If not, what does the title "Father" mean? Does it mean something patriarchal? When one examines the allusions and prior usages before the Gospels as well as in the Gospels themselves, one finds that this assertion to name-like status is not warranted. However, one does find a usage that advances a non-patriarchal meaning.

The Old Testament Backgrounds

Does "*Abba*" express intimacy beyond the word "Father"? As James Barr points out, "*Abba*" is not the same as "Daddy," a highly popularized misconception that goes back to Joachim Jeremias's article on the matter.[13] *Abba* seems to mean father in Aramaic. Either way, this is not a name per se, so much as a relational term and title of endearment. The question of whether Father language is unique to Jesus seems to be the condition proponents of exclusive Father language make. Following Jeremias, Robert Hammerton-Kelly makes the claim that Jesus' usage of "*Abba*, Father" is unique to Jesus and, thus, it qualifies as a revealed name.[14] (This is a strange claim given how sparsely "*Abba*" is actually used.) Similarly, Gerhard Kittel argues that *Abba* "far surpasses any possibilities of intimacy assumed in Judaism" and thus is "something which is wholly new."[15] While these are all fine studies, they all miss the fact that there are examples of prior usage, which offer occasions for how these names were functioning rhetorically in Jesus and the Gospel writers' usages.

The fact *Abba* means "father" in Aramaic suggests that what Jesus is saying is very much in continuity with the title "Father" in the Old Testament, especially since the Hebrew word for "Father" is *ab*. The title "Father" is implied in many places (e.g., the imago Dei in Genesis, the blessing of Abraham, the liberation of the nation of Israel), but the title itself is not used of God very frequently (only about sixteen times). It

---

13. See Jeremias, *The Prayers of Jesus*.
14. Hammerton-Kelly, *God the Father*, 72.
15. Kittel, "Abba," 5–6.

develops to speak about Israel as the child of God, which, despite disobedience, God still loves and promises to restore. However, more important for the New Testament, the title is used to speak about the kings of Israel, the line of David. David is understood as God's son, and God is a "father" to him and to all his successors in his line (2 Sam 7:12–14; this passage is alluded to in 1 Chr 17:13; 22:10; 28:6, but also in Ps 2:7 and more explicitly in Ps 89:27, as discussed in chapter 3). To understand these as applying to Jesus as God's Son is then to realize that the language has multiple facets. First, given the meaning of *Abba* and its similarity to its cognate in Hebrew, the uniqueness of the title as a novelty of Jesus is already disproved. Second, its connection to messianic promises means it is bound to the Old Testament frame of reference, where God is the "I Am," who appeals to multiple metaphors and analogies to self-communicate, *one* of which is the title, Father. The title then very much does come from a culture of patriarchy, as the line of David had no queen (with the brief and negative exception of queen Athaliah). The Israelite monarchy itself was based on the concession by God when Israel wanted a king so it could be like the nations (1 Sam 8:5). On the other hand, the Father symbol invoked here is one that holds the king accountable and is a part of the larger father symbolism where God the Father is a loving and compassionate father, despite Israel's waywardness. The New Testament uses these texts, both regarding Israel and David's line.

Intertestamental Developments

From the Old Testament, the title Father grows in usage, particularly in prayer, during the intertestamental period in the Targums of Genesis, the books of the Maccabees, and the Wisdom of Solomon.

All of these show an interesting foreshadowing of Jesus' usage as the title of God is called upon during times of persecution. For example, the intertestamental prayer found in 4Q372 reflects upon Joseph's cry for help in Genesis and its use of the language of God as Father:

> My father and my God do not abandon me into the hands of the nations;
> do justice for me lest the afflicted and the poor perish.
> You have no need for any nation or people for any help;
> Your finger is greater and stronger than anything in the world.[16]

---

16. 4Q372 1:16–18, translated in Schuller, "The Psalm of 4Q372 1," 67–79.

Intertestamental literature such as this shows several examples of the persecuted righteous praying to God, invoking God as Father and them as his children, against their persecutors, such that there is a reliance upon him to vindicate them. In Sir 51:10, Jesus Ben Sirach prays, "I cried out, 'Lord, you are my Father; do not forsake me in the days of trouble.'" 3 Maccabees 2:21 praises God as "overseer and the first father of all," and in 3 Macc 6:3–4, 6–7, Eliezer prays to God as Father in order to vindicate the children of Jacob against tyrants. Wisdom of Solomon similarly speaks about how the righteous are persecuted. The righteous man sees himself as a "child of the lord" (Wis 2:13) and that "God is his father" (Wis 2:16), who will rescue the righteous (Wis 2:17–18). In Wis 11:10, God tests his children like a father, and in Wis 14:3, God is like a father directing human fates with his providence. These form strong resemblances to the way Jesus invokes the language of the Father, which will be explored shortly.

Abba is not unique to Jesus, as it appears in the Targums of Genesis (written in Aramaic), and thus, the different translations of Genesis (the Hebrew, LXX, and its Aramaic Targum) demonstrate the synonymous nature of the words for father. These references form important aspects of the Gospel's language, particularly in the Gospel of Mark (14:36), which we will discuss shortly. As to whether Jesus is revealing from heaven the unique proper name of the first person of the Trinity, the matter is already falsified: Father and specifically *Abba* were used before Jesus, and Jesus seems to be, in part, using the language in a way consistent with the conventions proceeding him.

The Father in the New Testament

So then, what are Jesus and the New Testament writers' usages of the Father symbol? One should note the sparsity of references in Mark (four times) compared to the later Synoptics (twenty times in Luke, thirty times in Matthew) and then John (120 times). Clearly, there is a development of preference for the father symbol that Mark does not display, so tracing this snowball effect will be vital to understanding the meaning more clearly. Thus, to understand what this means, an investigation into Paul (the earliest writer), the Synoptics, and John's usages must be done.

TRINITY AND MUTUALITY

In Paul's theology, the Father symbol is important in the way believers relate to God through Jesus Christ,[17] but this does not ontologize "Father" as the name of the first member of the Trinity. The Father symbol is important but not exclusive. One can see Father language used consistently in a manner suggesting Jesus' deity. Paul's common opening of his epistles reads "God our Father and the Lord Jesus Christ," which suggests his early proto-trinitarian theology where lordship points to divinity and fatherhood points to the Son's messiahship, a complementary inherence of the divine identity. However, Paul refers to God as Father forty times but uses the general term "God" as a standalone term nearly five hundred times. Thompson confesses, "It is clear that Father is not the preferred designation for God in the Pauline writings."[18] Paul, at times, uses the Old Testament titles such as "Lord God Almighty," "God of Abraham, Isaac, and Jacob," "God of Israel," and "God Most High." This suggests that the Father symbol is one of several identifying references for God based on the Old Testament and is serving a certain function to understand the identity of Jesus and, as it will be shown, believers' identity to God.

God as Father, indeed, "*Abba*, Father," is tried together with the believer's experience of the Spirit coming upon them as the inheritance of blessing longed for in the Old Testament. Since Jesus is the "Son," believers are adopted into "sonship," which means all believers, notably male and female, have the inheritance of the blessing of the Spirit. Galatians 4:4–7 and Rom 8:14–17 are exemplary, and one can see how they are similar and consistent in Paul's thinking:

> But when the fullness of time had come, God sent his Son, born of a woman, born under the law, in order to redeem those who were under the law so that we might receive adoption as children. And because you are children, God has sent the Spirit of his Son into our hearts, crying, "*Abba*! Father!" 7 So you are no longer a slave but a child, and if a child then also an heir, through God. (Gal 4:4–7)

> For all who are led by the Spirit of God are children of God. For you did not receive a spirit of slavery to fall back into fear, but you have received a spirit of adoption. When we cry, "*Abba*! Father!" it is that very Spirit bearing witness with our spirit that we are children of God, and if children, then heirs, heirs of God

---

17. See Mengestu, *God as Father in Paul*.
18. Thompson, *The Promise of God the Father*, 118.

and joint-heirs with Christ—if, in fact, we suffer with him so that we may also be glorified with him. (Rom 8:14–17)

Gentiles are now Abraham's descendants in faith too (Rom 4:11–18). Abraham is the "ancestor of *all* who believe" (v. 11), and thus, through faith in the Spirit, gentiles are blessed and incorporated into the people of God. The fact that the language of adoption applies to both men and women, whom the Spirit comes upon fully without prejudice of ethnicity, gender, or status (Gal 3:28; 1 Cor 12:13; Col 3:11), forms another interesting example of how *a patriarchal concept* (only male children inherited in that culture) *becomes egalitarian in application.*

"*Abba*, Father" is a kind of early marker of the Spirit, but it is not an exclusive one. The confession of "*Abba*, Father" is not repeated as a marker outside Romans and Galatians in Paul's thinking, nor is it observed in Acts. In 1 John, the marker and test for an authentic spirit is one that confesses Christ has come in the flesh (1 John 4:2). The "*Abba*, Father" confessional marker seems to characterize early Jewish-influenced congregations' experience of the Spirit, pushing them to recognize the gentiles that confessed this as their own.

The Father symbol's social function is particularly emphasized in Ephesians, where the Spirit incorporates Jews and gentiles into the family of God:

> So, he came and proclaimed peace to you who were far off and peace to those who were near; for through him, both of us have access in one Spirit to the Father. So, then you are no longer strangers and aliens, but you are citizens with the saints and also members of the household of God, built upon the foundation of the apostles and prophets, with Christ Jesus himself as the cornerstone. In him, the whole structure is joined together and grows into a holy temple in the Lord, in whom you also are built together spiritually into a dwelling place for God. (Eph 2:17–22)

Notice the metaphorical nature, however, of these statements as believers are not only "citizens" but also "members of God's household" as well as a "structure, . . . a holy temple, . . . a dwelling place for God." This is part of the cosmic purpose of seeing all things in Christ that Ephesians envisions (1:10), which then means all humanity is renewed as a family in God. Thus, Paul prays, "For this reason, I bow my knees before the Father (*pros ton patera*), from whom every family (*pasa patria*) in heaven and on earth takes its name" (3:14). As stated previously, this passage is often incorrectly translated as "from whom all fatherhood . . . takes its name." This passage does not demonstrate that all true fatherhood is derived from God's fatherhood, nor is Father the name of God and all other fathers. Philippians 2 makes clear that the God revealed in Jesus, who is given the "name above every name," is still named the ineffable YHWH of the Hebrew Scriptures. Rather, Eph 3:14 offers a wordplay between Father (*patera*) and family (*patria*). The name in question is "family," *not* "fatherhood" (thus, the wordplay is lost in translation), which coalesces with Paul's argument: God is bringing humanity together back into one family just as God is one. The prayer continues to implore all believers to be bound together in the Spirit of God's love (vv. 16–19) so that they might take on the fullness of God (Eph 4:1–6). So, here, oneness and love are both descriptors of God and to be the unifying practice of the believers, which reflects the metaphor's ethical function well for all of Pauline thinking.

This means the Pauline usage of the term has layers. The Father symbol is bound up with witnessing the messianic and divine status of Jesus Christ, using the Old Testament figure of God being Father of the messianic son as a way of understanding Jesus' identity. However, this is not the exclusive way the first member of the Trinity is identified. Paul uses other Old Testament titles but understandably prioritizes the Father symbol to identify Jesus. Father language becomes expansive so as to include others in the family of God through this figure. Thus, it is central but not exclusive to the inclusion of the gentiles through the confession of "*Abba*, Father." As this usage continues, it seems to display a characteristically metaphorical quality, employing meanings from the culture to communicate the new reality of the church. In one sense, it does reflect the patriarchal structuring of the world around, as these metaphors are used to communicate to the Greco-Roman world, such as the function of the father for the family and how sonship worked for inheritance. It also uses Old Testament allusions back to Abraham, which also reflects a patriarchal world. So, the title is bound up with the metaphor of the father of the family but uses it expansively to show that gentiles are now Abraham's descendants in faith (Rom 4:11–18) and a part of the household of God (Eph 2:17–22). However, its employment is Christ-centred and therefore love-focused. It displays the expansiveness that the rule of narrative offers to metaphors. In that regard, it has a counter-patriarchal intention as it seeks to see all humanity, not just the biological tribes of this world ruled by their own patriarchs, as one entire human family.

Mark's employment of the Father symbol is quite sparse in comparison to the other New Testament authors, but its employments are powerfully illustrative. He uses it four times. Two are eschatological: Jesus says he is coming "in the glory of the Father" (Mark 8:38), but of the hour of his coming, no one knows except the Father (Mark 13:32). These have strong allusions to the coming of the Son of Man from Daniel 7. Also, Jesus speaks of forgiveness, "so that your Father in heaven may also forgive you our trespasses" (Mark 11:25), which strongly resembles what Matthew and Luke later write concerning the Lord's Prayer. Lastly, Jesus prays to "*Abba*, Father" in the Garden of Gethsemane (Mark 14:36).

This sparsity should indicate that its function is rather modest. It is not doing the functions many theologians place on it. Based on the above references in the intertestamental literature, one can see that Mark is coinciding with these references a good deal. God is "your Father" or commonly "the Father" (not "my Father") in a way that suggests the disciples already understood this truth apart from Jesus' teaching. There is no instantiation narrative for Jesus naming the Father, so the title is already assumed by his audience.

Jesus' usage of "*Abba*, Father" shows that when speaking of the cross he is invoking allusions to the sacrifice of Isaac in the Targum of Genesis, and his invocation of God as Father is coinciding with Jewish patterns of prayer for vindication in the midst of persecution, as already noted. Mark 14:36 reads, "And he [Jesus] said, '*Abba*, Father'" (*Abba*, 'o *pater*). Joseph Grassi notes how this brings together the Hebrew, LXX, and Targum, showing their terms to be much more similar than previously thought.[19] In the Hebrew Old Testament text, the Greek Septuagint, and the Aramaic Targums of this text, one sees the title translated:

> (Hebr.) And Isaac spoke to Abraham, his father, and he said, "My father." (*abi*)
>
> (LXX) And Isaac spoke to Abraham his father, saying, "father." (*pater*)
>
> (Targums) And Isaac spoke to Abraham, his father, and he said, "*Abba*." (*abba*)

Thus, while each of these words still carries slight differences in nuances, they share greater similarities than the assertion of Jeremias can account for.

---

19. Grassi, "*Abba*, Father (Mark 14:36): Another Approach," 450.

Also, for Jesus to use this line in the prayer at Gethsemane sets an important allusion for understanding his death as similar to the sacrifice of Isaac, compounded by the references just discussed from the other intertestamental literature. Jesus is like Isaac, only he is the perfect, willing sacrifice that God has provided. Joseph Grassi comments on this:

> Jesus' final trial in Gethsemane appears to be modeled on the supreme Abraham and Isaac. Despite his horror and anguish before the prospect of an imminent sacrificial death, Isaac calls to Abraham his *Abba* and, as a faithful son, obeys the voice of God speaking through his father. Parallel to this, Jesus says *Abba* to God in the same way that Isaac does to Abraham. In this context, *Abba* has the meaning of "father" in the sense of a relationship to a devoted and obedient son. In Jesus' supreme hour of trial, it is his trust and obedience to God as *Abba* that carries him through, even to the cross. This meaning of *Abba* may prompt further study of the significance of *son* in other NT texts to discover whether the obediential aspect may be more prominent than has been suspected. The father-son relationship in Genesis 22 may be a far-reaching New Testament model of that between Jesus and God.[20]

Grassi brings up important dimensions of the "*Abba*, Father" language that are tied together with very particular understandings of what Jesus is as the "Son."

Father-Son language carried additional cultural meaning in the context of imperial tyranny. While the "son of God" is a Davidic title, it also has a counter-imperial polemic to it as the emperor understood himself as the "son of God" as well. Coupled with the Father symbol, the titles strongly coincide with intertestamental usages where Father-Son language was part of the prayers of the persecuted righteous for divine deliverance (as explored in the previous section), where the persecuted righteous appealed to God as Father to vindicate them as they were God's sons. Mary D'Angelo writes,

> Jesus was a Jew who is likely to have drawn on the tradition in prayer. In light of his death at the hands of Rome and his role in a movement that expected and preached God's reign, it would not be surprising if Jesus and his companions preferred the use of "father" as an address to God that called Caesar's reign into question and made a special claim on God's protection, mercy,

---

20. Grassi, "*Abba*, Father (Mark 14:36): Another Approach," 455.

and providence. It cannot be argued that such a usage was unique or was characterized by special intimacy. Thus, Jesus's possible use of *Abba* or "father" cannot be used to defend the normative nature and primacy of "father" for twentieth-century theology and liturgy or to endow these words with special meaning.[21]

D'Angelo is overly dismissive of any uniqueness, but the comment is correct. The term *abba* is not novel to Jesus. When Jesus used it, the people understood the reference based on prior usages. Jesus does not have an instantiation narrative of the title. Again, this is not to say that there is nothing unique about Jesus' usage. What is unique about Jesus' terms is not the terms themselves but how Jesus *used* them and *redefined* them by his actions as the messianic Son.

Therefore, Mark's fatherhood theology is anchored in Jesus' Sonship, and Jesus' Sonship, both as Son of God and Son of Man, are linked to the cross of Christ. Jesus is introduced in the beginning as the "Son of God" (1:1), and the Gospel of Mark immediately begins with Jesus' baptism, where a "voice from heaven" says, "You are my Son, the Beloved; with you, I am well pleased" (Mark 1:11). This pronouncement of Sonship is an allusion back to Ps 2, where the Davidic monarch is declared the beloved son of God, and it is through him that the nations will be brought under complete divine rule. This sonship declaration is fundamental to the Gospel of Mark as it is repeated two other times, from the beginning, middle, and end of the book. Jesus is declared by the Father to be the beloved Son in the transfiguration (Mark 9:7) and then finally by the centurion at the cross (Mark 15:39). These sonship pronouncements are the driving force of the narrative and so also Mark's understanding of divine fatherhood. God is Father, which is a way of witnessing Jesus as the Davidic Messiah.

God is the Father, as in the Ancient of Days, who with the Son of Man (Jesus' most common self-designation in the Synoptics) will usher in the kingdom, and these usages converge in understanding Jesus' identity fundamentally through his cross and resurrection, where the first is last, but in becoming last, Jesus is resurrected first. "For even the Son of Man did not come to be served, but to serve, and to give his life as a ransom for many" (Mark 10:45). In other words, Mark's usage of the Father symbol does little to name the first member of the Trinity apart

---

21. D'Angelo, "Theology in Mark and Q," 173–74.

from how the audience would have already understood God from the Old Testament in general, nor does it function to develop a trinitarian doctrine in the way John's does. It serves, first and foremost, to identify Jesus as the Son of God. Even then, the Son of God theology stands alone often as primary. Notice that no Father references are used after the Garden of Gethsemane. The title of the Son, nevertheless, appears alongside an important reference to Dan 7, where the first member of the Trinity is "the Power": "Again the high priest asked him, 'Are you the Messiah, the Son of the Blessed One?' 'I am,' said Jesus. 'And you will see the Son of Man sitting at the right hand of the Power and coming on the clouds of heaven'" (Mark 14:61–62), alluding back to Dan 7.

Finally, the messianic identity stands on its own at the cross, where Mark has Jesus cry out, echoing Ps 22:1, "My God, my God, why have you forsaken me?" (This is a messianic psalm, but it does not use the Father title in it.) To which the centurion declares, "Surely this man was the Son of God!" (Mark 14:39). It would seem that if Mark was concerned with doing the things the conservative position sees the Father symbol doing, these narratives would have looked different.

Thus, Mark's Gospel does not really conform to the theological expectations of conservative trinitarian discourse concerning the Father symbol. The references are sparse, and they coincide strongly with the preceding conventions for how the language was used. Father language seems anchored to the messianic status of Jesus, as sonship is far more pronounced, and this is the case to the point where sonship language appears on its own.

Matthew and Luke-Acts use Mark as a source but clearly expand and elevate the usage of Father for what it means for believers. Thus, they are worth summarizing briefly, particularly in regard to the Lord's Prayer. Luke uses "God" 122 times in the Gospel and 168 times in Acts. He only uses Father twenty-four times in the Gospel and only three times in Acts (1:4, 7; 2:33).[22] Phrases are fairly evenly distributed between "my Father," "your Father," "the Father," and "Father." Luke is actually more restrained than Matthew in his Father references. Thompson notes three facets to Luke's theology of God as Father.[23]

First, Father language is used to display the unique relationship Jesus has as part of his messianic and divine identity. Luke shows that

22. Thompson, *The Promise of God the Father*, 92.

23. Thompson, *The Promise of God the Father*, 94. Also see Chen, *God as Father in Luke-Acts*.

Jesus has a distinct relationship with the Father. This has a dimension to it that is a part of Jesus being the messianic Son, as shown in Gabriel announcing that Jesus will sit on the throne of "his father David" (1:32). But this is juxtaposed as Jesus is found in the temple as a boy. As Mary and Joseph reprimand him, he replies, "Did you not know that I would be in my Father's house?" (2:49). In a statement that is very similar to the Johannine material, Luke speaks of the revelatory in-dwelling of Father and Son: "no one knows the Son except the Father, and no one knows the Father except the Son" (10:22).

Second, the disciples are included in this relationship through Jesus and, thus, are given similar provisions of care and forgiveness. Few passages showcase this more than the parable of the prodigal son (Luke 15:11–32). Jesus is the messianic bearer of the kingdom, which comes from the Father, similar to the revelatory relationship already mentioned: "I confer on you, just as my Father has conferred on me, a kingdom" (22:29). This kingdom is a constant invitation to the disciples from the Father through Christ. Luke includes the Lord's Prayer in a more simple form from Matthew, but its connection to the kingdom and the Father is present:

> Father, hallowed be your name.
> Your kingdom come
> Give us each day our daily bread.
> And forgive us our sins,
> For we ourselves forgive everyone indebted to us.
> And do not bring us to the time of trial (Luke 11:3–4)

As it will be noted in Matthew and Luke, the "name" here is not "Father," despite them being mentioned alongside each other. Typical of Jewish protocol, the name is the sacred, Yhwh, and goes unpronounced out of reverence. Father, then, is a title of address in keeping with the intertestamental prayers that invoke God as Father. This prayer is followed up with a call to trust in God when we pray, for God provides like a loving father would (11:11–13). This pattern of loving action by God the Father is an assurance of provision and an example to follow, particularly in caring for the poor:

> For it is the nations of the world that strive after all these things, and your Father knows that you need them. Instead, strive for his kingdom, and these things will be given to you as well. "Do not be afraid, little flock, for it is your Father's good pleasure

TRINITY AND MUTUALITY

to give you the kingdom. Sell your possessions, and give alms." (Luke 12:30-33)

The role of provision by the father in that culture is thus the basis for prayers for provision.

Third, the disciples are expected to have the character of Christ, emulating the character of the Father. This is expansive of Mark's axiom on forgiveness: "so that your Father in heaven may also forgive you our trespasses" (Mark 11:25), which Luke places in the Lord's Prayer (Luke 11:4). It is an ongoing theme in many of the parables of Jesus in Luke that God has mercy that the believer is invited into a merciful kingdom: "But love your enemies, do good, and lend, expecting nothing in return. Your reward will be great, and you will be children of the Most High, for he is kind to the ungrateful and the wicked. Be merciful as your Father is merciful" (6:35-36).

Father language in Matthew strongly coincides with Mark, as Matthew uses Mark as one of its sources. Matthew uses the phrases "my Father" and "your Father" in equal measure (around fifteen times each). Matthew and Luke both include infancy narratives of Jesus, which are intended to clarify and deepen Jesus' status as the messianic Son. Matthew shows that the virginal conception portrays the son of David as "God with us, Immanuel" (Matt 1:23). Matthew also includes a narrative of Jesus' escape to Egypt (Matt 2:15). This is meant as a fulfillment of the text, "out of Egypt I called my son" (Hos 11:1). Here sonship is portrayed as Jesus fulfilling not only messianic descriptions but embodying Israel's story, as Hos 11 is intended to describe Israel as the child of God liberated out of Egypt. Jesus is the messianic fulfillment of Israel. Coinciding with the other Synoptic books, then, the title Father heavily coincides with the messianic description of Jesus as the Son. As Peter confesses: "You are the Messiah, the Son of the living God" (Matt 16:16).

It is in the Sermon on the Mount that Jesus makes reference to the first member of the Trinity as Father, and it is used to speak of emulation of God's character. Here, Jesus uses the phrase "your Father," not "my Father," and uses it to talk about the ethical character of the disciples: "Let your light shine before others, so that they may see your good works and give glory to your Father in heaven" (Matt 5:16). This, again, suggests that the title is a known convention. More than that, Matthew's expansion applies the Father-child relationship to the believers as they emulate the Father's character: "Blessed are the peacemakers, for they will be called children of God" (Matt 5:9). The sermon continues on to say, "Love your enemies and pray for those who persecute you, so that you may be children of your Father in heaven; for he makes his sun rise on the evil and on the good, and sends rain on the righteous and on the unrighteous.... Be perfect, therefore, as your heavenly Father is perfect" (Matt 5: 44-45, 48).[24] This is further used to reiterate the family nature of disciples. Jesus states when told his mother and siblings want to speak with him, "For whoever does the will of my Father in heaven is my brother and sister and mother" (Matt 12:50). This notion is expanded to the point where the Father titles are reserved for God alone so as to prevent anyone claiming the level of teaching authority concerning God's will that Jesus conveys (Matt 23:8-10).

Matthew includes in the Sermon on the Mount the Lord's Prayer, which opens with "Our Father in heaven, hallowed be your name" (Matt 6:9). Again, this is often assumed to mean that Father is the name, but one must remember that Matthew and the other New Testament authors follow the Jewish custom of not saying or writing out the sacred name of God (YHWH). Here "your name" does not refer to "Father" but is a substitute for YHWH.

Particularly emphasized in Matthew is the prophetic themes of fatherhood found in Jeremiah. Jeremiah 3:19 reads, "I thought that you would call me, My Father, and would not turn from following me," as well as Jer 31:9: "I have become a father to Israel, and Ephraim is my firstborn." Father is not disclosing the name of the first member of the Trinity, but Jesus is using this in his messianic teaching to show the fulfillment of an OT longing for forgiveness and renewed relationship (cf. Jer 31:31-35). The prayers for provision in the Lord's Prayer coincide with the rest of Matt 6, where the fatherly quality of God is the basis of provision. The prayer also says, "Your kingdom come," and this coincides with the eschatological dimension of the Father symbol.

John offers perhaps the most developed and explicit trinitarian theology in the New Testament. The Father is mentioned 120 times. Similar to the other Gospels, the Father symbol is used to identify Jesus as the Son, but this is done in some distinct ways.

One can see the overt usage of the Father symbol from the very first chapter. God is the Father of Jesus, the Son, who reveals the Father and allows others to become children of God:

---

24. Other examples include 5:16; 7:21; 12:50; 21:31; 25:34, 41.

> But to all who received him, who believed in his name, he gave power to become children of God, who were born, not of blood or of the will of the flesh or of the will of man, but of God. And the Word became flesh and lived among us, and we have seen his glory, the glory as of a father's only son, full of grace and truth.... No one has ever seen God. It is God the only Son, who is close to the Father's heart, who has made him known. (John 1:12–14, 18)

One should note the difference from the other Gospels: John begins with the incarnation. While Mark begins at the baptism of Jesus and offers little material on the birth circumstances of Jesus, Matthew and Luke both include their virginal conception accounts and genealogies, both intent on demonstrating Jesus as the messianic Son through a Davidic lineage. John has no such concern. Jesus is the Son because of his unique relationship to the Father. John moves on to the baptism of Jesus, where John testifies that Jesus has the dove of the Holy Spirit descend on him. This leads him to testify that Jesus is the Son of God (John 1:34, unlike the Synoptics, no voice from heaven is reported as the emphasis is focused on John the Baptist).

The relationship between the Father and the Son is stressed to the point of emphasizing Jesus' divinity. While many are the children of God, Jesus is the "only begotten Son" (John 3:16). What the Father does, Jesus does: "My Father is still working, and I also am working" (John 5:17). Jesus' usage of the title "Father" inflames the Pharisees because of its divine connotation: "For this reason, the Jews were seeking all the more to kill him, because he was not only breaking the Sabbath but was also calling God his own Father, thereby making himself equal to God" (John 5:18). This also reflects a point of contention as tensions grew between the church and synagogue. The theology of fatherhood is used to polemicize the Pharisees' understanding of how they were children of Jacob and Abraham (John 4:12; 8:56). The Jews saw God as their Father (John 8:41), but Jesus responded, "If God were your Father, you would love me" (John 8:42).

The Father is the origin, sender, witness, and thus vindicator of Jesus' identity in glory, to whom he ascends. Many of these themes are displayed in chapter 5:

> Jesus said to them, "Very truly, I tell you, the Son can do nothing on his own, but only what he sees the Father doing; for whatever the Father does, the Son does likewise. The Father loves the Son

> and shows him all that he himself is doing, and he will show him greater works than these, so that you will be astonished. Indeed, just as the Father raises the dead and gives them life, so also the Son gives life to whomever he wishes. The Father judges no one but has given all judgment to the Son so that all may honor the Son just as they honor the Father. Anyone who does not honor the Son does not honor the Father who sent him. Very truly, I tell you, anyone who hears my word and believes him who sent me has eternal life, and does not come under judgment, but has passed from death to life. Very truly, I tell you, the hour is coming, and is now here, when the dead will hear the voice of the Son of God, and those who hear will live. For just as the Father has life in himself, so he has granted the Son also to have life in himself; and he has given him authority to execute judgment, because he is the Son of Man." (John 5:19–27, cf. 12:48–49)

However, this continues as the Father testifies to the Son: "I testify on my own behalf, and the Father who sent me testifies on my behalf" (John 8:18). The Father vindicates the Son as the Son is obedient to the Father's will: "For this reason, the Father loves me because I lay down my life in order to take it up again. . . . I have received this command from my Father" (John 10:17–18). As Jesus is faithful to the Father, the Father glories the Son. Jesus prays, "Now my soul is troubled. And what should I say—'Father, save me from this hour'? No, it is for this reason that I have come to this hour. Father, glorify your name." John records, "Then a voice came from heaven, 'I have glorified it, and I will glorify it again'" (John 12:27–28). Thus, the Father gives "all things" to the Son (John 3:35, cf. 13:3; 17:1–2). After the crucifixion, Jesus appears to the women and disciples, and then he states that he is ascending to the Father and he confers the Holy Spirit by breathing on the disciples (John 20:17).

John has an explicit and well-developed early trinitarian theology, where the Father is the source and destination of Jesus' identity and mission, with the Spirit flowing from Father to Son to the disciples. The Father and Son are bound together as one in love, and this love is something the believers are invited into through the Spirit. There is a revelatory in-dwelling similar to Luke: "Do you not believe that I am in the Father and the Father is in me?" (John 14:10). Jesus then extends this relationship to the disciples through the Spirit:

> And I will ask the Father, and he will give you another Advocate to be with you forever. This is the Spirit of truth, whom the world cannot receive, because it neither sees him nor knows

> him. You know him, because he abides with you, and he will be in you.... On that day, you will know that I am in my Father, and you in me, and I in you. (John 14:15–17, 20)

The oneness that the Father and Son share ("The Father and I are one," John 10:30), which alludes back to the oneness of God in the *Shema* (Deut 6:4) and the reciprocal nuptial mystery (Gen 2:24; Song 2:16). The disciples are to abide in this relationship through emulating Jesus' example of love. Note that while the Synoptics give extended treatments of Jesus' teachings and parables, John does not. John merely reiterates that Jesus gives a new commandment to love, and this love looks like the self-giving love that Jesus models in going to the cross:

> As the Father has loved me, so I have loved you; abide in my love. If you keep my commandments, you will abide in my love, just as I have kept my Father's commandments and abide in his love.... This is my commandment, that you love one another as I have loved you. No one has greater love than this, to lay down one's life for one's friends. (John 15:9–10, 12–13)

Thus, John's theology of Father and Son is the most explicitly trinitarian. John certainly uses the messianic themes that the Synoptics use but employs them to emphasize that Jesus is the Son through the Father, not his lineage to David. Jesus is the Son because of the obedience and love he shows in laying down his life for others, which the Father vindicates and glorifies. This movement of love forms an invitation to the disciples to believe in Jesus and allow the Holy Spirit to work in the midst of the believers.

Thus, the title Father is certainly important for the New Testament writers. However, the title does not become a proper name the way male-exclusive language proponents have argued. For Paul and Mark, it certainly is not even the primary way of referring. Its usage is, however, deeply important to the structuring of the New Testament and is intentionally counter-patriarchal, both in its messianic reference to Jesus as the Son and how it uses the household metaphor to open up deeper lines of care for members of the church community.

THE MEANING OF FATHER FOR TRINITARIAN THEOLOGY

Since we have nuanced the meaning of the Father symbol to demonstrate that it is not the *name* of the first member of the Trinity, the question might be, then, what does it mean? Some constructive statements are worth summarizing here as to what this means for gender-inclusive language and the non-patriarchal usage of the symbol.

The Father symbol cannot be literalized. Catholic Gerald O'Collins summarizes this well:

> When the Trinity is named, God the Father functions validly if we align ourselves with the meanings communicated in that metaphor by the biblical witnesses (above all, by Jesus himself) and refuse to literalize it. . . . In these days, we may need more than ever some alternatives to prevent our "Father" language from collapsing into crass literalism.[25]

If it was literalized, it would mean either the first member of the Trinity would be reduced to the creation or be temporally and ontologically prior to the second member. It has often been argued that the Father does not mean a biological relation, nor does it mean gender, but one must be careful what it does mean. The symbols of the Father and Son are male symbols in the history of this relationship, going back to the Davidic covenant and cultural analogy from the family. However, this is why the Father must not be taken as an ontological name in the way many have argued. The metaphor very much suggests gender as it is a title linked to a male relationship, and it is accompanied by male pronouns. To insist the Father symbol is the name, suggestive of genderlessness, would be to ignore the fact that it very much does come from human convention, thus projecting and reifying the very thing into God that conservatives worry about. However, if taken as analogical references clarified through narrative usage and context, a more productive meaning is ascribed.

In early church theology, the title "Father" was rightly not literalized. Arius used the notion that God is the Father of Jesus to imply that there was a time when the Son was not since no son is the same age as their father. To this, the title "Father" and the language of being "begotten" had to be abstracted and qualified to respect the divinity of the Son.[26] The

---

25. O'Collins, *The Tripersonal God*, 127, 130.

26. For further exposition on early church views of the Father-Son relationship, see Widdicome, "The Fathers on the Father in the Gospel of John."

Father "begot" the Son, but not literally; the Son is "eternally begotten," suggesting simultaneity. Similarly, today, these male ways of referring have to be contextualized and qualified in order to prevent projecting maleness into God and violating God's ineffability. Father is an analogical title that Jesus used to speak of his messianic status, suggesting a pattern Christians are to use today in following Jesus' example of prayer, but it is not naming the first member of the Trinity.

Some have even argued that the Father (or the Father, Son, and Holy Spirit together) replace the tetragrammaton as the name of God in the New Testament.[27] To reiterate, again, "Father" is not the name of the first member of the Trinity, just as "Son" is not Jesus' given name. God's primary name, as R. Kendall Soulen points out, is and remains the ineffable Yhwh. Father, Son, and Spirit are, as he calls them, "inflections" that reveal relational roles that bear witness to how the oneness of the "I Am" has three personal identities revealed in the biblical narrative.[28]

The Father is a symbol for understanding Jesus as Messiah. In this regard, sonship, based on the Davidic promises, drives fatherhood language. In the case of the Gospel of Mark, sonship is more dominant. These identities act as a coordinating witness in Jesus' baptism, ministry of proclaiming the kingdom, his transfiguration, and especially his cross and resurrection. They are relational roles identifying the narrative character of God's ineffable love. The fact that the Father and the Spirit are identified with male pronouns is not a reification of God's gender so much as witnesses of God's identification with Jesus Christ's work, whose own maleness has already been explained in chapter 4. Jesus is the (male) messianic king in history, who, unlike patriarchal kings, empties himself of his power in service to others. In this, the incarnation creates a space to understand God and thus be pictured in all flesh.

More broadly, the Father is a symbol of how Jesus fulfills the Old Testament portrait of God. Through this layer, the title Father is showing not the gender of the first member of the Trinity, nor even a biological relation between Father and Son, but Jesus as the fulfillment of the character of the God of the Old Testament, and while Father is used in the Gospels, as previously noted, the portraits of God in the Old Testament were not exclusively male. Thus, the vindication of God's identity in Jesus is shown through the "Father," but this action is not exclusively bound

27. Kimel, "The God Who Likes His Name," 191: "The Father, Son, and Spirit is our deity's *proper name*" (italics original).

28. Soulen, "The Name of the Holy Trinity: A Triune Name," 244–61.

or understood exclusively through one word. Recall that Jesus was also identified through the figure of Wisdom in Matthew and Luke.

If the Father symbol functions to show Jesus' fulfillment of the whole Old Testament, where there are motherly metaphors and analogies used as well, these other references are permitted for us to use in our attempts to understand Jesus. We have charted the motherly metaphors and analogies for God in a previous chapter where it was noted that God's name, moral attributes, and redeeming acts are illustrated with the appeal to fatherly and motherly analogies, and if this is the case, the mother imagery can serve as a means to identify the first member of the Trinity as it has served analogically and metaphorically in the Old Testament. Jesus primarily used the Father symbol, and so believers ought to continue to use it too, but not exclusively.

Thus, while the Father is not a name for the first member of the Trinity, and so alternatives are permitted (which will be discussed shortly), it should also be emphasized that the Father is a way of witnessing the centrality of Jesus Christ, the messianic Son.

ALTERNATIVE WAYS OF REFERRING TO THE TRINITY

In what ways can people further refer to the Trinity that *supplement* the standard language of Father, Son, and Spirit? There are other possibilities that can be employed to speak of the Triune God, which, in turn, augment and reinforce the Triune reality Christians confess.

The very possibility of this notion of further naming is seen in the use of the word "Trinity" itself. "Trinity," it should be noted, is not a word found in the Bible. It is the innovation proposed first by Tertullian, who also suggested a "three persons and one being" vocabulary that later thinkers further developed. This vocabulary is also not explicitly mentioned in the Bible, nor are other terms of creedal orthodoxy. If the term Trinity is acceptable to refer to God in worship, this speaks of the possibility of extrabiblical description that, while not literally stated in the text, has the capacity to encapsulate the whole meaning of the biblical message in a single term.[29] In worship, churches sing "Blessed Trinity," and it seems that the "Trinity" is able to offer a name-like title that accurately describes what God has revealed despite it being a post-biblical

---

29. Fiddes, *Participating in God*, 5.

description. Thus, if this is true, in encountering God and being invited to respond, there is a kind of doxological capacity to further name God in ways that coincide with biblical revelation.

Wolfhart Pannenberg reminds us that God accepts language spoken in prayer and praise.[30] Thus, speech for God is speech permitted to God. Gail Ramshaw has taken Pannenberg's insight and shown its usefulness in allowing for feminine expression in worship.[31] In doxology, we can praise God for the qualities the events of revelation display and the titles these experiences suggest. While Yahweh is the proper name of God and Jesus the name of the apex of God's historical revelation, this does not mean all attempts to use alternative and supplementary language are subjective preferential assertions or projections. Rather, as Paul Fiddes notes, it affirms the revelation of God that is the condition of all human experience:

> Rather, our experience of ourselves and others must always be understood in the context of a God who is present in the world, offering self-communication that springs from boundless love. It is this self-gift of God that already shapes both our experience of being in the world and our language with which we configure our experiences. In taking a path from experience to doctrine we are retracing a journey that God has already taken towards us. Theology is doxology, worship called out from those who have received the self-offering and self-opening of the triune God.[32]

And to speak "'Father' or 'Mother' to God," Fiddes notes, "we are being enticed into a movement of speech—responding, obeying, glorifying—that is already there before us."[33] It is possible, then, doxologically and experientially, to name God in ways that are faithful to what the Bible presents. However, this is a response to the revelation of God. In other words, Scripture norms it and empowers it.

Perhaps one of the earliest and most beautiful examples of this doxological dynamic is when God rescues Hagar after Abraham cast her out. Genesis reports that she names the Lord, who spoke with her, "El-roi," which means the "One Who Sees" (Gen 16:13). If what Hagar has done

---

30. See Pannenberg, "Analogy and Doxology," in *Basic Questions in Theology*, 2:212–38.

31. Ramshaw, *God Beyond Gender*, 1–2.

32. Fiddes, *Participating in God*, 8–9.

33. Fiddes, *Participating in God*, 42.

is legitimate, this suggests that believers then are able to view the acts of God and are permitted to form names of God that praise God, congruent with canonical revelation. As this project has been insisting, while Father language is normative in convention, it need not be viewed as exclusive.

What is the notion of Trinity attempting to communicate? While the grammar of three personal identities cannot be shoved aside as secondary, the Trinity is intended to provide a witness to the identity and character of Jesus Christ. Jesus Christ, in turn, is the incarnation of God's character that is abounding in steadfast love. As Augustine showed, the trinitarian relationships speak of God's essential identity as love. Augustine interpreted the trinitarian relationships as displaying God as a lover, beloved, and the gift of love itself.[34] God is agapeic love, and love is the founding reality by which gendered metaphors are employed as illustrations. Not that love is God literally, but that agapeic love bears witness to God's character and presence shown throughout Scripture and especially in the cross and resurrection of Christ. Nevertheless, Augustine was insistent that love formed a way to know God.[35] To further the analogical way of speaking of God, where there is agapeic action, its goodness is from and participates in God's agapeic goodness. The Trinity is a conceptual rendering of something that can only be lived, the movement of the relationship of God beyond, beside, and within, moving to fully unite all things with God.

If the Trinity is a grammar that attempts to faithfully communicate the saving love revealed in the biblical narrative, admitting that a part of this descriptive activity is understanding God's actions to be indescribable, the pattern of Father, Son, and Spirit surely has a cherished and enduring place for aiding believers to understand God's love, but this does not prevent other patterns that can reinforce and reiterate this truth in creative ways. Indeed, one need only look as far as Andrei Rublev's icon of *The Trinity* (also called *The Hospitality of Abraham*, ca. 1411) as evidence. While this may be the most well-known icon of the Trinity (see fig. 6.1), powerful in its symbolism and arrangement of colors to designate the different members (gold for the Father, brown for the humanity of the incarnation, green for the life of the Spirit, and blue for their unity) the three angelic members do not appear to be male. Their

---

34. Augustine, *The Trinity*, 8:5:10,14.
35. Augustine, *On the Psalms*, 18.11.

hair and clothing suggest femininity. This is not a novel notion in church history, and so, three examples are worth mentioning.

Fig. 6.1

First, some might simply opt for more gender-neutral ways of referring to God. While there are certainly different trinitarian metaphors to use, if left to their own, they can sound modalistic (or simply less specific). It has been the prescription offered in previous chapters that while female language is possible, one should be careful to not surmount historical revelation, particularly around Jesus Christ. What could this mean for something like baptism? While Matthew 28 uses that language of the name of "Father, Son, and Holy Spirt," this does not create a proper or exclusive name to pronounce baptism. Those who treat this formulation as having a kind of legal status to administrate baptism neglect how the church in Acts simply baptized in the name of Jesus (Acts 2:38). Thus,

Ruth Duck offers one proposal. She notes that in the early church, as recorded in the *Apostolic Traditions* of Hippolytus, a proto version of the Apostles Creed was used as a confession statement of the one baptized, three questions of "Do you believe in . . . ?" based on the three trinitarian articles.[36] She notes then that baptismal rhetoric is confessional before it is declarative. In other words, the person is confessing their faith in Jesus, not the baptizer, who declares them legally in the eyes of the church to be a Christian. The guiding principle is not rigid adherence to one form but whether the person baptized knows they are redeemed in Jesus Christ. Duck's own project tends to see male language as problematic and thus moves to suggest gender-neutral options. As previously stated, male language is not inherently offensive, but whenever it is insisted upon as the exclusive option, there is cause for worry. Duck offers her own proposal, one that retains baptism in the name of Jesus Christ. While she sees the Father language as promoting the patriarchy that has hurt many women, she does not think moving away from the historical Jesus is helpful. Thus, her baptismal liturgy reads as follows:

> Do you believe in God, the Source, the fountain of life?
> I believe.
> Do you believe in Christ, the offspring of God embodied in Jesus of Nazareth and in the church?
> I believe.
> Do you believe in the liberating Spirit of God, the wellspring of new life?
> I believe.
> N, through the power of God, you have been baptized into a new relationship with God and this community. You have put on Christ. "Whoever is in Christ is a new creation. The old has passed away. The new has come." You have passed through the waters of new life. Together we join in an exodus from injustice and sin of this world toward God's new age.[37]

While Duck's own approach is stated in gender-neutral terms here in regards to the first person of the Trinity, the baptismal liturgy retains the trinitarian form, drawing off of the narratives of Scripture and the name of Jesus as the foci of particularity. There are many variations of what might be called the God–Christ–Spirit pattern, and they reflect the

---

36. Duck, *Gender and the Name of God*, 131.
37. Duck, *Gender and the Name of God*, 185–86.

often Pauline way of speaking.[38] Some might use more traditional imagery, while others might use more neutral imagery. Both are to be used with recognition of the fallibility of the words: the Son is not literally the offspring of the Father (nor "begotten" in the biological, procreative sense) when these words are used, and similarly, the first member of the Trinity is more than "the Source" as there is no temporality like this in the imminent Trinity nor is the Father's relationship the Son merely that of being the Source. The strength of Duck's approach is its recovery of a confessional approach to Jesus Christ as the fundamental principle. However, as Catherine Lacugna argues, while another language is permitted to correct the pervasive distortions of the meaning of the Father symbol, "to refuse to use 'Father' as a personal name for God concedes that God the Father is male as patriarchy has defined it."[39] In this regard, there is no set baptismal formula, although many will still use the Matthean form. Whatever a church's choice, the governing grammar will be to offer confessional content that identifies the triune God centered in Jesus Christ within the biblical narrative of love and redemption, seeking to invite the individual coming forward for baptism with questions about what a redeemed life truly means.

The second way of thinking about female imagery in the Trinity is with the title Mother. As we have been noting, God's love is described as motherly (e.g., Isa 66:13), Christ's love is specifically described as a motherly love (e.g., Matt 24:37), and the Spirit's actions are that of birthing (e.g., John 3:5), the notion that God's love toward humans takes on a mother-like role warrants the title Mother in reference to the Trinity. The clearest example of maternal imagery for the Trinity is in the writings of Julian of Norwich (d. 1416), who famously referred to Christ as her Mother while not trying to revise his maleness: "he is our Mother."[40] She also applied motherhood to the Trinity: "The high might of the Trinity is our Father and the deep wisdom of the Trinity is our Mother, and the great love of the Trinity is our Lord."[41] She refers to the entirety of the Trinity as having the properties of fatherliness, motherliness, and lordship while referring to Jesus as "Mother Christ."

Supposing that self-sacrificial love is the central characteristic that trinitarian theology witnesses to in Jesus Christ, this frees the preacher to

38. For examples, see Johnson, *She Who Is*, 210.
39. LaCugna, "The Baptismal Formula," 243.
40. Julian of Norwich, *Showings* (long version), ch. 58.
41. Julian of Norwich, *Showings* (long version), ch. 58.

use creative illustrations to witness to the love of God. Both the fatherly love and the motherly love that sacrifices for one's children speak of the entire being of God, naming the action of all members of the Trinity, not just one. "Mother" need not be a title that replaces Father in the classic baptismal formula or Lord's Prayer if they are understood in their counter-patriarchal intention, but "Mother" can be a way of identifying the love characteristic of each member and their whole being. Joe Jones have advocated a significant middle ground benediction: "In the name of the Father, Son, and Holy Spirit, One God, Mother to us all."[42] Jones recognizes the patriarchal dimension of male language while respecting its place in the canon, supplementing it with "Mother" as a way, similar to Julian, of naming the love of God's whole being. One can see different pathways as to how the first member of the Trinity or the whole being of the Trinity can take on female imagery.

A third way of referring to the Trinity in feminine ways is by revisiting the figure of Sophia. The figure of Sophia has already been discussed, but here, this figure can be incorporated into trinitarian discourse more fully. The Spirit is most consistently identified with the figure of Sophia in intertestamental literature. However, Sophia is also equated with Christ in the New Testament. Hildegard of Bingen (1098–1179) provides an important medieval example of a Sophia doctrine of the Trinity. In the codex of her *Scivias*, this text contains a picture entitled "Trinity" (fig. 6.2). It is a female figure who is the eternal love of God that made creation. Creation is depicted as the circles flowing outward, the outer rings signifying the planets, sun, and stars.

---

42. Jones, *Grammar of Christian Faith*, 1:158–66. This line has its origins in the debates around inclusive language at Riverside Baptist Church and was first proposed by James Kay, "In Whose Name?," 524–33.

TRINITY AND MUTUALITY

Fig. 6.2

Now, Bingen's picture, like many pictures of the Trinity, shows a characteristic inability to render the Trinity fully, as a single figure with circles is limited in what it conveys just as classic icons of three persons, whether in heaven or in different Gospel scenes, often fails to depict the oneness of being. Nevertheless, for Bingen, Wisdom is the imminent providence of God, the love that formed and empowered creation. However, Wisdom is also linked with the figures of Mary, the church, and Love itself, and so, Wisdom is the unfolding of creation from God as well as the enfolding back of creation to Christ. Barbara Newman comments:

> But the trope remains irrepressibly feminine in context. The three archetypal mothers in Hildegard's visions—Caritas, Mary, Ecclesia—all bring God into the world in the flesh. Thus, Christ is predestined of eternal love, who creates the world to provide the substance of his body; in the fullness of time he is born once of the Virgin and continually of the church, until his mystical body is fulfilled. Through these concordant images of maternity, Hildegard expressed her conviction that the universe exists for the sake of the incarnate Christ. The eternal feminine, in

her several guises, links God's coming into the world with the world's own coming to be.[43]

In modern theology, Bulgakov suggests in a more systematic exposition that Sophia is the Glory of God's being, God's *ousia*; thus, similar to how God had Spirit as well as is Spirit, God has Sophia and is Sophia. The Father connotes the origin principle, the Son as the Logos of Wisdom, and the Spirit as the breath of life and the revealer of the Son, the love between Father and Son, even Love, Truth, and Beauty itself. As these things, the Spirit is the site of creation and God coming together, God's glory. Thus, "in summing up, we can say that the entire Holy Trinity in its tri-unity 'is Sophia,' just as all three hypostases are in their separateness."[44]

Whether in gender-neutral terms, in creative uses of motherly imagery, or the figure of Wisdom, there are supplementary patterns of language churches can use that can add depth to the trinitarian expression of the Christian life, ones that reiterate the Christ-centred character of revelation, the loving essence of God, and the presence of God's saving initiative with all creation.

LIVING THE TRINITY

As the previous sections already suggest, the way Christians refer to the Trinity prompts a certain way of living. Here, reference suggests usage. The Father symbol cannot be taken to promote hierarchal relations between men and women, and it will be necessary to comment briefly on several texts to offer this clarification. The movements of the Trinity suggest an ethic of mutuality that humans are to participate in, and so, the love of the Trinity shown in different titles can inspire this oneness.

Trinity without Hierarchy

The Father cannot mean an ontological hierarchy in God's being, nor does it suggest one for humans to live out. Scriptures such as 1 Cor 15:28 ("When all things are subjected to him, then the Son himself will also be subjected to the one who put all things in subjection under him, so that God may be all in all") speak of Christ's subjection to the Father, and

---

43. Newman, *Sister of Wisdom*, ch. 2.
44. Bulgakov, *Sophia*, 53.

this is often coupled with Eph 5 to suggest that the male occupies the position of Christ (or God), and the female occupies the position of the church in submission to its head. However, it must be clarified what this means in the scope of Pauline thought and the wider New Testament.

There is a dynamic in the persons of the Trinity that makes a hierarchal construal of human gender problematic. If to be Lord is to have authority, there is no authority one member has that the others do not. To merely say that the Father has authority or power over the Son runs the risk of suggesting two wills within God. The implication is multiple gods. Or, to say that divinity has attributes of authority and power and the Father has authority that the Son does not is to espouse a type of semi-Arianism where the Father is more God than the Son.[45] Why does the Father not "submit" to the Son then? It seems that for Paul, the Father is not subject to the Son because the Father remains transcendent from history, functioning as the reference point to Jewish monotheism that Jesus fulfills. Thus, the subjection of Christ is framed this way as part of his kenosis of the incarnation in history. As Phil 2 says, Jesus,

> who, though he existed in the form of God,
> did not regard equality with God
> as something to be grasped,
> but emptied himself,
> taking the form of a slave,
> assuming human likeness.
> And being found in appearance as a human,
> he humbled himself
> and became obedient to the point of death—
> even death on a cross. (Phil 2:6–8)

The language of "taking on the form of a slave" and "becoming obedient" because he assumed "human likeness" is pivotal. Philippians 2 continues, "Therefore God exalted him even more highly and gave him the name that is above every other name" (Phil 2:9). Subordination again cannot be understood as a description of the immanent Trinity, as the name that Jesus is given (an allusion to Isa 45:23) is the very name of God. Jesus did not become divine in the exaltation any more than Jesus was subordinate to God before creation. He "took on the form of a slave," but in so doing, is revealed in the plane of history to be the very Wisdom and Power of God (1 Cor 1:24). In other words, there is a historical kenosis, but this

---

45. This is the warning of Giles, "The Trinity Argument for Women's Subordination." Also see Erickson, *Whose Tampering with the Trinity?*

is not Jesus becoming less divine. It is the narrative display of giving up prerogatives of status and power for the sake of humanity that reveals the eternal essence of God. Paul employs this hierarchal framing to explain the mission of the Son, but in so doing, also overturns subordination as the Son and Spirit (cf. 2 Cor 3:17) are fully Lord.[46]

To overemphasize the pattern of authority from Father to Son as to suggest a hierarchy in the very being of God is to fail to see the theme of mutuality and reciprocity used to describe the Trinity, which both seem to be the most applicable dimension of trinitarian language for gendered relations and more closely approximates the immanent Trinity. In the Garden, the man sees the woman and proclaims she is bone of his bones and flesh of his flesh (Gen 2:23), to have her described as the one he "clings to," leaving his father and mother to become "one flesh," all suggests a repudiation of hierarchy: that man needs his other, rescuing him from loneliness, depending on her for strength, seeing his identity in her. This ideal is broken in the curse of sin as the relationship now is characterized by domination and power over (Gen 3:16). However, this ideal of reciprocity and mutuality is recaptured in the Song of Songs, where the bride says, "My beloved is mine, and I am his" (Song 2:16). This is a relationship of mutual procession, not hierarchy, and it is this ideal that comes through in Paul's description of marriage in 1 Cor 7 in addressing sexual immorality in the church:

> But because of cases of sexual immorality, each man should have his own wife and each woman her own husband. The husband should give to his wife what is due her and likewise, the wife to her husband. For the wife does not have authority over her own body, but the husband does; likewise, the husband does not have authority over his own body, but the wife does. (1 Cor 7:2–4)

Meanwhile, this dynamic is used to describe the relationship between Father and Son in John's Gospel. Jesus says, "Believe me that I am in the Father and the Father is in me" (John 14:10) as well as "All mine are yours, and yours are mine" (John 17:10—notice the difference John's framing is from Paul's in 1 Cor 15). This reciprocal relationship suggests that while the Son is subordinate to the Father as a human being in history, doing his will as the servant Messiah, showing the pattern to follow for his disciples, as the imminent revelation of the transcendent God, Jesus and the Father are one (John 10:30) to the point that when one looks at the Son

---

46. A point made by Hill, *Paul and the Trinity*, ch. 4.

the Father is seen. All that one has, the other has also. Just as Paul emphasizes both Son and Spirit are truly Lord, the Johannine emphasis suggests they are persons *through* each other in ways human persons are not but are called to emulate, as we can see from the use of imagery. Within the Trinity, the persons are not individuals, as humans are enclosed centers of consciousness. There is something mysterious about "persons" in the God who transcends created things and ultimately is not divided, composite, or anything material the way humans are persons with brains and bodies. God's persons (*hypostases*) are one in being (*ousia*), and thus, this being is understood as centres of relationship and interaction that reveal the oneness of God's love in a narrative of threefold dynamism. In this oneness of being, there is a "perichoresis" of the persons in each other and through each other that believers are invited into.[47] To use the title "Father" is to recognize that the first member of the Trinity is identified with a relationship: the Father is the Father through the Son and with the Son, eternally. The persons are "subsistent relationships."[48] However, as already stated, this relationship cannot be literalized as to suggest a human correlate: the Son is the Word of the Father (John 1:1), and the Son is the visible image of the invisible God (Col 1:15). The Father does not exercise authority in the human sense over the Son, since the Son is the very being of the Father's will, one transcendent and the other imminent to history. Again, there is no correlation between male and female human persons (unless a complementarian is satisfied with a man withdrawing and exercising no other agency other than through his wife).

Thus, while Paul does use a hierarchal framing to discuss the Trinity's position of persons vis-à-vis history, the import of human relationships actually minimizes hierarchy. We have already noted that the Father symbol functions in a patriarchal culture to expand the scope of family relations, positing God's universal human family coming together in the church over divided tribal human families. Within the New Testament, the conventions of the family (where the father is the provider) are used in an ideal way to speak about God as providing. This conventional metaphor is then expanded to identify others as being a part of the family of God, and the Father symbol, as defined by the love of God in Christ, reinfuses the metaphor to be an imperative of moral action for believers to emulate as children of God. This is an important way that by setting up

---

47. Fiddes, *Participating in God*, 71–78.
48. Fiddes, *Participating in God*, 34.

the Father as vertically "over" humanity, there is a horizontal extension of love beyond the patriarchs' reach.

Furthermore, in 1 Corinthians, the hierarchal framing is also used in chapter 11: "Christ is the head of every man, and the man is the head of the woman, and God is the head of Christ" (1 Cor 11:3). It should be noted that "head" (Gk. *kalephe*) is used more often to suggest source like the head of a river as the one line suggests: "For just as woman came from man, so man comes through woman, but all things come from God" (1 Cor 11:12). However, headship certainly coincides with authority, and while this passage has been used to set up a hierarchy of men over women, the point of this passage is the opposite. In keeping with proper cultural decorum (cf. 1 Cor 11:16), women ought to have a head covering as a sign of their authority on their heads (a logic that Paul admits is not universal in the churches, only in this local, cf. 1 Cor 11:16). This does not speak of their subjection, however, as Paul describes women "praying and prophesying" (1 Cor 11:5) and thus, women are with authority, not under authority. As Cynthia Westfall points out, this passage is very similar in content to 1 Esd 4:11–17, which speaks of the Jewish concept of how women are the glory of men, not in the sense of "glorifying" men as superior in authority, but rather suggesting a form of power women have over men as their glory.[49] Paul's discussion on headship, hair, origins, shame, and authority—logic that is lost to contemporary readers as it relates to Corinthian customs—is that "in the Lord woman is not independent of man or man independent of woman" (1 Cor 11:11), reiterating the same logic of mutuality as 1 Cor 7:2–4 only through a reciprocal notion of headship and glory.

Similarly, in Eph 5, while this passage recommends the wife submitting to the husband "as to the Lord, for the husband is the head of the wife just as Christ is the head of the church, his body, and is himself its Savior" (Eph 5:22–23) this hierarchal framing in context minimizes male domination compared to the culture, suggesting mutuality is the trans-cultural principle. In the passage before it, the task of submission is not just for women but for everyone: "Submit to one another out of reverence for Christ" (5:21). Similarly, at the top of this whole discourse in the passage, everyone is to "walk in the way of love, just as Christ loved us and gave himself up for us" (5:2). In other words, wives submitting to men and men loving their wives are just mirrored examples of

---

49. Westfall, *Paul and Gender*, 67.

both being called to love in a Christlike way. The guiding principle of this passage is that all Christians submit and love one another, regardless of gender. While the contemporary reader tends to feel the force of the statements on submission (and it was argued in chapter 4 why these should not be absolutized unless the possibility of resurrection liberation is denied in our context), this is not what would have been the rhetorical force for the original audience. Ephesians 5–6 is very likely framed as a household code like the one in Aristotle's *Politics*, where Aristotle argues that a proper household is one where women submit to men, children to parents, and slaves to masters. It reads,

> Of household management, we have seen that there are three parts—one is the rule of a master over slaves, . . . another of a father, and the third of a husband. A husband and father rules over wife and children, both free, but the rule differs, the rule over his children being a royal, over his wife a constitutional rule. For although there may be exceptions to the order of nature, the male is by nature fitter for command than the female, just as the older and full-grown is superior to the younger and more immature. . . . [W]hen one rules and the other is ruled we endeavor to create a difference of outward forms and names and titles of respect. . . . The relation of the male to the female is of this kind, but there the inequality is permanent.[50]

The difference between the two is fundamental. Aristotle believes in a state of permanent inequality; Paul uses the framing of a household code that his culture would understand but he emphasizes reciprocity through it. The accountability of the Ephesian household code is altogether absent in the household codes of Greek culture, suggesting this is the transcultural element. Ephesians adds that men must love their wives self-sacrificially like their very body (5:28), parents must not embitter their children (6:4), and masters must respect their slaves the same way the slaves ought to toward them (6:9), knowing that they have a master to be accountable to (6:9).

It seems that Paul uses hierarchal frames in order to polemicize them (and thus deconstruct them), yet so often modern complementarians gravitate to the former while forgetting the later.

---

50. Aristotle, *Politics*, Book I; ch. 12, in *The Complete Works of Aristotle*.

Mutuality in Self-Giving Love

Thus, in looking at the dynamic of mutual procession and in-dwelling in the Trinity, people, whether the church in general or individuals in marriage, are not called to fit into a Father-Son trinitarian relationship but are called to participate in the dynamic of self-giving love that the Son reveals to humanity as the very essence of God. John writes,

> As you, Father, are in me and I am in you, may they also be in us, so that the world may believe that you have sent me. The glory that you have given me I have given them, so that they may be one, as we are one, I in them and you in me, that they may become completely one. (John 17:21–23)

John suggests that the *oneness* of the Father and Son is what is to be emulated by the church, and this is a oneness of self-giving love for one another.

The closest approximation that the New Testament writers are surmising in their cultural context may be what Desmond Tutu spoke of in using the African proverb "ubuntu."[51] Ubuntu means that people are people through other people. This is not the same as the notion of perichoretic personhood in the Trinity, but it may be the closest analogy. Tutu utilized this in his own context to communicate the notion that racial division undermined common humanity and that the only victory possible was through seeing the success of the other as fundamental to one's own success, that there could be no betterment of society that excluded another or left another behind. For John's Gospel to implore the church to see itself as one as God is one, for marriage to be a oneness of flesh in a similar sense, and ultimately for this to influence all relationships in society, longing for God to be all in all, means seeing mutuality and reciprocity, the giving of oneself for the sake of the other and the receiving of help from the other to be more fully oneself, as the call to live a manner of godliness that resembles the Triune God's love.

To see that marriage approximates the oneness of God in becoming "one flesh" (Eph 5:31) invites the intimacy of marriage and the intimacy of God to form a mutually enriching interplay. As Rowan Williams explains, this invites human relationships into the movements of Triune love, where the interaction of bodies forms occasions of grace through acts of trust, acceptance, delight, and care. He writes,

---

51. Tutu, "Ubuntu," in *God Is Not a Christian*, 21–24.

> Grace, for the Christian believer, is a transformation that depends in large part on knowing yourself to be seen in a certain way: as significant, as wanted. The whole story of creation, incarnation, and our incorporation into the fellowship of Christ's body tells us that God desires us, *as if we were God*, as if we were that unconditional response to God's giving that God's self makes in the life of the Trinity. We are created so that we may be caught up in this, so that we may grow into the wholehearted love of God by learning that God loves us as God loves God. The life of the Christian community has as its rationale—if not invariably its practical reality—the task of teaching us to so order our relations that humans beings may see themselves as desired, as the occasion of joy.[52]

This suggests a self in-process where the true self is found in the other, coming to a particular focus in marriage but also in the family-like bonds of community. As suggested in an earlier chapter, this is what Stanley Grenz called the "ecclesial self," where the meaning of oneself is worked out in a relationship with others in the process of anticipating the final day of God being all in all.[53]

Toward this end, the New Testament's language of Father and Son communicates a form of love that points to the cross where the Son reveals the very essence of God as self-giving: the pattern for both men and women. God is for sinful humanity, unreservedly. Sadly, this language has been misunderstood as suggesting that the male is positioned over the female, which is fundamentally out of step with the reciprocal oneness described in Genesis and Song of Songs, as well as the kind of kenotic love the Son showed for humanity.

Furthermore, there is a way of understanding the Trinity that often characterizes humanity as inconsequential to God. Yet, Jesus uses the parable of the lost coin, likening God to a poor, desperate woman trying to find money (Luke 15:8–10). Perhaps it is the sum of her savings or her dowry. Either way, the money is crucial to her sustenance and future. While God is free as the living God, irreducible to creation, God is also the God who freely binds Godself to creation, becoming one with sinful humanity at the cross. While the classical language implies this, the Bible reiterates this also with feminine and motherly metaphors: "Can a woman forget her nursing child or show no compassion for the child of

---

52. See Williams, "The Body's Grace," 311–12.
53. Grenz, *Social God and Relational Self*, 322.

her womb? Even these might forget, yet I will not forget you" (Isa 49:15). If Christ died in the position of a sinner, becoming a curse (Gal 3:13), the sinner *qua* sinner is loved with the same love that the Father has for the Son, so perfect that even if a mother may forget her child, God the perfect Mother does not.

Emphasis on the Wisdom of God also reiterates this. If the Spirit is the Spirit of life, the basis of all things, Bulgakov insists that what he calls "creaturely Sophia" (that is, creation existing through the Spirit, even creation in estrangement from the Father) is, by God's free choice, not to be forsaken by God's salvific will. While true Wisdom is freely chosen, Bulgakov's use of Sophia reiterates the desire of God for "the complete penetration of the creature by Wisdom, the manifestation of the power of Divine-humanity in the whole world."[54] That is to say that by affirming the full extent of Sophia for the Trinity, Bulgakov reminds the church that God desires all things to be redeemed with a love the sees God's self in all that is not God. If gendered metaphors can open our eyes to God and enable humans to participate in this kind of love—and Scripture and tradition insist they can—then such love can be communicated and fostered through both male and female imagery. While New Testament use of Father language is not intended to support or reinforce patriarchy, Sophia or motherly references interrupt the kind of patriarchal usage that is sadly commonplace.

Thus, the use of Father language, as well as Mother and Sophia supplements, suggest the opposite of domination or a hierarchy within the genders. The deepest contours of trinitarian thought suggest the essence of God is perfect love, a love that refuses to abandon humanity, inspiring a way of life where mutuality and reciprocity are constitutive to what it means to be human.

CONCLUSION

The word Father in its trinitarian presentation in the Bible is a title that has layers of meaning. To address God as Father is to use the analogy that begins in the Old Testament and develops into a prayer convention in intertestamental times. When Jesus uses it, it indicates his identity as the messianic "Son." In this regard, Father language is not inherently offensive and is important for understanding the redemptive—indeed, the

54. Bulgakov, *Sophia*, 147.

counter-patriarchal—contour of the Bible. The metaphor shows ethically expansive dimensions, particularly important for the inclusion of the gentiles in Paul's congregations. Understood in the full canonical context, it does not bolster patriarchy but rather speaks of God's self-giving love, a mutuality that human relationships are called to emulate. While the title Father is standard for the New Testament, it is not exclusive. As that trinitarian language flows from the doxological activities of the church, believers are at liberty to praise God using alternative scriptural vocabularies that speak of God's loving, redemptive activity in their lives. Three examples are offered here (gender-neutral terms, the title Mother, and the figure of Wisdom), but there are surely more.

7

Conclusion

How do we speak of God with gendered language? Is it possible to speak of God with feminine language? How do these patterns of language affect us as gendered people? It has been the work of this project to explore and clarify how this is possible. In pursuing this task, we have looked at two sides. One side has insisted on exclusively male language, and the other has sought to replace male language with female language, seeing male language as inherently patriarchal. What this project has insisted on is that male language is not inherently offensive, but it also ought not be exclusive. Meanwhile, female language is biblically possible, a notion many in church history have expanded upon.

A RECAP OF THE ARGUMENTS

In the first chapter, it was shown that Christian speech is possible because of revelation. However, Christian speech is intended to be liberating also, and this debate is really caused by a clash between these two rules. Conservatives defend male-exclusive language because they see it as biblical; meanwhile, feminists defend feminine language because it is liberating. However, this presents a false dichotomy between reference and pragmatics. In understanding this, this book sets out to analyze the "grammar" of speech about God, recognizing that Scripture offers multiple grammars, and thus figures and pathways, to think and speak about God. Understanding the embodied site of language, the interplay between reference and usage, Scripture and experience, offers a holistic path forward.

In the second chapter, it was shown that both sides appeal to the notion that God is ineffable and transcendent to build their case. One states that if God is transcendent, only the words of Scripture may be used to refer to God; the other argues that if God is ineffable, words fail and could be particularly idolatrous if intending to render God as male. We saw that a certain allergy on the part of some to the mystical is unwarranted. In fact, God's ineffability is the content of revelation, not something that bypasses it. Looking to Dionysius, one of the most important minds in mystical theology, language can and must be used in theology, but there must also be an awareness that all language falls short. Often negation with an opposite is a common strategy for understanding the fuller sense of the mystical. Could Father language be idolatrous? It was shown that the things of God can be misused, and so, the question becomes, what is the strategy to counter the idolatrous: reiterate a non-idolatrous understanding or negate it in an act of iconoclasm? The two camps appeal to their preferred strategy. What these say, however, to human nature is important. The very root of the soul is God's Spirit, the breath of life, and it is one echo that causes humans to long for divine union. Patriarchy, in reducing God to the creation and elevating male power to god-like status, is idolatrous and causes spiritual death. Thus, to negate idolatrous images of God will cause and must involve the negation of distorted images of the self.

Chapter 3 explored the nature of metaphor, analogy, and narrative in contemplating God. Again, while different theologians appeal to these structures in different ways, certain impasses arise. Looking further at the notion of metaphor gave the clarification that metaphorical language need not be viewed as a de-actualizing revelation. On the other hand, the claim that God cannot, analogically, be understood in feminine and motherly ways fundamentally undermines the created goodness of these things, let alone the fact that both men and women are in God's image. What was found is that Aquinas's analogical way is a powerful linguistic operation to reflect on God's being, but Aquinas's own theology improperly prioritized the masculine, albeit not to the degree that Aristotle did. There are both feminine and motherly analogies and metaphors in Scripture that warrant attention and reflection. However, the objection has been that analogies and metaphors can be prone to projection. To this, we noted that the biblical narrative offers the context where the saving acts of God are the basis of realistic reference. This does not mean Christians appeal to the narrative as frozen or static; rather, the story of Scripture opens one up to the nature of God, that is, the truth of every truth. Thus, it is through the biblical narrative that human experience can be incorporated into and configured by divine love. It is the narrative travail of Scripture that offers the best context for understanding the fatherly love of God as well, a title that is in its beginning an accommodation to the culture of patriarchy but moves redemptively forward in the covenant of David and the claiming of Israel as God's children, despite their waywardness. These form the vital context for and center point in the next rule of grammar.

Chapter 4 examined the Christological figure as the apex of Christian speech. Some see Jesus' maleness as the ultimate defeater of female language for God, while others see the maleness of Jesus as inessential, something that must be surmounted. Similarly, some see the cross of Jesus as a symbol of submission, while some feminists see the cross as abusive and needs to be abandoned. Here, we say that Christology is very much founded on the historical Jesus, but Jesus' maleness is properly counter-patriarchal, for he is the Servant King who empties himself. Moreover, the very structure of the incarnation, as Clement of Alexandria pointed out, shows that God's presence is upon all flesh, making female Christological references possible, as long as they do not intend to ignore the historical Jesus. Instead, artistic depictions, such as Edwina Sandys's *Christa*, may aid in countering distorted understandings of the cross, ones that continue the scapegoating of women.

Chapter 5 examines the discourses around the Holy Spirit, particularly the figure often identified with the Spirit, Sophia or Lady Wisdom. By far the most multifaceted grammar, the Spirit is connected to the breath of life, the Shekinah, the presence of motherly love, and the presence of truth, beauty, love, etc., which have their own ramifications for gendered speech. However, it is Sophia that is the most complicated as Sophia is a figure that develops significantly from Proverbs and texts like the Wisdom of Solomon into the New Testament. Yet, it is this figure that offers the most significant evidence of female language for God, particularly on the lips of Jesus. Thus, while the Spirit is the Spirit of Christ, warranting male language, there are other patterns throughout Scripture and church history that suggest feminine usages as well, ones that can be used to dignify the experience of women as well as speak of the truth of the Spirit in other cultures.

CONCLUSION

Chapter 6 brings previous chapters together in looking at the trinitarian framing of Christian discourse. By this, it is meant that in the narrative of the Bible, revelation displays three identities in a relationship. As we saw, the first member of the Trinity is sometimes argued to be "named" the Father, but when the Gospels are investigated, this is clarified: it is not a name but rather an analogical title rooted in the grammar discussed in chapter 3. However, the title takes on a unique usage in Jesus' life, referring to Jesus' messianic Sonship, as well as the Christian community, where believers are adopted into a new family. Understood this way, Father language is not offensive, but, again, it is not exclusive. Father language ought not to suggest a hierarchy in the imminent Trinity nor one in human gendered relations. Supplementary language is explored, such as motherly references or the figure of Sophia, both of which can reiterate the essence of the triune God, which is self-giving love for all.

Revisiting Grammars of Revelation and Liberation in Communal Practice

As chapter 1 noted, this debate has largely been the result of a perceived clash between the rules of revelation and liberation in the Christian community's speech about God. Now, at the end of this study, it is appropriate to briefly revisit how these grammars are shown in the lived practice of Bible study and discernment, worship and prayer, as well as what a fuller picture of liberation then looks like.

The pathway to better language about God is not to discard the Bible but to reflect on it and appreciate all its richness and roughness, discerning its deeper grammar beyond proof-texting methods. This book, then, implicitly prescribes certain pathways in studying Scripture as a community discerns the experience of its members. The grammar sketched out suggests the following emphases as disciples gather around the Scripture: (1) Begin with the fundamentals of God's character: God is ineffable and transcendent, and so, God is beyond creation and gender. God cannot be reduced to these things, but when God is, this forms the potential for an idol. Yet, God is love, and God freely draws near to humanity, refuting any agnosticism on the issue. God has spoken, and God has revealed. (2) Thus, the Bible shows that the goodness of creation speaks of God's goodness, and more specifically, humanity—made in God's image, male and female—reflects God. Human experience and creation can form metaphors and analogies that communicate God's love. How do we know that a metaphor or analogy is being faithful? The narrative of God's action with humanity offers the particularity and context that fleshes out the meaning of these. The narratives of Scripture, as we noted, are polysemous and multilayered. As the church is invited to reflect on the goodness of God's character in the narratives, so also a church needs to reflect on the "dark" passages, such as the narratives of Hagar, Tamar, Jephthah's daughter, and such like. Both the dark and ambiguous passages, as well as the clear passages, need to be read. In this regard, the Bible reflects the human condition as it both records our fallenness and encourages us in the journey to God's redemption, inviting our stories to join and be transformed by God's Great Story. (3) God is known in Jesus Christ, and so, the example of Jesus spurs us on: his kingdom raises up the marginalized and warns the proud and the privileged they must humble themselves and become servants; he demonstrates the elevated status of women; his love is shown in the cross and he is revealed as the victor of sin in the resurrection. Jesus helps expose who our victims are. Moreover, (4) in looking at the figures of the Spirit and Sophia, particular how Jesus mentions her, the most solid case is made for understanding femininity in God. It is from these figures also that we reckon with the experience of life, love, and liberation, teaching us to accept truth whereever we find it as the truth of Christ. (5) By recovering a full-fledged trinitarian way of thinking in the church, the church is best equipped to use language that shows the full dignity of people by the fullness of God's revelation. Jesus' address to God as Father provides the avenue of rebuke against patriarchal meanings in a culture that still gravitates to patriarchy. The Trinity encourages life to be shaped by mutuality and reciprocity not hierarchy, and different pathways of language, whether motherly language or Sophia language, can further reiterate the unconditional love of God where conventional figures have been misused.

As the biblical work is being done, this project has insisted that feminine language is not the invention of modern liberalism. There are examples of theologians, mystics, and artists who have reflected on God using both genders. They have been mentioned along the way in this project. The icons and artwork offer powerful visual cues. Inclusive language is more about recovery than revision. It is not about taking offense at Father language; it is about saying and discovering that there is more to the story in Scripture and church history.

CONCLUSION

Understanding these different grammars means that scriptural interpretation must be done through communal discernment. Matthew 18:18, 1 John 4:1–3, and 1 Corinthians 14:29 suggest practices where the church had to discern prophecy and spiritual experiences using wise criteria.[1] We see an important example of this when the Jerusalem church decided to loosen the restrictions on gentile believers. While circumcision was a pivotal ordinance for the Hebrew people, the church discerned the presence of the Spirit and saw that this law's function was no longer applicable. The Spirit was poured out on all flesh, and the only criteria for this were not the observance of the Torah in its minutia. Rather, it was trusting in the grace of God revealed in Jesus Christ. For the church to decide this, one cannot overestimate its radicality. Today, communities are faced with discerning experiences of men and women in all sorts of issues. The voice of women and the ramifications of gender are our present subjects. Scripture does not shut down human experience but welcomes it into prayerful dialogue. No experience is infallible or obvious in meaning, just as no interpretation of Scripture or prophesy is, and that is why communal discernment is a necessary virtue. Communal discernment is one where every believer is able to speak and be heard. This stands both on the notion that all believers are priests, fully capable of representing Christ to each other, each person having soul liberty and reasonability to interpret according to their consciences, and each congregation is led by the Spirit to listen to the least of those in society as the community seeks to live out the kingdom of God.

This communal dimension is what first allowed women to preach in the Baptist churches of my own tradition.[2] As Freeman, McClendon, and Ewell note, "All believers are priests and so may pray for others, comfort the afflicted, or proclaim the gospel. But when it comes to speaking about God, this conviction has too often lacked a practice to sustain it."[3] Thus, they recommend the practice be used to its fullest measure in opening up the church to the voices of the marginalized, allowing them to speak on equal footing. This does not prevent bias and mob rule, but such a

---

1. Molly Marshall has exposited the nature of discernment quite helpfully in "Reading Scripture with the Spirit," 17–33.

2. See Freeman, *A Company of Women Preachers*.

3. Freeman, McClendon, and Ewell, *Baptist Roots*, 8. Also see Chilton and Harmon, eds., *Sources of Light: Resources for Baptist Churches Practicing Theology*. These are baptistic resources, but their practices of congregational reading are relevant to any Christian community.

practice is in sharp contrast with hierarchical approaches that have reinforced patriarchy and isolationism.

Communal discernment does not mean whatever a community decides is the new status quo, nor does it give a community the right to decide against the Word of God. Rather, it recognizes that the grammar of Christian speech and practice is diverse, multifaceted, fallible, and contextual. It means that incorporating feminine imagery into worship will not be based on a denominational authority or committee legislating it but rather on believers wrestling with each other, the Bible, the voices of the past, and the longings for the future. It will not move in heavy-handed unilateral ways but local ways, as a community reads texts together, prays at the liberty of the Spirit, and sings. The church will undergo an ongoing process of dealing with patriarchy and dignifying the marginalized, one that is never finished. Luke Timothy Johnson has described the process eloquently:

> We must let go of any fantasy concerning the church as a stable, predictable, well-regulated organization. If the church is truly the place in the world where the experience of God is brought to the level of narrative and discernment, then the church will always be disorderly, a family living under stress because it will as a community always be in transition between partial closure and openness, between the idolatry of institutional self-preservation and the obedience of faith in the living God. We must let go of the desire for theology to be a finished product or complete conceptual symmetry. If theology is, in fact, the attempt to understand living faith, then it must always be an unfinished process, for the data continues to come in, as the Living God persists in working through the lives of people and being revealed in their stories. We must let go of any pretense of closing of the New Testament within some comprehensive, all-purpose, singular reading which reduces its complexity to simplicity.... We must recognize our tendency to seek a stable package of meaning that we can then apply to other situations or fit within our systematic theological constructs so that, ideally, we need never really read the texts again. A conversion to an understanding of church theology and the reading of Scripture which is appropriate to faith in the Living God is one that is fully committed (though never fully realized, because the inertia of idolatry always pulls us backward) to the risk-filled, tricky, and unpredictable freedom of the Spirit.[4]

---

4. Johnson, *Scripture and Discernment*, 55.

CONCLUSION

All of this is done as a community, as disciples read Scripture honestly together. The church is not owned by the pastor or priest. The church is the people of God, the family of God gathered as disciples seeking to better themselves and each other in the leading of the Spirit. While the Spirit gives the church elders, teachers, and prophets, ultimately, the Spirit working in the entire community, not any one member, is the teacher.

Liberation, then, is not the projected preference of individuals nor merely the physical or political liberation as some would have it. The grammars of each chapter have suggested a fuller understanding of liberation, where we find our true selves in authentic relationship with God and others. Liberation is union with the God who is ineffable, from whom we know our souls, our whole persons, were meant for more. Liberation is the freedom of self that is no longer seen as an object to have power over or worthy only because one has power. It is freedom from idolatry and sin. Liberation is the dignity that is prompted when all of the goodness of created life is seen for what it is, reflecting the goodness of God. Liberation is the result of any practice that upholds the full dignity of the person as made in the image of God. Liberation is what God enacts in the narratives of Scripture, such as the exodus and resurrection. Liberation is when the way of Christ is taken up, whether the powerful emptying themselves of privilege or the promise of the resurrection breaking in, lifting the lowly up. Liberation is the new possibilities of life that are breathed into us from the Spirit, inspiring new wise ways of effectively following God in love and truth. Liberation is participating in the relationship of the Triune God; oneness like God is being one in the love of the other, the kind of love that God has between Father and Son, an often mother-like love that refuses to let God's children go. In the love of the Triune God, liberation is living out the flow of self-giving love that seeks the success of the self in and through the success of all people. Liberation is understood *through* the figures of Scriptures, not despite them. Liberation looks like the exodus rescue, kingdom empowerment, effective wisdom, cross-shaped solidarity, resurrection hope, Triune love, and Spirit-filled joy.

As suggested, the seeking of liberation, as it is guided by the figures of Scripture, similarly forms the lived data for discerning the correct reading of the Scriptures. Again, this occurs in a community that is prepared to discern, and one manner that is essential to this endeavor is forming the kind of community that listened in a mode of gentleness. It is not enough to disavow violence as a Christian way of life for coercion can take the form of things like exclusion, intimidation, gaslighting, and other forms of emotional manipulation. Liberation is chosen in communities where there is a practice that contends with differences, with the deliberate restraint from attempts to control, such that a person is valued despite their views. This should not mean the refusal of measures to protect vulnerable people, but it does suggest that the only kind of transformation than truly corresponds to the grammars discussed is one within a community that practices love, acceptance, and forgiveness in a radical, noncoercive way.[5]

Of course, seeing the acts of God in Scripture and in the midst of our communities ought to move us to worship. What this project envisions is the liberty in contemplation, prayer, and worship to use the imagery and language delineated in previous chapters to express union with God with the full measure of authenticity the reality of God and the human condition permits. This, again, reflect my own Baptistic sensibilities where the way a community worships will not be the result of committee deciding the prescribed language, but rather, the creative privilege of the people of God to worship in a way that expresses how God has acted in their midst, whether this is through a person contemplating in private, praying publicly according to their conscience, or the community hearing and responding to hymns and other aspects of the liturgy that reflects their discernment of Scripture. Again, the argument of this book is that there are good, non-patriarchal ways of referring to God, whether the Father, Son, or Spirit, yet there are multiple grammars that offer possibilities of female language which believers and congregations are at liberty to use as they feel called.

For many, the use of feminine language and imagery will be used primarily in contemplation, something discussed already in chapters 2 and 3. While many churches might not use feminine language in their liturgies, the encouragement of contemplating the ineffability of God over all gender and also feminine images of God will aid in realizing God's goodness in all that is good. To contemplate these images in all their benefits is perhaps the most important task of these grammars, and the least controversial.

What this project envisions is the liberty in contemplation, prayer, and worship to use the imagery and language delineated in previous chapters to express union with God with the full measure of authenticity

---

5. See Parker Palmer, *The Hidden Wholeness*.

the reality of God and the human condition permits. Prayer and worship, the very acts of speaking with God, can be done according to the grammar sketched out: we pray acknowledging God's revelation and transcendence; we worship ascribing God with analogical titles to praise God as the Good of every good; we sing responding to how God is revealed in Jesus Christ—the incarnation (Christ's presence in all flesh), cross, and resurrection; we praise in the Spirit, who is identified with Lady Wisdom, with Christ; we pray in Trinitarian manner, identifying God's movements of love.

Examples of what these prayers and worship could look like have been noted. Recall from the previous chapters that there is feminine imagery for God in worship. There are examples of prayers and artwork that reflect the members of the Trinity in feminine ways. In fact, some of the oldest hymns of the church in the *Odes of Solomon* did include feminine references for God, particularly God as Spirit. Recall that John Chrysostom uses the benediction, "Thou art my Father, thou art my Mother, thou my Brother, thou art Friend, thou art Servant, thou art House-keeper; thou art the All, and the All is in thee; thou art Being, and there is nothing that is, except thou."[6] Recall also that Anselm of Canterbury prayed, acknowledging Jesus as a mother.[7] This project has also noted pieces of art and iconography that have displayed feminine characteristics. More recent examples include William Cleary's work *Prayers to She Who Is*, which was inspired by the work of Elizabeth Johnson and stands as a wonderful collection of prayers, theological and scripturally rich. There have been inclusive hymnals, notably the work of Ruth Duck, whose work has been celebrated for its passion for justice.[8] In the last chapter, it was suggested a significant middle ground benediction is possible: "In the name of the Father, Son, and Holy Spirit, One God, Mother to us all."[9] This preserves the concern for the classic historical pattern of titles but also supplements it with feminine language, although since Father is not a name, there are many non-gendered ways of speaking that can still witness to the triune redemption in Christ. All of this suggests not

---

6. John Chrysostom, "Homilies on the Gospel of Saint Matthew," 447.

7. Anslem of Canterbury in "Prayers to Saint Paul," 396–98, in *The Prayers and Meditations of Saint Anselm with the Proslogion*, 153.

8. Ruth Duck has also written on accessibility and worship, which, while it is beyond the scope of this project, is still deeply connected. See her *Worship for the Whole People of God*.

9. Jones, *Grammar of Christian Faith*, 1:158–66.

so much that the worship of the church needs to be forgotten so much as continually supplemented with the creativity of God's people, and, ironically, adopting feminine language in prayer and worship is actually being faithful to the richness of tradition.

It was cautioned not to do so in a way that sought "re-symbolization" but rather scripturally normed supplementation. In other words, churches do not need to do away with male language, cease praying the "Our Father" and no longer baptizing in the "name of Father, Son, and Spirit," but churches can find creative ways of incorporating the richness of scriptural language, primed by the examples shown in church history. This is best done in scriptural discernment and in contemplation and prayer, not as mere individual practices but as communal practices that invite reflection, dialogue, discovery, and the liberty for people to express their faith in the context of a listening community. This encourages practices that seek liberation from the sin of patriarchy in the church, whether the work of enabling children to resist gender stereotyping and biblical literalism, supporting women's ordination and better representation in governments, or seeking support for childcare, one of the most common ways women are disadvantaged in society. There are, of course, many other ways, but these seem to be the most immediate. Whatever else this entails is up to the people of God to discern together.

FURTHER RESEARCH

This book has, admittedly, primarily focused on the grammar for speech about God and only suggested in a cursory manner what this means for human gender. However, with these grammars clarified, further work, both scholarly and practical, can be anticipated. Four seem most obvious for this researcher moving forward:

Throughout this work, feminist theology has been engaged. Radical forms have been critiqued, but more robust forms have been warmly embraced. While it is not my place to exposit the meaning of femininity (the grammar delineated in this book is intended to open a space of liberty), the meaning of masculinity and fatherhood is much more pertinent and applicable to me. Feminism has often not appreciated masculinity nor delineated it in the most helpful of ways. Similarly, the symbols of fatherhood still hold immense cultural importance, whether for good or for ill. All of this signals a greater theological exploration of the nature of masculinity and fatherhood in how both function in modern cultures and the church and how they ought to look when configured by these grammars.

While this project has focused on gender as a delimitation, along the way, an intersectional approach has been acknowledged, realizing that gender intersects with class, race, ability, etc. Patriarchy is a phenomenon of sin that intersects with cultural forces like racism, ableism, classism, nationalism, capitalism, colonialism, militarism, etc. As it has been stated, merely changing the church's language may or may not cause the deep kinds of transformation that lie deep in a community's institutional practices, ones that are practiced habitually but often not verbalized. Thus, the further work of a theology of gendered language for God is cultural criticism, integrating the work here with others in order to expose the ways patriarchy affects institutions and culture, both in and outside the church.

This project coincides with my work for an organization called the Atlantic Society for Biblical Equality, which was founded to primarily advocate for women's ordination in Atlantic Baptist circles, although its scope is now multidenominational. In the summer of 2023, as this draft was being written, the Canadian Baptists in the Atlantic elected their first female executive minister, Reneé MacVicar, who will lead a team of denomination-wide ministry leaders. The vote in affirmation was overwhelming (96 percent in favor), and it was announced with jubilation. It was truly a spiritual moment as people started singing hymns, and the whole assembly joined in. However, it is suspected that a large group of churches did not attend that year, and while many of the pastors (who are usually the delegates for the denominational assembly from the churches) are egalitarians, very few churches are led by a female pastor, indicating that there is still much the work to be done for advancing women's leadership in churches.

This work has only scratched the surface of a much larger and more complicated conversation on the nature of human gender. What does this language have to say about the realities of transgender and intersex individuals? I have used the notion of "strategic essentialism" in regards to male and female identities but also recognized that this binary can be, in many cases, an unhelpful construct as people pursue deeper forms of authenticity with God. What this means, admittedly, needs further exploration. Thus, this project is meant to be in many ways preliminary, anticipating further work.

A CONCLUDING PERSONAL POSTSCRIPT

I conclude with the story of how I came to contemplate God using feminine imagery. I have said that one ought not to impose experience onto or against the Bible but rather to allow Scripture to invite all our experiences into conversation with God's word. Mine is a very strange experience to share, both in that it is a deeply personal dimension of an often abstract and technical debate and also since my experience often does not fit the expectations.[10] Most people have bad relationships with their fathers, and that is why they gravitate toward Mother language for God, or so that assumption goes.

"All theology is biographical," the Baptist theologian James McClendon once said. Theology always happens from a particular place, a particular story. I recall the first time someone suggested that God was a mother. I was twenty or so and in seminary. I had never heard the suggestion until that time, twenty years after growing up in the church. At the time, I was ardently opposed to women's ordination. I was raised in a Baptist denomination (although we went to a number of evangelical churches through the years). My mother insisted on enrolling us in Bible camp and vacation Bible school, and I loved going. My grandfather helped form the Baptist denomination (the Fellowship of Evangelical Baptists), and it prided itself on its complementarianism, the conviction that men, by the nature of the gender, ought to have positional authority over women, whether in the home, in church (disallowing women from being ordained), or in the wider world. There was an order to things, male and female, and those who did not like this order were rebelling against the things that God designed to bring happiness. Men were supposed to be happy working and making decisions, whereas women were supposed to be happy mothering and submitting. This denomination also boasted of its high view of Scripture. The Bible was inerrant, and it could be understood with a high degree of certainty and clarity very quickly as assisted with prayer or the direction of some wiser pastoral teacher. Education in the Bible was not seen as a bad thing per se, provided it was done with close supervision and clear parameters. Otherwise, education causes doubt. When a friend of mine, whose soul I was a bit concerned about, suggested to me, while we were talking about a novel called *The Shack*, that God could be a "Mother" or even a "she," the notion struck

---

10. The following is a piece of a larger, forthcoming biographical work, *Faith in Fragments*, on my faith through what many call deconstruction.

me as ridiculous and dangerous. The unfamiliar is often dismissed this way. The person pointed out that the Holy Spirit in Proverbs is female—Lady Wisdom. I thought that was plainly absurd, a verse stretched out of context. I have learned that Scripture speaks true enough, but it takes years to listen, to listen past all the filtering one has inherited, and that the work of listening is never finished.

Not all was well at home growing up. My mother and father divorced during my teen years, and it was messy. My mother forced my dad out under a pretense as she was beginning to pursue another relationship. Several years later, she remarried a man who turned out to be abusive. He was charming at first, but the truth slowly emerged as arguments turned to screaming matches between my mother and him. This man was a bigot who believed his authority in the home was God-ordained and that women were, as he often would say, "stupid." He would belittle my mother and threaten to beat her.

My mother got cancer when I was in grade 12. My stepfather did not think she would live, and so he drained money from their accounts so that my mother would not use this money on health spending, and he could be "taken care of" after she was gone. However, the cancer went into remission, and she found out about that missing money. At the time, I was in Bible college, and I was very reluctant to think that any divorce was allowable except on the basis of adultery. However, one night, he and my mother were fighting. She was trying to convince him that they should get a divorce. It was getting quite heated, so my mother invited me into the room. I think she was afraid. In the end, I argued that it was best that he should go. He complained that he did nothing wrong. He defended himself by using the Bible. Divorce was unbiblical, where his ways were merely exercising his God-given authority. He had not cheated on her. In reality, he said, he was the one getting his heart broken. She was the one sinning, not him. Oddly, for whatever truncated reason, he had a regard for my pastoral training, and he and I talked. I convinced him that leaving would be the "peaceable" thing to do. He left, but since he and my mother co-owned a business, it made for several years of bitter legal fighting. The police were called on several occasions.

At the time, I did not connect complementarianism with the abusive ways of my stepfather. If anything, I reckoned, he was why real men need to be truly godly and Christlike in their leadership in the home. I was quite impressed with the theology of John Piper at the time. It had not occurred to me just how much an exclusively male depiction of God implicitly facilitates this vision of how the male is God in terms of authority and power used in the home. It is something that one really does not see until one sees alternatives to it.

As I continued on in seminary, I was influenced by the teaching of William Webb. Admittedly, I was deeply opposed to taking a class with him at first. He had written a book that called for the possibility of a dynamic reading of the Bible, a reading where the Bible's own movement permits and necessitates equality.[11] He called this approach "Redemptive-Movement Hermeneutic." This, I felt, was the worst form of liberalism, imposing a culture of feminism upon Scripture. In fact, as embarrassing as it is to admit, I wrote a paper for a class in my undergrad on why the college should fire him. I thought I was being courageous for the truth, but the professor of that class graciously invited me to rewrite the paper.

As you can imagine, as I continued on in seminary, I was working through a lot of issues in my thinking and in my life, the two being intertwined. I have always been a good student, and so I got through my undergrad in two and a half years. That also meant I had to take Dr. Webb's hermeneutics class at the graduate level. I recall pelting that poor man with question after question. He responded gently with careful exegesis and deliberation on not merely what the Bible says—as the approach I was raised with could easily shut down a conversation with a quick proof text—but also with why the Bible says what it says. I came to agree with the conviction that women could be ordained. This, I knew, would get me in trouble.

I did not think of myself as a fundamentalist at the time, but looking back, I realize I was (I recall thinking that I actually did agree with just about everything fundamentalists believed, but I didn't think I was as unreasonable or angry as they were). Similarly, no racist or sexist person ever thinks they are racist or sexist when they mask and justify these concerns with what they feel is the truth or what they think is right. I realized, looking back, that my "fundamentalism" took a mortal blow those days. Education can do that, but then again, some people come to seminary remarkably set on not learning anything new.

In my reading, I was deeply impressed by Dr. Webb's book, but also Stanley Grenz and Denise Muir Kjesbo's book, *Women in the Church*. I found myself convinced that the Bible, properly understood, supports the equality of women. Passages that I had read dozens of times appeared in a new light.

---

11. See Webb, *Slaves, Women, and Homosexuals*.

CONCLUSION

I had a good relationship with my father. My father worked the night shift and was not around so often. After my parents split up, I saw him less, but through high school, I started going to church with him and my stepmother, usually spending Sundays at his house. We got to be quite close. My father was the kind of person who, as he once said, was unconditionally proud as a father. I later found out it might have had something to do with how discouraging his own father was to him. Apparently, my grandfather, the fundamentalist Baptist preacher, was not a particularly warm parent. In the last year of my undergrad, my father came down with pancreatic cancer. He lived long enough to see me graduate.

Meanwhile, my mother left Christianity, seeing it as too narrow-minded. I felt that was strange in one regard, as the pastor of the church our family attended was very clear in his disapproval of her ex-husband and very supportive of my mother, along with a large community of Christians in my hometown. My mother grew increasingly erratic. She began to rant about conspiracies. She ran an alternative medicine clinic and slowly dived deeper and deeper into New Age practices. She considered the Christian faith too repressive, so she embarked on a journey of what she saw as self-liberation. She spent any money she could find on new-age medicine and natural supplements and went on cruises and trips. She began dating several men at the same time, one of which got her involved in the New Age group, the Unity Church. We argued often. She thought I was too narrow-minded as a Christian. Looking back, I associated her carefree libertine mentality with feminism.

In the fall of 2009, my mother's cancer finally prevailed after being in remission for a few years. My sister, who lived at home, would care for her through the week, while my wife and I tried our best to take care of her on the weekends. She died on December 17, and we had her funeral on the day before Christmas Eve.

In the days that followed, we found out the extent of both my mother's love interests and the amount of debts she accumulated. She owed money to people who did not think her passing away was any reason why they should come and collect the money from us instead. I had a lot of hurt and confused anger about the whole thing. As I said before, many think about God through the lens of a bad relationship with their father. Mine was the opposite.

Meanwhile, while my thinking was expanding, my denomination was intent on getting more closed. I got a job as a pastoral intern at Bradford Baptist Church during my studies. I also learned that Dr. Webb's contract was not renewed at the seminary. The suspicions as to why were obvious. Members of the board of the college were a part of the association I pastored in, and they bragged openly to their buddies about how they "got rid of the liberal."

I piped up one time over lunch at an association meeting: "But what about Junia? It seems fairly clear that she is listed as an apostle in Romans 16." I did not know at the time that the preferred translation of complementarianism was now the ESV, which modified that passage. But when I voiced what it stated in Greek, one leader asked me, in turn, deeply concerned, "So, when did the demon of feminism first infect your mind?"

At the time, I was working toward becoming a church planter, but when denominational leaders found out I was in support of women in ministry, I received several clear ultimatums. I recall having coffee with one denominational leader, and I protested the notion that the denomination should take such hard-line stances on these kinds of things rather than let the individual churches decide. At the time, I was content to see doctrine coming before ethics, a dichotomy that I have realized is unsupportable (as this book shows). Thus, I said, "Why can't we let doctrines like the Trinity define us rather than fighting about gender roles?" To which I was told, "Spencer, for our denomination, gender roles are more important to the gospel than the Trinity." Shocked, I protested further, "You know I used to hold what you hold. Who's to say that if you read and studied what I have studied, you won't agree with me?" The person I was speaking with prided themselves in not reading books of any academic nature (despite somehow having a doctor of ministry from an evangelical seminary). Nevertheless, he responded, "Spencer, the Bible is clear when you have the Holy Spirit. I don't need to read anything else." The implication was, of course, that I did not have the Holy Spirit. The conversation ended with an ultimatum: if I continued to talk about women's equality, my funding as a church planter would be cut. When I got home, I told my wife that I was going to have to leave this denomination. I knew my internship contract was about up, so I began applying elsewhere. For our young family, money was tight; my wife and I were already working several jobs each to pay the bills, and the notion of not having work, or not enough work, was terrifying, but we knew that this was something that had to be done. That day reiterated to me just how much gender and God, language and action, are very much intertwined.

By this time, I was working on doctoral studies at Wycliffe College, University of Toronto. There, I found myself exploring other Christian traditions. I wanted nothing to do with the fundamentalism I was raised with. I took philosophy courses at the university and at an affiliate institution, the Institute for Christian Studies, where I studied post-structuralism, critical theory, and hermeneutics. I realized that I loved reading philosophy, but I was, at the end of the day, a theologian. I found myself gravitating toward thinkers like Karl Barth, Wolfhart Pannenberg, Robert Jenson, and Jürgen Moltmann. At Wycliffe, we read George Lindbeck and Hans Frei, and I was introduced to the term "postliberal," a term that named my growing concerns as I explored the liberal side of theology. I was not a conservative, but I also realized I was not a liberal either. I recall taking George Sumner's class on Pannenberg, where one week, an extended discussion occurred regarding Pannenberg's disapproval of female language for God. I recall feeling uneasy about the arguments made, even those that were quite familiar, but it was this class that got me thinking more about the present topic in a more academic sense. Reading feminists—or at least reading feminists well—was a long way off, I must confess, as I still had a deep allergic reaction to the place of experience in theology (the irony is that kind of sensibility is often based on a very particular set of experiences also). For many years I inhabited comfortably many of the views that have been surveyed and critiqued in this project. But, as Clark Pinnock would say, in the journey of theology, some are settlers, while others are pilgrims. It seems like I just could not stay in one place.

People process anger in strange ways. I found myself retreating into my studies as an escape at times, but life and thought for someone with a personality like mine always have a way of joining back together. Reading Jürgen Moltmann's *Crucified God* taught me how to mourn, as odd as that may sound. Many times, I would just sit in the courtyards of the university and just reflect and process my grief. One of the best courses I took was on Christian mystics, which I took toward the end of my coursework. I got to read through Dionysus and Gregory of Nyssa (names that have turned up in this project for good reason). These writers taught me there was something unspeakable about God, and that insight was so needed in times when I did not know what to think or say about God.

In particular, it was Julian of Norwich's *Showings* that really struck me. I simply did not know what to do with her visions of God as Mother. I had a deep regard for her person, a saint of the church, but how could she say these things? In my mind, I was an egalitarian, not a feminist.

There was a difference, and calling God Mother was one of them. But what if this respected saint of the church was correct? It was an odd thing. I was supportive of women in ministry, but because of my experiences with my mother and because so much of my paradigm for thinking about God was the result of my complementarian upbringing, I had a deep suspicion toward feminism and anything that could be associated with it (feminism being something that devalued men and rejected the Bible). This was, however, an unfair assumption to make. But Norwich's ideas were seeds planted. I remember praying, "God, you are a Father. You aren't a mother. Are you?"

Later on, I was at our family's home, going through some old boxes of stuff from my childhood that I had left there when I went away to college. My sister was living there now and wanted all the clutter cleaned out. Going through an old box of books, I happened upon the book *Love You Forever* by Robert Munch. It is about a mother who would sing this song to her child at night through all the difficult stages of that boy's life: infancy, being a rambunctious toddler, a rebellious teenager, etc. She would sing,

> I love you forever,
> I like you for always,
> As long as I am living,
> My baby you'll be.

It was a book that my mother had read many times to me, and as I read it, I cried. I knew then that all the turmoil that happened at the end of my mother's life was forgivable. It was not her fault, and the stuff that was her fault simply did not take away from the fact that I knew she loved us kids. It also struck me that the love she had was a gift from God. Where there was the gift of love, there was God's very being. I remember praying, "Thank you, God, for my mother. Thank you for her love in my life, which was also your love. Thank you for your perfect love revealed in Jesus Christ. Thank you, God, that you are the perfect Mother to us all. Amen." From that day, I began to explore the arguments for feminine language for God in more detail, seeing, as I have shown, that certain arguments work and others do not.

When I began pastoring First Baptist Church of Sudbury and was also brought on two years later to the faculty of an Anglican institution there, Thorneloe University, I realized it was time to grapple with feminist thinking, to engage in some "faith seeking understanding" in regard to a sensibility that was long past due for me to sit and unpack and reflect on. This project grew out of thoughts developed during this time as I continued to read and reread Jürgen Moltmann and Wolfhart Pannenberg, as well as Elizabeth Johnson and Sarah Coakley, while preparing sermons and Bible studies, all while reflecting on what these mean for gender.

This book reflects something steeped deeply in my intellectual curiosities as well as a preacher and pastor but also as a person with a messy upbringing. Thus, it reflects an intertwined journey of working out my theological convictions with research and specific argumentation but also trying to work out what effect patriarchy has had on me and on the church. This has been a pursuit of wholeness and authenticity, and I hope anyone reading this will find concepts that help them to do so, too. It is a lifelong journey we must all go on.

Bibliography

Abelson, J. *The Immanence of God in Rabbinical Literature*. London: Macmillan, 1912.
Achtemeier, Elizabeth. "Exchanging God for 'No Gods': A Discussion of Female Language for God." In *Speaking the Christian God*, edited by Alvin Kimel, 1–16. Grand Rapids: Eerdmans, 1992.
Aghiorgoussis, Maximos. *Women Priests?* Brookline, MA: Holy Cross Orthodox, 1976.
Aldredge-Clanton, Jann. *In Search of Christ-Sophia*. Fort Worth, TX: Eeakin, 2004.
Allert, Craig. *A High View of Scripture?* Grand Rapids: Baker, 2007.
Allison, Dale, Jr. *The Historical Christ and the Theological Jesus*. Grand Rapids: Eerdmans, 2009.
Alter, Robert. *The Art of Biblical Narrative*. New York: Basic, 1981.
Anderson, Ray. "The Incarnation of God in Feminist Christology: A Theological Critique." In *Speaking the Christian God*, edited by Alvin Kimel, 288–312. Grand Rapids: Eerdmans, 1992.
Anselm of Canterbury. *The Prayers and Meditations of Saint Anselm with the Proslogion*. Translated by Sister Benedicta Ward. New York: Penguin, 1997.
Aquinas, Thomas. *Summa Contra Gentiles*. Translated by Anton Pegis. Notre Dame, IN: University of Notre Dame, 1955.
———. *The Summa Theologiæ of St. Thomas Aquinas*. 2nd ed. Translated by Fathers of the English Dominican Province. Online ed. Kevin Knight. *New Advent* (2017): https://www.newadvent.org/summa/.
Athanasius. *Four Discourses against the Arians*. In *The Nicene and Post-Nicene Fathers of the Christian Church*, vol. 4, edited by P. Schaff and H. Wace. Grand Rapids: Eerdmans, 1971.
Auerbach, Erich. *Mimesis*. Translated by William Trask. Princeton: Princeton University Press, 1953.
Augustine. *On the Psalms*. Translated by R. G. MacMullen. In *Nicene and Post-Nicene Fathers*, first series, vol. 8, edited by Philip Schaff. Buffalo, NY: Christian Literature, 1888.
———. *Sermons on the New Testament*. Translated by R. G. MacMullen. In *Nicene and Post-Nicene Fathers*, first series, vol. 6, edited by Philip Schaff. Buffalo, NY: Christian Literature Publishing Co., 1888.
———. *The Trinity*. 2nd ed. Translated by Edmund Hill. New York: New City, 2015.
Baker, Mark, and Joel Green. *Recovering the Scandal of the Cross*. 2nd ed. Downers Grove, IL: InterVarsity, 2011.

Ballen, Sian, Lesley Hauge, and Jeff Hirsch. "Interview with Edwina Sandys." *New York Social Diary*, November 18, 2011. https://www.newyorksocialdiary.com/edwina-sandys/.

Balthasar, Hans Urs von. *Mary for Today*. Translated by Robert Nowell. San Francisco: Ignatius, 1987.

Barron, James. "An 'Evolving' Episcopal Church Invites Back a Controversial Sculpture." *New York Times*, Oct. 4, 2016. https://www.nytimes.com/2016/10/05/nyregion/an-evolving-episcopal-church-invites-back-a-controversial-sculpture.html.

Barron, Joshua Robert. "My God Is enkAi: A Reflection of Vernacular Theology." *Journal of Language, Culture, and Religion* 2.1 (2021) 1–20.

Barth, Karl. *Church Dogmatics*. 14 vols. Translated by G. W. Bromiley. London: T. & T. Clark, 2009.

Bashaw, Jennifer Garcia. *Scapegoats: The Gospel through the Eyes of Victims*. Minneapolis: Fortress, 2022.

Basil. *Epistle 234*. Translated by Blomfield Jackson. In *Nicene and Post-Nicene Fathers*, second series, vol. 8, edited by Philip Schaff and Henry Wace. Buffalo, NY: Christian Literature, 1895.

Basil. *On the Holy Spirit*. Translated by Stephen Hildebrand. Yonkers, NY: St. Vladimir's Seminary Press, 2011.

Bauckham, Richard. *Jesus and the Eyewitnesses*. 2nd ed. Grand Rapids: Eerdmans, 2017.

———. *Jesus and the God of Israel*. Milton Keynes, UK: Paternoster, 2008.

———. *Who Is God?* Grand Rapids: Baker, 2020.

Bedard, Stephen Stanley Porter. *Unmasking the Pagan Christ*. Toronto: Clements, 2006.

Bellville, Linda. "Women Leaders in the Bible." In *Discovering Biblical Equality*, edited by Ronald Pierce and Cynthian Long Westfall, 70–89. Downers Grove, IL: InterVarsity, 2021.

Belonick, Deborah Malacky. "Revelation and Metaphors: The Significance of the Trinitarians Names, Father, Son and Holy Spirit." *Union Seminary Quarterly Review* 40.3 (1985) 31–42.

Biale, David. "The God with Breasts: El Shaddai in the Bible." *History of Religions* 21.3 (1982) 240–56.

Bishops' Council of the Russian Orthodox Church Abroad. "Decision of the Bishops' Council of the Russian Orthodox Church Abroad of the 17/30 October 1935 concerning the new teaching of Archpriest Sergei Bulgakov on Sophia, the Wisdom of God." (1935).

Bloesch, Donald G. *Battle for the Trinity*. Ann Arbor, MI: Vine, 1985.

———. *Is the Bible Sexist? Beyond Feminism and Patriarchalism*. 1982. Reprint, Eugene, OR: Wipf and Stock, 2001.

———. *A Theology of Word and Spirit: Authority and Method in Theology*. Carlisle, UK: Paternoster, 1992.

Boersma, Spencer Miles. "Beyond Literalism and Liberalism: Understanding the Grammar of Gendered Language about God." *McMaster Journal of Theology and Ministry* 21 (2019–20) 111–57.

———. "Father and the Feminine." *Priscilla Papers*, August 9, 2022. https://www.cbeinternational.org/resource/the-father-and-the-feminine-assessing-the-grammar-of-gender-inclusive-god-language/.

———. "The Motherly Love of God: Theological Reflections on Mother's Day." Spencer Boersma, Friend of Radicals, May 27, 2015. https://spencerboersma.com/2015/05/27/the-motherly-love-of-god/.

Boff, Leonardo. *Come Holy Spirit*. Translated by Margaret Wilde. Maryknoll, NY: Orbis, 2015.

———. *Holy Trinity, Perfect Community*. Maryknoll, NY: Orbis, 2000.

———. *The Maternal Face of God: The Feminine in Its Religious Expressions*. San Francisco: Harper and Row, 1987.

Boulais-Duong, Lindsey. "The Power of a Pronoun: How What We Call God Affects Everything." *Mutuality*, Oct. 8, 2019. https://www.cbeinternational.org/resource/article/mutuality-blog-magazine/power-pronoun-how-what-we-call-god-affects-everything.

Borg, Marcus. *Jesus: Uncovering the Life, Teachings, and Relevance of a Religious Revolutionary*. New York: Harper San Francisco, 2006.

Boyd, Gregory. *Inspired Imperfection*. Minneapolis: Fortress, 2020.

Brannan, Rick, trans. *The Apostolic Fathers*. Bellingham, WA: Lexham, 2017.

Briggs, Richard S. "Gender and God-Talk: Can We Call God 'Mother'?" *Themelios* 29.2 (2004). https://www.thegospelcoalition.org/themelios/article/gender-and-god-talk-can-we-call-god-mother/.

Brown, Joanne Carlson, and Rebecca Parker. "For God So Loved the World?" In *Christianity, Patriarchy, and Abuse*, edited by Joanne Carlson Brown and Carole Bohn, 1–31. Cleveland, OH: Pilgrim, 1989.

Brown, Raymond. *The Sensus Plenior of Sacred Scripture*. 1955. Reprint, Eugene, OR: Wipf and Stock, 2008.

Brueggemann, Walter. *Old Testament Theology*. Minneapolis: Fortress, 1997.

Bulgakov, Sergei. *Sophia: The Wisdom of God*. Translated by Patrick Thompson, O. Fielding Clarke, and Xenia Braikevitc. Hudson, NY: Lindisfarne, 1993.

Butler, Judith. "Bodies That Matter." Ch. 16 in *Understanding Inequality: The Intersection of Race/Ethnicity, Class, and Gender*, edited by Barbara Arrighi. 2nd ed. New York: Rowman and Littlefield, 2007.

———. *Gender Trouble*. London: Routledge, 1990.

Bynum, Caroline Walker. *Jesus as Mother: Studies in the Spirituality of the High Middle Ages*. Berkeley: University of California Press, 1982.

Calvin, John. *Commentary on Isaiah*. 5 vols. Translated by William Pringle. Grand Rapids: Christian Classics Ethereal Library.

Camp, Claudia. "Feminist Theological Hermeneutics: Canon and Identity." In *Searching the Scriptures*, vol. 1, edited by Elizabeth Schüssler Fiorenza, 154–71. New York: Herder and Herder, 1997.

———. *Wisdom and the Feminine in the Book of Proverbs*. Sheffield, UK: Almond, 1985.

Carr, Anne. *Transforming Grace*. San Francisco: Harper and Row, 1988.

Charles, H. R., trans. *The Apocrypha and Pseudepigrapha of the Old Testament*. Oxford: Clarendon, 2004.

Charleston, Steven. *The Four Vision Quests of Jesus*. New York: Morehouse, 2015.

Charlesworth, James H., trans. *The Odes of Solomon*. Missoula, MT: Scholars, 1977.

Chen, Diane. *God as Father in Luke-Acts*. New York: Lang, 2005.

"Child Injured in Apt. Fire Dies." *Fox16*. Jan. 15, 2015. https://www.fox16.com/news/child-injured-in-harrison-apt-fire-dies/.

BIBLIOGRAPHY

Chilton, Amy, and Steven Harmon, eds. *Sources of Light: Resources for Baptist Churches Practicing Theology*. Macon, GA: Mercer University Press, 2020.

Chrysostom, John. "Homilies on the Gospel of Saint Matthew." In *The Nicene and Post Nicene Fathers*, vol. 10, edited by Philip Schaff. Grand Rapids: Eerdmans, 1956.

Cleary, William. *Prayers to She Who Is*. New York: Crossroad, 1995.

Clement of Alexandria. *Christ the Educator*. Translated by Simon Wood. New York: Fathers of the Church, 1954.

———. *Stomata*. Translated by William Wilson. In *Ante-Nicene Fathers*, vol. 2, edited by Alexander Roberts, James Donaldson, and A. Cleveland Coxe. Buffalo, NY: Christian Literature, 1885.

———. *Who Is the Rich Man That Shall Be Saved?* Translated by G. W. Butterworth. Cambridge: Harvard University Press, 1953.

———. "Who Is the Rich Man That Shall Be Saved?" Translated by William Wilson. In *Ante-Nicene Fathers*, vol. 2, edited by Alexander Roberts, James Donaldson, and A. Cleveland Coxe. Buffalo, NY: Christian Literature, 1885.

Clines, David J. A. "Alleged Female Language about the Deity in the Hebrew Bible." *Journal of Biblical Literature* 140.2 (2021) 229–49.

Coakley, Sarah. *God, Sexuality, and the Self*. Cambridge: Cambridge University Press, 2013.

———. *Powers and Submissions*. Oxford: Blackwell, 2002.

Comblin, Jose. *The Holy Spirit and Liberation*. Translated by Paul Burns. 1989. Reprint, Eugene, OR: Wipf and Stock, 2004.

Cone, James. *The Cross and the Lynching Tree*. Maryknoll, NY: Orbis, 2011.

———. *God of the Oppressed*. Maryknoll, NY: Orbis, 2007.

Congar, Yves. *I Believe in the Holy Spirit*. 3 vols. New York: Herder & Herder, 1983.

Cooper, John. *Our Father in Heaven: Christian Faith and Inclusive Language for God*. Grand Rapids: Baker, 1998.

Copeland, M. Shawn. *Knowing Christ Crucified*. Maryknoll, NY: Orbis, 2017.

Cornwall, Susannah. *Constructive Theology and Gender Variance: Transformative Creatures*. Cambridge: Cambridge University Press, 2023.

Craig, William Lane. *The Son Rises: The Historical Evidence for the Resurrection of Jesus*. 1981. Reprint, Eugene, OR: Wipf and Stock, 2000.

Crossan, John Dominic. *God and Empire*. New York: Harper One, 2007.

Curtis, Edward. "Idol, Idolatry." In *Anchor Bible Dictionary*, vol. 3, edited by David Noel Freedman, 376–81. New York: Doubleday, 1992.

Daly, Mary. *Beyond God the Father: Towards a Philosophy of Women's Liberation*. Boston: Beacon, 1973.

———. *The Church and the Second Sex*. New York: Harper & Row, 1968.

———. *Gyn/Ecology: The Metaethics of Radical Feminism*. Boston: Beacon, 1978.

D'Angelo, Mary. "Theology in Mark and Q: Abba and 'Father' in Context." *Harvard Theological Review* 85.2 (1992) 149–74.

Daniel, Lillian. *Tell It Like It Is: Reclaiming the Practice of Testimony*. Hendron, VA: The Alban Institute, 2006.

Day, John. "Foreign Semitic Influence on the Wisdom of Israel and Its Appropriation in the Book of Proverbs." In *Wisdom in Ancient Israel: Essays in Honor of J. A. Emerton*, edited by John Day et al., 55–70. Cambridge: Cambridge University Press, 1995.

BIBLIOGRAPHY

"Declaration *Inter Insigniores* on the Question of Admission of Women to the Ministerial Priesthood." *Sacred Congregation for the Doctrine of the Faith*, October 15, 1976.

Dewey, Joanna. "Gospel of Mark." In *Searching the Scriptures*, vol. 2, edited by Elizabeth Schüssler Fiorenza, 470–509. New York: Herder and Herder, 1994.

DiNoia, J. A. "Knowing and Naming the Triune God." In *Speaking the Christian God*, edited by Alvin Kimel, 162–87. Grand Rapids: Eerdmans, 1992.

Dionysius (Pseudo). *Pseudo-Dionysius: The Complete Works*. Translated by Colm Luibheid. New York: Paulist, 1987.

Douglas, Kelly Brown. *The Black Christ*. Maryknoll, NY: Orbis, 1994.

Douglas, Sally. *Jesus Sophia: Returning to Woman Wisdom in the Bible, Practice, and Prayer*. Eugene, OR: Cascade, 2023.

Duck, Ruth. *Gender and the Name of God: The Trinitarian Baptismal Formula*. New York: Pilgrim, 1991.

———. *Worship for the Whole People of God*. 2nd ed. Louisville, KY: Westminster John Knox, 2021.

du Mez, Kristin Kobe. *Jesus and John Wayne*. New York: Liveright, 2021.

Dunn, James D. G. *The Oral Gospel Tradition*. Grand Rapids: Eerdmans, 2013.

Durrell, F. X. *Holy Spirit of God*. London: Geoffrey Chapman, 1986.

Erickson, Millard. *Whose Tampering with the Trinity?* Grand Rapids: Kregel Academic, 2009.

Evans, James. *We Have Been Believers*. 2nd ed. Minneapolis: Fortress, 2012.

Fee, Gordon. "The Cultural Context of Ephesians 5:18—6:9." *Priscilla Papers*, Jan. 31, 2002. https://www.cbeinternational.org/resource/cultural-context-ephesians-518-69/.

———. *Pauline Christology*. Grand Rapids: Baker Academic, 2007.

Fiddes, Paul S. *Participating in God*. Louisville, KY: Westminster John Knox, 2000.

———. *Past Event and Present Salvation*. Louisville, KY: Westminster John Knox, 1989.

Florensky, Pavel. *The Pillar and Ground of Truth*. Translated by Boris Jakim. Princeton: Princeton University Press, 1997.

Fodor, James. "Postliberal Theology." In *The Modern Theologians*, edited by David Ford and Rachel Muirs, 229–49. Oxford: Blackwell, 2005.

Ford, David, and Rachel Muirs, eds. *The Modern Theologians*. Oxford: Blackwell, 2005.

Fox, Matthew. *The Hidden Spirituality of Men: Ten Metaphors to Awaken the Sacred Masculine*. Navato, CA: New World Library, 2008.

Freedman, David Noel, ed. *Anchor Bible Dictionary*. 6 vols. New York: Doubleday, 1992.

Freeman, Curtis, ed. *A Company of Women Preachers*. Waco, TX: Baylor University Press, 2011.

———. *Contesting Catholicity*. Waco, TX: Baylor University Press, 2014.

Freeman, Curtis, James Wm. McClendon Jr., and C. Rosalee Velloso Ewell, eds. *Baptist Roots: A Reader in the Theology of a Christian People*. King of Prussia, PA: Judson, 1999.

Frei, Hans. *The Bible and the Narrative Tradition*. Edited by Frank McConnell. New York: Oxford University Press, 1986.

———. *The Identity of Jesus Christ*. Reprint, Eugene, OR: Wipf and Stock, 1997.

———. *Reading Faithfully*. 2 vols. Edited by Mike Higton and Mark Alan Bowald. Eugene, OR: Cascade: 2015.

Frye, Northrop. *The Great Code*. Toronto: Academic, 1981.

Frye, Roland. "Language for God and Feminist Language." In *Speaking the Christian God*, edited by Alvin Kimel, 17–44. Grand Rapids: Eerdmans, 1992.

BIBLIOGRAPHY

Garcia-Johnson, Oscar. "In Search of Indigenous Pneumatologies in the Americas." In *Spirit over the Earth*, edited by Gene L. Green, Stephen T. Perdue, K. K. Yeo, 142–64. Carlisle: Langham, 2016.

Gelpi, Donald. *The Divine Mother: Trinitarian Theology of the Holy Spirit*. New York: University Press of America, 1984.

Gerhardt, Elizabeth. *The Cross and Gendercide*. Downers Grove, IL: InterVarsity, 2014.

Gibson, J. "Could Christ Have Been Born a Woman?" *Journal of Feminist Studies* 8 (1982) 65–82.

Giles, Kevin. *The Headship of Men and the Abuse of Women*. Eugene, OR: Cascade, 2020.

———. "The Trinity Argument for Woman's Subordination." In *Discovering Biblical Equality*, edited by Ronald Pierce and Cynthian Long Westfall, 351–71. 3rd ed. Downers Grove, IL: InterVarsity, 2021.

Girard, Rene. *The Scapegoat*. Baltimore: Johns Hopkins University Press, 1986.

Goldingay, John. *Models for Scripture*. Grand Rapids: Eerdmans, 1994.

Goossen, Rachel Waltner. "A Failure to Bind and Loose: Responses to Yoder's Sexual Abuse." *Anabaptist World*, January 3, 2015. https://anabaptistworld.org/failure-bind-loose-responses-john-howard-yoders-sexual-abuse/.

Grassi, Joseph. "*Abba*, Father (Mark 14:36): Another Approach." *Journal of the American Academy of Religion* 50.3 (1982) 449–58.

Green-McCreight, Kathryn. *Feminist Reconstructions of Christian Doctrine*. Oxford: Oxford University Press, 2000.

Greenley, A. M. *The Mary Myth: On the Femininity of God*. New York: Seabury, 1977.

Gregory of Nazianzus. *Oration 28*. Translated by Charles Gordon Browne and James Edward Swallow. In *Nicene and Post-Nicene Fathers*, second series, vol. 7, edited by Philip Schaff and Henry Wace. Buffalo, NY: Christian Literature, 1894.

Grenz, Stanley. *The Named God and the Question of Being*. Louisville, KY: Westminster John Knox, 2005.

———. *The Social God and the Relational Self*. Louisville, KY: Westminster John Knox, 2001.

Grenz, Stanley, and John Franke. *Beyond Foundationalism: Shaping Theology in a Postmodern Context*. Louisville, KY: Westminster John Knox, 2001.

Grudem, Wayne. *Systematic Theology*. Grand Rapids: Zondervan, 2000.

Grudem, Wayne, and John Piper, eds. *Recovering Biblical Manhood and Womanhood*. Wheaton, IL: Crossway, 2012.

Gunton, Colin. *Actuality of the Atonement*. Edinburgh: T. & T. Clark, 1988.

———. "Proteus and Procrustes: A Study in the Dialectic of Language in Disagreement with Sallie McFague." In *Speaking the Christian God*, edited by Alvin Kimel, 65–81. Grand Rapids: Eerdmans, 1992.

Gushee, David. *The Sacredness of Human Life*. Grand Rapids: Eerdmans, 2013.

Gushee, David, and Glen Stassen. *Kingdom Ethics*. 2nd ed. Grand Rapids: Eerdmans, 2012.

Haddad, Mimi. "Evidence for and Significance of Feminine God Language from the Church Fathers to the Modern Era." *Priscilla Papers*, July 30, 2004. https://www.cbeinternational.org/resource/article/priscilla-papers-academic-journal/evidence-and-significance-feminine-god-language?page=5.

Hadewijch. *Hadewijch: The Complete Works*. Translated by Mother Columba Hart. New York: Paulist, 1980.

Hamerton-Kelly, Robert. *God the Father: Theology and Patriarchy in the Teachings of Jesus*. Minneapolis: Fortress, 1979.
Hampson, Daphne. *Theology and Feminism*. Oxford: Blackwell, 1990.
Hanson, Paul. "Masculine Metaphors for God and Sex-Discrimination in the Old Testament." *Ecumenical Review* 27.4 (1975) 316–24.
Harmon, Steven. *Towards Baptist Catholicity*. Studies in Baptist History and Thought. Milton Keynes, UK: Paternoster, 2006.
Harvey, Susan Ashbrook. "Feminine Imagery for the Divine: The Holy Spirit, the Odes of Solomon, and Early Syriac Tradition." *St. Vladimir's Theological Quarterly* 37 (1993) 111–39.
Hauerwas, Stanley. *Unleashing the Scripture*. Nashville: Abingdon, 1993.
Hays, Richard B. *Reading Backwards: Figural Christology and the Fourfold Gospel Witness*. Waco, TX: Baylor University, 2014.
Heimmel, Jennifer P. "'God Is Our Mother': Julian of Norwich and the Medieval Image of Christian Feminine Divinity." PhD diss., St. John's University, New York, 1980.
Hennecke, E., W. Schneemelcher, and P. Vielhauer, trans. *New Testament Apocrypha*. 2 vols. Philadelphia: Westminster, 1963.
Heschel, Abraham Joshua. *The Prophets*. 2 vols. New York: Harper and Row, 1962.
———. *The Sabbath*. New York: Farrar, Straus and Giroux, 2005.
Heschel, Susanna. *The Aryan Jesus*. Princeton: Princeton University Press, 2008.
Heyward, Carter. *Our Passion for Justice*. New York: Pilgrim, 1984.
Hildegard of Bingen. *Book of Divine Works*. Edited by Matthew Fox. Translated by Robert Cunningham. Santa Fe: Bear, 1987.
Hill, Wesley. *Paul and the Trinity: Persons, Relations, and the Pauline Letter*. Grand Rapids: Eerdmans, 2015.
Hooft, W. A. Visser't. *The Fatherhood of God in an Age of Emancipation*. Philadelphia: Westminster, 1982.
hooks, bell. *The Will to Change*. New York: Atria, 2004.
Hopko, Thomas. "Apophatic Theology and the Naming of God in Eastern Orthodox Tradition." In *Speaking the Christian God*, edited by Alvin Kimel, 144–61. Grand Rapids: Eerdmans, 1992.
———. "On the Male Character of Christian Priesthood." In *Women and the Priesthood*, edited by Thomas Hopko, 97–134. New York: St. Vladimir's Seminar Press, 1983.
———, ed. *Women and the Priesthood*. Crestwood, NY: St. Vladimir's Seminary Press, 1983.
"Inclusive Language Guidelines." Anglican Diocese of Toronto. 2010. www.toronto.anglican.ca.
An Inclusive Language Lectionary: Readings for Year A. Rev. ed. Louisville, KY: Westminster John Knox, 1986.
An Inclusive Language Lectionary: Readings for Year B. Rev. ed. Louisville, KY: Westminster John Knox, 1987.
An Inclusive Language Lectionary: Readings for Year C. Rev. ed. Louisville, KY: Westminster John Knox, 1988.
Irenaeus. *Against Heresies*. Translated by Philip Schaff. Grand Rapids: Eerdmans, 2016.
Irigaray, Luce. *I Love to You*. London: Routledge, 1996.
James, Carolyn Custis. *Malestrom: How Jesus Dismantles Patriarchy and Redefines Manhood*. Grand Rapids: Zondervan, 2022.

Jenson, Blanche. "The Movement and the Story: What Happened to 'Her'?" In *Speaking the Christian God*, edited by Alvin Kimel, 276–88. Grand Rapids: Eerdmans, 1992.
Jenson, Robert W. *The Triune Identity*. Philadelphia: Fortress, 1982.
Jeremias, Joachim. *The Prayers of Jesus*. London: SCM, 1967.
Jewett, Paul K. *God, Creation, and Revelation*. Grand Rapids: Eerdmans, 1991.
John of Damascus. *Exposition of the Orthodox Faith*. Translated by S. D. F. Salmond. Hawthorne, CA: Aeterna, 2016.
Johnson, Elizabeth. *Abounding in Kindness*. Maryknoll, NY: Orbis, 2015.
———. *Consider Jesus*. New York: Crossroads, 1990.
———. "The Incomprehensibility of God and the Image of God as Male and Female." *Theological Studies* 43 (1984) 441–65.
———. *She Who Is*. New York: Crossroad, 1993.
Johnson, Luke Timothy. *The Real Jesus*. New York: HarperCollins, 1996.
———. *Scripture and Discernment: Decision Making in the Church*. Nashville: Abingdon, 1983.
Johnston, Robert K. *God's Wider Presence: Reconsidering General Revelation*. Grand Rapids: Baker, 2014.
Jones, Joe. *Grammar of Christian Faith*. 2 vols. Lanham, MD: Rowman and Littlefield, 2002.
Jones, Serene. *Feminist Theory and Christian Theology*. Minneapolis: Fortress, 2000.
Julian of Norwich. *Showings*. Translated by Edmund Colledge. New York: Paulist, 1978.
Justin Martyr. *First Apology*. Translated by Marcus Dods and George Reith. In *Ante-Nicene Fathers*, vol. 1, edited by Alexander Roberts, James Donaldson, and A. Cleveland Coxe. Buffalo, NY: Christian Literature, 1885.
Kaufman, Gordon. Review of *Models of God: Theology for an Ecological, Nuclear Age*, by Sallie McFague. *Theology Today* 45.1 (1988) 95–101.
Kay, James. "In Whose Name? Feminism and the Trinitarian Baptismal Formula." *Theology Today* 9.4 (1993) 524–33.
Keating, Thomas. *Open Mind, Open Heart: Contemplative Dimension of the Gospel*. London: Bloomsbury, 2006.
Keener, Craig. *Christobiography: Memory, History, and the Reliability of the Gospels*. Grand Rapids: Eerdmans, 2020.
———. "Mutual Submission Frames the Household Codes." *Priscilla Papers*, July 31, 2021. https://www.cbeinternational.org/resource/mutual-submission-frames-household-codes.
———. *Spirit Hermeneutics: Reading Scripture in Light of Pentecost*. Grand Rapids: Eerdmans, 2016.
Kim, Grace Ji-Sun. *Embracing the Other: The Transformative Spirit of Love*. Grand Rapids: Eerdmans, 2015.
———. *The Grace of Sophia: A Korean North American Women's Christology*. Cleveland, OH: Pilgrim, 2002.
Kim, Grace Ji-Sun, and Susan Shaw. *Intersectional Theology*. Minneapolis: Fortress, 2018.
Kimel, Alvin, Jr., ed. "It Could Have Been. . . ." *Pro Ecclesia* 3 (1994) 389–94.
———. *Speaking the Christian God*. Grand Rapids: Eerdmans, 1992.
King, Ursula, ed. *Feminist Theology from the Third World: A Reader*. Maryknoll, NY: Orbis, 1994.

Kittel, Gerhard. "Abba." In *Theological Dictionary of the New Testament*, edited by Gerhard Kittel, Geoffrey Bromiley and Gerhard Friedrich. 10 vols. Grand Rapids: Eerdmans, 1964–76.
Kloppenborg, John. "Isis and Sophia in the Book of Wisdom." *Harvard Theology Review* 75.1 (1982) 57–85.
LaCugna, Catherine Mowry. "The Baptismal Formula, Feminist Objections, and Trinitarian Theology." *Journal of Ecumenical Studies* 26.2 (1989) 235–50.
———, ed. *Freeing Theology: The Essentials of Theology in Feminist Perspective*. New York: HarperCollins, 1993.
———. *God for Us: The Trinity and Christian Life*. New York: Harper Collins, 1991.
———. Review of *Speaking the Christian God: The Holy Trinity and the Challenge of Feminism*, by Alvin F. Kimel Jr. *Pro Ecclesia* 3 (1994) 114–16.
Lanzetta, Beverly. *Radical Wisdom*. Minneapolis: Fortress, 2005.
Lau, Holning. *Sexual Orientation and Gender Identity Discrimination*. Boston: Brill, 2018.
Layton, B., trans. *The Gnostic Scriptures*. Garden City, NY: Doubleday, 1987.
Lindbeck, George. *Nature of Doctrine*. Louisville, KY: Westminster John Knox, 1984.
Lloyd, Genevieve. "Augustine and Aquinas." In *Feminist Theology: A Reader*, edited by Ann Loades, 90–99. London: SPCK, 1990.
Loades, Ann, ed. *Feminist Theology: A Reader*. London: SPCK, 1990.
Lodahl, Michael. *Shekinah/Spirit: Divine Presence in Jewish and Christian Religion*. New York: Paulist, 1992.
Long, D. Stephen. *Speaking of God: Theology, Language, and Truth*. Grand Rapids: Eerdmans, 2009.
Lorder, Judith. *Gender Inequality: Feminist Theories and Politics*. Oxford: Oxford University Press, 2012.
Lu, She-Min. "Woman's Role in New Testament Household Codes: Transforming First-Century Roman Culture." *Priscilla Papers*, Jan. 30, 2016. https://www.cbeinternational.org/resource/womans-role-new-testament-household-codes.
Lyotard, Jean-Francois. *The Postmodern Condition*. Minneapolis: University of Minnesota Press, 1984.
MacIntyre, Alasdair. *After Virtue: A Study in Moral Theory*. 2nd ed. Notre Dame, IN: University of Notre Dame Press, 1984.
Matthis, David. "Why Jesus Was Not a Woman." *Desiring God*, Oct. 11, 2020. https://www.desiringgod.org/articles/why-jesus-was-not-a-woman.
Marriage, Alwyn. *Life-Giving Spirit*. London: SPCK, 1989.
Marshall, Molly. "Reading Scripture with the Spirit, II. Discerning Reading: Winnowing the Harvest." *Baptistic Theologies* 3.2 (2011) 17–33.
McClendon, James Wm., Jr. *The Collected Works of James Wm. McClendon, Jr.* 2 vols. Edited by Ryan Andrew Newson and Andrew Wright. Waco, TX: Baylor University Press, 2014.
———. *Systematic Theology*. 3 vols. Ethics, Doctrine, Witness. Waco, TX: Baylor University Press, 2012.
McClendon, James Wm., Jr., and James M. Smith. *Convictions: Defusing Religious Relativism*. 1994. Rev. ed. Eugene, OR: Wipf and Stock, 2002.
McFague, Sallie. *The Body of God*. Minneapolis: Fortress, 1993.
———. *Metaphorical Theology*. Philadelphia: Fortress, 1982.
———. *Models of God*. Minneapolis: Fortress, 1988.

———. *Speaking in Parables: A Study in Metaphor and Theology*. Philadelphia: Fortress, 1975.
McGregor-Wright, R. K. "God, Metaphor and Gender: Is the God of the Bible a Male Deity?" In *Discovering Biblical Equality*, edited by Ronald Pierce and Rebecca Merrill Groothuis, 287–301. 2nd ed. Downer's Grove, IL: InterVarsity, 2005.
Meehan, Brenda. "Wisdom/Sophia, Russian Identity, and Western Feminist Theology." *Cross Currents* 46.2 (1996) 149–68.
Mengestu, Abera. *God as Father in Paul: Kinship Language and Identity Formation in Early Christianity*. Eugene, OR: Pickwick, 2013.
Merton, Thomas. *New Seeds of Contemplation*. New York: New Directions, 2007.
Metz, Johannes-Baptist, and Edward Schillebeeckx, eds. *God as Father?* New York: Seabury, 1981.
Metzger, Bruce. *Canon of the New Testament*. Oxford: Oxford University Press, 1997.
Migliore, Daniel. "'The Trinity: God's Love Overflowing'; A Study Paper Received by the 217th General Assembly of the PCUSA." Presbyterian Church (USA), March 17, 2010. https://www.presbyterianmission.org/resource/trinity-gods-love-overflowing.
Mohler, Albert. "The God Who Names Himself." Albert Mohler's blog, June 21, 2006. https://albertmohler.com/2006/06/21/the-god-who-names-himself.
Mollenkott, Virginia Ramsey. *The Divine Feminine: The Biblical Imagery of God as Female*. 1987. Reprint, Eugene, OR: Wipf and Stock, 2014.
Molnar, Paul. *Divine Freedom and the Doctrine of the Immanent Trinity*. London: T. & T. Clark, 2002.
Moltmann, Jürgen. *Experiences in Theology*. Translated by Margaret Kohl. Minneapolis: Fortress, 2000.
———. *Spirit of Life*. Translated by Margaret Kohl. Minneapolis: Fortress, 2001.
Montague, George. *The Holy Spirit*. New York: Paulist, 1976.
Montero, Roman. *All Things in Common: The Economic Practices of the Early Christians*. Eugene, OR: Resource, 2017.
Munch, Robert. *Love You Forever*. Toronto: Firefly, 1986.
Murashko, Alex. "John Piper: God Gave Christianity a 'Masculine Feel.'" *Christian Post*, Feb. 1, 2012. https://www.christianpost.com/news/john-piper-god-gave-christianity-a-masculine-feel.html.
Musurillo, Herbert. *The Acts of the Christian Martyrs*. Oxford: Clarendon, 1972.
Myers, Ched. *Binding the Strong Man: A Political Reading of Mark's Story of Jesus*. Maryknoll, NY: Orbis, 2008.
Newman, Barbara. *God and the Goddesses: Vision, Poetry, and Belief in the Middle Ages*. Philadelphia: University of Pennsylvania Press, 2003.
———. *Sister of Wisdom: St. Hildegard's Theology of the Feminine*. Berkeley: University of California Press, 1998.
Novick, Leah. *On the Wings of Shekinah*. Wheaton, IL: Quest, 2008.
O'Collins, Gerald. *Christology*. 2nd ed. Oxford: Oxford University Press, 2009.
———. *The Tripersonal God*. 2nd ed. New York: Paulist, 2014.
O'Donnell, John J. *The Mystery of the Triune God*. London: Sheed & Ward, 1988.
Origen. *On First Principles*. Translated by G. W. Butterfield. Gloucester, MA: Peter Smith, 1973.

Ostrander, Tina. "Who Is Sophia?" *Priscilla Papers*, April 30, 1994. https://www.cbe international.org/resource/article/priscilla-papers-academic-journal/who-sophia.
Packer, J. I. *Knowing God*. Downers Grove, IL: InterVarsity, 1973.
Palmer, Parker J. *A Hidden Wholeness: The Journey toward an Undivided Life*. San Francisco: Jossey Bass, 2003.
Pannenberg, Wolfhart. "Analogy and Doxology." Translated by George Kelm. In *Basic Questions in Theology*, 1:212–38. Minneapolis: Fortress, 1970.
———. *Basic Questions in Theology*. 2 vols. Translated by George Kelm. Minneapolis: Fortress, 1970.
———. *Systematic Theology*. 3 vols. Translated by Geoffrey Bromiley. Grand Rapids: Eerdmans, 1997.
Parson, Susan Frank, ed. *Cambridge Companion to Feminist Theology*. Cambridge: Cambridge University Press, 2002.
Peeler, Amy. *Women and the Gender of God*. Grand Rapids: Eerdmans, 2022.
Pelican, Jaroslav. *Mary through the Centuries*. New Haven, CT: Yale University Press, 1996.
Perdue, Leo G. *Wisdom and Creation: The Theology of the Wisdom Literature*. Nashville: Abingdon, 1994.
Peterson, Jordan. *12 Rules for Life*. Toronto: Random House, 2018.
Pierce, Ronald, and Rebecca Merrill Groothuis, eds. *Discovering Biblical Equality: Complementarity without Hierarchy*. Downers Grove, IL: InterVarsity, 2005.
Pierce, Ronald, Cynthia Long Westfall, Christa McKirkland, eds. *Discovering Biblical Equality*. 3rd ed. Downers Grove, IL: InterVarsity, 2021.
Pinnock, Clark. *Flame of Love: A Theology of the Holy Spirit*. Downers Grove, IL: InterVarsity, 1996.
Poole, Stafford. *Our Lady of Guadalupe: The Origins and Sources of a Mexican National Symbol, 1531–1797*. Rev. ed. Tucson: University of Arizona Press 2017.
Powell, Mark Allan. *Jesus as a Figure in History*. 2nd ed. Louisville, KY: Westminster John Knox, 2013.
Poythress, Vern Sheridan. "The Church as Family: Why Male Leadership in the Family Requires Male Leadership in the Church." In *Recovering Biblical Manhood and Womanhood*, edited by John Piper and Wayne Grudem, 307–25. Wheaton, IL: Crossway, 2021.
Pramuk, Christopher. *Sophia: The Hidden Christ of Thomas Merton*. Collegeville, MN: Liturgical, 2009.
Procter-Smith, Marjorie. "Feminist Interpretation and Liturgical Proclamation." In *Searching the Scriptures*, vol. 1, edited by Elizabeth Schüssler Fiorenza, 313–25. New York: Herder and Herder, 1997.
Rad, Gerhard von. *Old Testament Theology*. 2 vols. Translated by D. M. G. Stalker. New York: Harper & Row, 1962–65.
Ramshaw, Gail. *God Beyond Gender*. Minneapolis: Fortress, 1995.
Ramshaw-Schmidt, Gail. "De Divinis Nominibus: The Gender of God." *Worship* 56 (1982) 117–31.
———. "An Inclusive Language Lectionary." *Worship* 58 (1984) 29–36.
———. "Lutheran Liturgical Prayer and God as Mother." *Worship* 52 (1978) 517–42.
———. "Naming the Trinity: Orthodoxy and Inclusivity." *Worship* 60 (1986) 491–98.

Raschke, Carl, and Susan Doughty Raschke. *The Engendering God: Male and Female Faces of God*. Nashville: Westminster John Knox, 1995.
Reynolds, Nettie. "Christa Interview with Edwina Sandys by Nettie Reynolds." *Feminism and Religion*, October 6, 2015. https://feminismandreligion.com/2015/10/06/christa-interview-with-edwina-sandys-by-nettie-reynolds/.
Rhodes, Deborah. *Justice and Gender: Sex Discrimination and the Law*. Cambridge: Harvard University Press, 1989.
Ricoeur, Paul. *Conflict in Interpretations*. Evanston, IL: Northwestern University Press, 1979.
———. *Figuring the Sacred*. Edited by Richard Kearney. Minneapolis: Augsburg, 1995.
———. *The Rule of Metaphor: Multi-Disciplinary Studies in the Creation of Meaning in Language*. Toronto: University of Toronto Press, 1978.
Rogers, Eugene, Jr. *Essentials of Christian Thought*. Minneapolis: Fortress, 2021.
———, ed. *Theology and Sexuality*. Oxford: Blackwell, 2002.
Ruether, Rosemary Radford. *Gaia and God: An Ecofeminist Theology of Earth Healing*. New York: HarperCollins, 1994.
———. *Goddesses and the Divine Feminine*. Berkeley: University of California Press, 2005.
———. "The Liberation of Christology from Patriarchy." In *Feminist Theology: A Reader*, edited by Ann Loades, 138–47. London: SPCK, 1990.
———. *Mary—The Feminine Face of the Church*. Philadelphia: Westminster, 1977.
———. *My Quests for Hope and Meaning: An Autobiography*. Eugene, OR: Cascade, 2013.
———. *Sexism and God-Talk*. Boston: Beacon, 1983.
Russell, Letty. *Human Liberation in Feminist Perspective—A Theology*. Philadelphia: Westminster, 1974.
Rutledge, Fleming. *The Crucifixion: Understanding the Death of Jesus Christ*. Grand Rapids: Eerdmans, 2017.
Sabia-Tanis, Justin. *Trans-Gender: Theology, Ministry, and Communities of Faith*. 2003. Reprint, Eugene, OR: Wipf and Stock, 2018.
Sachs-Shmueli, Leore. "Shekinah and the Revivial of Feminine God Language." *Modern Judaism* 39.3 (2019) 347–69.
"SBC Executive Committee Revision of Report of Committee on Resolutions." *SBC Bulletin*, June 1992.
Schneiders, Sandra. "The Bible and Feminism: Biblical Theology." In *Freeing Theology*, edited by Catherine Mowry LaCugna, 31–58. San Francisco: HarperSanFrancisco, 1993.
Schuller, Eileen. "The Psalm of 4Q372 1 within the Context of Second Temple Prayer." *Catholic Biblical Quarterly* 54 (1992) 67–79.
Schüssler Fiorenza, Elizabeth. *But She Said: Feminist Practices of Biblical Interpretation*. Boston: Beacon, 1993.
———. *In Memory of Her: A Feminist Theological Reconstruction of Christian Origins*. New York: Crossroad, 1983.
———. *Jesus: Miriam's Child, Sophia's Prophet*. London: T. & T. Clark, 2015.
———, ed. *Searching the Scriptures*. Vol. 2. New York: Herder and Herder, 1994.
———. *Wisdom Ways: Introducing Feminist Biblical Interpretation*. Maryknoll, NY: Orbis, 2001.
Smith, Paul. *Is It Okay to Call God "Mother"?* Peabody, MA: Hendrickson, 1993.

Snodgrass, Klyne. *Ephesians*. NIV Application COmmentary. Grand Rapids: Eerdmans, 1996.

Solovyov, Vladimir. *Lectures on Divine Humanity*. Translated by P. Zouboff, edited by B. Jakim. Hudson, NY: Lindisfarne, 1995.

———. *The Meaning of Love*. Translated by Tomas Beyer Jr. Hudson, NY: Lindisfarne, 1985.

———. *The Religious Poetry of Vladimir Solovyov*. Edited by Boris Jakim. Kettering, UK: Angelico, 2014.

Soskice, Janet Martin. "Can a Feminist Call God 'Father'?" In *Speaking the Christian God*, edited by Alvin Kimel, 81–94. Grand Rapids: Eerdmans, 1992.

———. *Metaphor and Religious Language*. Oxford: Clarendon, 1985.

———. *Naming God: Addressing the Divine in Philosophy, Theology and Scripture*. Cambridge: Cambridge University Press, 2023.

———. "Trinity and Feminism." In *Cambridge Companion to Feminist Theology*, edited by Susan Frank Parsons, 135–50. Cambridge: Cambridge University Press, 2002.

Soulen, R. Kendall. "The Name of the Holy Trinity: A Triune Name." *Modern Theology* 59.2 (2002) 244–61.

Sparks, Kenton. "Gospel as Conquest: Mosaic Typology in Matt. 28:16–20." *Catholic Biblical Quarterly* 68 (2006) 651–63.

Strauss, Mark. *Distorting Scripture? The Challenge of Bible Translations and Gender Accuracy*. Downers Grove, IL: InterVarsity, 1998.

Sumner, George. "Contra Washington: Ten Theses." The Episcopal Diocese of Dallas, Feb. 15, 2018. https://edod.org/bishops-blog/contra-washington-ten-theses.

Tamez, Elsa. "Reliving Our Histories: Racial and Cultural Revelations of God." In *New Visions for the Americas: Religious Engagement and Transformation*, edited by David Batstone, 33–56. Minneapolis: Fortress, 1993.

Tasker, David Russell. "The Fatherhood of God: An Exegetical Study from the Hebrew Scriptures." PhD diss., Andrews University, Berrien Springs, 2002.

Taylor, John V. *The Go-Between God: The Holy Spirit and the Christian Mission*. 1972. Reprint, Eugene, OR: Wipf and Stock, 2015.

Teresa of Avila. *Interior Castle*. Translated by K. Kavanaugh and O. Rodriguez. New York: Paulist, 1979.

Terrien, Samuel. *Till the Heart Sings*. Grand Rapids: Eerdmans, 2004.

Thiselton, Anthony. *The Holy Spirit*. Grand Rapids: Eerdmans, 2013.

Thompson, Marianne Meye. *The Promise of God the Father: Jesus and God in the New Testament*. Louisville, KY: Westminster John Knox, 2000.

Thurman, Howard. *Jesus and the Disinherited*. Boston: Beacon, 1976.

Titizano, Cecilia. "Mama Pacha: Creator and Sustainer Spirit of God." *Decolonial Horizons* 3 (2017) 127–59.

Torrance, Thomas F. "The Christian Apprehension of God the Father." In *Speaking the Christian God*, edited by Alvin Kimel, 120–43. Grand Rapids: Eerdmans, 1992.

———. *Reality and Evangelical Theology*. 1982. Reprint, Eugene, OR: Wipf and Stock, 2003.

———. *Space, Time and Resurrection*. Edinburgh: T. & T. Clark, 1976.

Trible, Phyllis. "Feminist Hermeneutics and Biblical Studies." In *Feminist Theology: A Reader*, edited by Ann Loades, 23–28. London: SPCK, 1990.

———. *Texts of Terror: Literary-Feminist Readings of Biblical Narratives*. Minneapolis: Fortress, 1984.

Tutu, Desmond. *God Is Not a Christian and Other Provocations*. Edited by John Allen. New York: Harper One, 2011.

van Oort, Johannes. "The Holy Spirit as Feminine: Early Christian Testimonies and Their Interpretation." *Theological Studies* 72.1 (2016). https://hts.org.za/index.php/hts/article/view/3225/7763.

Volf, Miroslav. *Exclusion and Embrace: A Theological Exploration of Identity, Otherness, and Reconciliation*. Nashville: Abingdon, 1996.

Wainwright, Geoffery. *Doxology: The Praise of God in Worship, Doctrine, and Life*. Oxford: Oxford University Press, 1980.

Walters, Margaret. *Feminism: A Very Short Introduction*. Oxford: Oxford University Press, 2005.

Webb, William J. *Slaves, Women, and Homosexuals: Exploring the Hermeneutics of Transcultural Analysis*. Downers Grove, IL: InterVarsity, 2001.

Webster, John. *Holy Scriptures: A Dogmatic Sketch*. Cambridge: Cambridge University Press, 2003.

Westfall, Cynthia Long. *Paul and Gender*. Grand Rapids: Baker, 2016.

Widdicombe, Peter. "The Fathers on the Father in the Gospel of John." *Semeia* 53 (1999) 105–25.

Williams, Rowan. "The Body's Grace." In *Theology and Sexuality*, edited by Eugene Rogers, 309–21. Oxford: Blackwell, 2002.

———. *Christ the Heart of Creation*. London: Bloomsbury, 2018.

———. *On Christian Theology*. Oxford: Blackwell, 2000.

———. *Resurrection*. London: Darton, Longman, and Todd, 2002.

Wink, Walter. *Engaging the Powers*. Minneapolis: Fortress, 1992.

———. *The Powers That Be*. New York: Random House, 1998.

Winner, Lauren. *The Dangers of Christian Practice*. New Haven, CT: Yale University Press, 2018.

Witt, William. *Icons of Christ*. Waco, TX: Baylor University Press, 2021.

Wittgenstein, Ludwig. *Philosophical Investigations*. Translated by G. E. M. Anscombe. Oxford: Blackwell, 1953.

Wright, G. Ernst. *God Who Acts: Biblical Theology as Recital*. Naperville: Alec Allenson, 1960.

Yoder, John Howard. *The Politics of Jesus*. 2nd ed. Grand Rapids: Eerdmans, 1994.

Yong, Amos. *Discerning the Spirit(s): A Pentecostal-Charismatic Contribution to Christian Theology of Religions*. 2000. Reprint, Eugene, OR: Wipf and Stock, 2019.

Young, Pamela Dickey. *Feminist Theology / Christian Theology: In Search of Method*. Minneapolis: Fortress, 1990.

Young, Williams Paul. *The Shack*. Los Angeles: Wind Blown, 2007.

Zolotarev, Sergey. "Interpretation of Sophia, the Wisdom of God in Russian Philosophical Sophiology." *Journal of Visual Theology* 4.2 (2022) 170–81.

www.ingramcontent.com/pod-product-compliance
Lightning Source LLC
Chambersburg PA
CBHW031726230426
43669CB00007B/257